James E. Clark
Wichita State University

Janet L. Wolcutt
Wichita State University

Study Guide

Macroeconomics

Fifth Edition
Boyes/Melvin

Houghton Mifflin Company   Boston   New York

Sponsoring Editor: Ann West
Assistant Editor: Jennifer Di Domenico
Senior Manufacturing Coordinator: Marie Barnes
Marketing Manager: Barbara LeBuhn

Copyright © 2002 by Houghton Mifflin Company. All rights reserved.

No part of this work may be reproduced or transmitted in any form or by any means, electronic or mechanical, including photocopying and recording, or by any information storage or retrieval system without the prior written permission of Houghton Mifflin Company unless such copying is expressly permitted by federal copyright law. Address inquiries to College Permissions, Houghton Mifflin Company, 222 Berkeley Street, Boston, MA 02116-3764.

Printed in the U.S.A.

ISBN: 0-618-12796-8

123456789-VG-05 04 03 02 01

Contents

	Correlation Chart	v
	Using the Study Guide	vii
Chapter 1	Economics: The World Around You	1
	Appendix: Working with Graphs	13
Chapter 2	Choice, Opportunity Costs, and Specialization	21
Chapter 3	Markets, Demand and Supply, and the Price System	39
Chapter 4	The Market System and the Private Sector	81
Chapter 5	The Public Sector	95
	Sample Test for Chapters 1–5	111
Chapter 6	National Income Accounting	117
Chapter 7	An Introduction to the Foreign Exchange Market and the Balance of Payments	133
Chapter 8	Unemployment and Inflation	149
Chapter 9	Macroeconomic Equilibrium: Aggregate Demand and Supply	165
Chapter 10	Aggregate Expenditures	189
	Appendix: An Algebraic Model of Aggregate Expenditures	213
Chapter 11	Income and Expenditures Equilibrium	217
	Appendix: An Algebraic Model of Income and Expenditures Equilibrium	239
	Sample Tests for Chapters 6–11	243
Chapter 12	Fiscal Policy	257
	Appendix: An Algebraic Examination of the Balanced-Budget Change in Fiscal Policy	277
Chapter 13	Money and Banking	281
Chapter 14	Monetary Policy	299
Chapter 15	Macroeconomic Policy: Tradeoffs, Expectations, Credibility, and Sources of Business Cycles	315
Chapter 16	Macroeconomic Viewpoints: New Keynesian, Monetarist, and New Classical	331
Chapter 17	Macroeconomic Links Between Countries	345
	Sample Tests for Chapters 12–17	363

Chapter 18	Economic Growth	375
Chapter 19	Development Economics	389
	Sample Test for Chapters 18–19	405
Chapter 20	World Trade Equilibrium	409
Chapter 21	International Trade Restrictions	429
Chapter 22	Exchange-Rate Systems and Practices	443
	Sample Test for Chapters 20–22	457

Correlation Chart

Boyes and Melvin, *Macroeconomics*, Fifth Edition
Boyes and Melvin, *Economics*, Fifth Edition

Chapter Title	Chapter Number in *Macroeconomics*	Chapter Number in *Economics*
Introduction to the Price System		
Economics: The World Around You	1	1
Appendix: Working with Graphs	1A	1A
Choice, Opportunity Costs, and Specialization	2	2
Markets, Demand and Supply, and the Price System	3	3
The Market System and the Private Sector	4	4
The Public Sector	5	5
Macroeconomic Basics		
National Income Accounting	6	6
An Introduction to the Foreign Exchange Market and the Balance of Payments	7	7
Unemployment and Inflation	8	8
Macroeconomic Equilibrium: Aggregate Demand and Supply	9	9
Aggregate Expenditures	10	10
Appendix: An Algebraic Model of Aggregate Expenditures	10A	10A
Income and Expenditures Equilibrium	11	11
Appendix: An Algebraic Model of Income and Expenditures Equilibrium	11A	11A
Macroeconomic Policy		
Fiscal Policy	12	12
Appendix: An Algebraic Examination of the Balanced-Budget Change in Fiscal Policy	12A	12A
Money and Banking	13	13
Monetary Policy	14	14
Macroeconomic Policy: Tradeoffs, Expectations, Credibility, and Sources of Business Cycles	15	15
Macroeconomic Viewpoints: New Keynesian, Monetarist, and New Classical	16	16
Macroeconomic Links Between Countries	17	17
Economic Growth and Development		
Economic Growth	18	18
Development Economics	19	19
Issues in International Trade and Finance		
World Trade Equilibrium	20	35
International Trade Restrictions	21	36
Exchange-Rate Systems and Practices	22	37

Using the Study Guide

What's in the Study Guide

All Study Guide chapters are organized the same way; each includes the following:

- *Fundamental Questions* are repeated from the text chapter and are briefly answered. The questions and their answers give you an overview of the chapter's main points.
- *Key Terms* from the chapter are listed to remind you of new vocabulary presented in the chapter.
- A *Quick-Check Quiz* focuses on vocabulary and key concepts from the chapter. These multiple-choice questions allow you to see whether you understand the material and are ready to move on or whether you need to review some of the text before continuing.
- *Practice Questions and Problems* provide in-depth coverage of important ideas from the chapter and give you the opportunity to apply concepts and work out problems.
- The *Thinking About and Applying* section covers one or more topics in greater depth and will help you learn to apply economics to real-world situations. This section will also show you how various economic concepts are related to one another and, as a result, will help you to think economically.
- *Homework Problems* may be assigned by your instructor and can be carefully removed from the Study Guide and handed in if requested. Answers to the Homework Problems are included in the Instructor's Resource Manual.
- The *Answers* section may be the most important part of the Study Guide. Answers to all questions and problems are provided with explanations of how to arrive at the correct answer. In many cases, explanations are given for what you did wrong if you arrived at certain wrong answers.
- *Sample Tests* appear at the end of each Study Guide part and provide students with a number of questions resembling test bank questions. Taking the Sample Tests will help you determine whether you're really prepared for exams.

How to Study Economics

No one ever said that economics is an easy subject, and many students tell us it is the most challenging subject they have studied. Despite the challenge, most students manage to learn a great deal of economics, and we're sure you can too. But doing well in economics requires a commitment from you to *keep up* your studying and to *study properly*.

Keeping up: Although there may be subjects that can be learned reasonably well by cramming the night before an exam, economics is *not* one of them. Learning economics is like building a house: first you need to lay a solid foundation, and then you must carefully build the walls. To master economics, you must first learn the early concepts, vocabulary, and ideas; if you do not, the later ones will not make any sense.

Studying properly: Listening in class, reading the text, and going through the Study Guide are not really enough to learn economics—you must also organize your studying. The textbook and the Study Guide have been designed to help you organize your thinking and your studying. Used together, they will help you learn.

We recommend following these steps for each chapter:

1. Skim the text chapter before your instructor discusses it in class to get a general idea of what the chapter covers.
   a. Read through the Fundamental Questions and the Preview to get a sense of what is to come.
   b. Skim through the chapter, looking only at the section headings and the section Recaps.
   c. Read the chapter Summary. By this point, you should have a good idea of what topics the chapter covers.

2. Read the text chapter and Study Guide one section at a time. Both the text and the Study Guide break down each chapter into several sections so that you will not need to juggle too many new ideas at once.
   a. Read through one section of the text chapter. Pay attention to the marginal notes containing definitions of Key Terms, highlights of important concepts, and Fundamental Questions.
   b. Study the section Recap. If parts of the Recap are not clear to you, review those parts of the section.
   c. In the Study Guide, read the answers to the Fundamental Questions covered in the section you are studying.
   d. Take the Quick-Check Quiz for the section. Write your answers on a separate sheet of paper so that you can use the quiz again later. If you missed any questions, review the applicable section in the text.
   e. Work through the Practice Questions and Problems for the section, writing your answers in the spaces provided. Check your answers, and then review what you missed. Read through the explanations in the Answers section, even if you answered the question or problem correctly.
   f. If there are ideas that are not clear or problems you do not understand, talk to your instructor. Economics instructors are interested in helping their students.

3. Review the chapter as a whole. Although each section should initially be studied alone, you will need to put the pieces together.
   a. Read through the chapter again, paying special attention to the Fundamental Questions, the section Recaps, the Economic Insight boxes, and the chapter Summary. If you like to outline chapters on paper, now is the time to do so. The section headings and subheadings provide an ideal framework for outlining the text.
   b. In the Study Guide, read through the Fundamental Questions and their answers.
   c. Review the list of Key Terms. Write down the definition of each one at this point, and check your definitions against the marginal notes or the glossary. Study any terms you missed.
   d. Work through the Exercises at the end of the text chapter.
   e. Read through the Economically Speaking section in the text to see how the real world contains examples of economic thinking.
   f. Work through the Thinking About and Applying section of the Study Guide.
   g. Complete the Homework section of the Study Guide and hand it in if your instructor requests it; otherwise, save it for exam review.

4. Ideally, studying for exams should be a repetition of steps 1, 2, and 3. However, economists recognize the existence of opportunity costs, and you have many other things to do with your time in addition to studying economics. If you cannot study for an exam as thoroughly as you should, you can use some techniques to help refresh your memory. These techniques assume that you *did* study the materials at least once (there is no magic way to learn economics without doing some serious studying).
   a. Review the Fundamental Questions, the section Recaps, the Key Terms lists, and the chapter Summaries in the text.
   b. Read again the Fundamental Questions and their answers in the Study Guide.
   c. Take the Quick-Check Quiz again, writing your answers in the Study Guide this time. Questions that you miss will direct you to the areas you need to study most.

d. Take a Sample Test, found at the end of each part in the Study Guide. These questions are likely to resemble closely the questions you'll see on your exam. They cover one part's worth of chapters in one test, because you are likely to be tested this way. Check your answers against the answer key; review the appropriate sections of the text if you answer any of the questions incorrectly.

If you follow these suggestions, you are sure to meet with success in your study of economics.

Use the Text as a System

The text presents all the key concepts of economics. In addition it explains how people use these concepts—in business, in government, and in ordinary households. In both the world of theory and the real world of application, knowing the relationships of ideas is crucial. No one can move about in either world without knowing the pathways that relationships form. The features of the text provide these pathways; taking advantage of them will help your studying immensely. The *Fundamental Questions* point to main issues and help you categorize details, examples, and theories accordingly. Colors in the *graphs* help you classify curves and see relationships to data in the *tables*. The *Recaps* reinforce overarching ideas; they orient you before you go on to the next big section. The *system of referencing* sections and headings by number will help you group concepts and also keep track of what level of ideas you are working with. If you use the features of the text, the text can be more than an authoritative source of information—it can be a system for comprehension.

Take More than One View

As you work through the chapters of this book, you will examine in close-up each particular concept. Yet to understand the material and to get a feel for how economists think, you need to have a second point of view too—an overview. Keeping yourself "up above it" at the same time you are "down in it" will help you remember what you are reading much better and also help you understand and use the concepts you learn more easily. Taking more than one view of your subject has another benefit; it is an ingredient of good critical thinking.

J.E.C.
J.L.W.

Chapter 1

ECONOMICS: THE WORLD AROUND YOU

FUNDAMENTAL QUESTIONS

1. What is economics?

    Economics is the study of how people choose to allocate scarce **resources** to satisfy their unlimited wants. There are several words in this definition that should be emphasized. First, people allocate *scarce* resources. If there was enough of a resource to go around so that everyone could have as much as he or she wanted, there would be no need to allocate.

    The definition states that people have *unlimited wants*. Notice that it says *wants*, not *needs*. People *act* on the basis of their wants, not necessarily on the basis of their needs. (Otherwise they would not buy strawberry sundaes.) If each of us made a list right now of the top ten things we would like to have and our fairy godmother popped out of the air and gave us what we wanted, most of us immediately would find that there are ten *more* things we'd like to have. Because resources are scarce and wants are unlimited, economics studies the best way to allocate resources so that none are wasted.

2. What is the economic way of thinking?

    The economic way of thinking focuses on **positive,** as opposed to **normative, analysis,** and applies the five-step **scientific method:** (1) recognize the problem, (2) cut away unnecessary detail by making **assumptions,** (3) develop a **model** or story, (4) make predictions, and (5) test the model.

Key Terms

scarcity
economic good
free good
economic bad
resources
factors of production
inputs
land

labor
capital
rational self-interest
positive analysis
normative analysis
scientific method
theory
model

assumptions
ceteris paribus
test
fallacy of composition
association as causation
microeconomics
macroeconomics

Quick-Check Quiz

Section 1: The Definition of Economics

1. Which of the following is *not* an economic good?
   a. wine
   b. bicycles
   c. refrigerators
   d. air pollution
   e. education

2. Which of the following is *not* one of the three categories of resources?
   a. land
   b. automobiles
   c. capital
   d. labor
   e. None of the above are categories for resources.

3. The payment for capital is called
   a. rent.
   b. wages.
   c. salaries.
   d. interest.
   e. profit.

4. If an item is scarce,
   a. it is not an economic good.
   b. at a zero price the amount of the item that people want is less than the amount that is available.
   c. there is not enough of the item to satisfy everyone who wants it.
   d. there is enough to satisfy wants even at a zero price.
   e. it must be a resource as opposed to an input.

5. Which of the following is a free good?
   a. clean air
   b. water from a river
   c. education
   d. golf lessons
   e. None of the above is a free good.

6. The payment for land is called
   a. wages and salaries.
   b. rent.
   c. interest.
   d. profit.
   e. financial capital.

7. Rational self-interest
   a. dictates that individuals with the same information will make identical choices.
   b. means that people are completely selfish.
   c. explains why people give money to charitable organizations.
   d. explains why all drivers wear seat belts.
   e. means that people choose options that they think will give them the smallest amount of satisfaction.

Section 2: The Economic Approach

1. Analysis that does not impose the value judgments of one individual on the decision of others is called _____ analysis.
   a. positive
   b. normative
   c. economic
   d. noneconomic
   e. the scientific method of

2. Which of the following is *not* one of the five steps in the scientific method?
   a. Recognize the problem.
   b. Make assumptions in order to cut away unnecessary detail.
   c. Develop a model of the problem.
   d. Test the hypothesis.
   e. Make a value judgment based on the results of the hypothesis test.

3. If an individual decides to save more, he or she can save more. Therefore, if society as a whole decides to save more, it will be able to save more. This reasoning is faulty and as such is an example of
   a. *ceteris paribus*.
   b. the fallacy of composition.
   c. the interpretation of association as causation.
   d. the scientific method.
   e. none of the above—this reasoning is not faulty.

4. Tim has noticed that every time he washes his car in the morning, it rains that afternoon. Because he believes he can cause it to rain by washing his car, he has decided to sell his services to farmers in drought-stricken areas. This reasoning is mistaken and as such is an example of
   a. *ceteris paribus*.
   b. the fallacy of composition.
   c. the mistaken interpretation of association as causation.
   d. the scientific method.
   e. none of the above—Tim's reasoning is not faulty.

5. Which of the following is a normative statement?
   a. Lower interest rates encourage people to borrow.
   b. Higher prices for cigarettes discourage people from buying cigarettes.
   c. If the price of eggs fell, people probably would buy more eggs.
   d. There should be a higher tax on cigarettes, alcohol, and other "sin" items to discourage people from buying them.
   e. A higher interest rate encourages people to save more.

6. Microeconomics includes the study of
   a. how an individual firm decides the price of its product.
   b. inflation in the United States.
   c. how much output will be produced in the U.S. economy.
   d. how many workers will be unemployed in the U.S. economy.
   e. how the U.S. banking system works.

Practice Questions and Problems

Section 1: The Definition of Economics

1. _____ exists when less of something is available than people want at a zero price.

2. Any good that is scarce is a(n) _____ good.

3. If there is enough of a good available at a zero price to satisfy wants, the good is called a(n) _____ good.

4. A good that people will pay to have less of is called an economic _____ .

5. People use scarce resources to satisfy their _____ wants.

6. _____ means that people make the choices that they think will give them the greatest amount of satisfaction.

7. List the three categories of resources and the payments associated with each.
   _____
   _____
   _____

8. _____ includes all natural resources, such as minerals, timber, and water, as well as the land itself.

9. _____ refers to the physical and intellectual services of people.

10. _____ is a manufactured or created product used solely to produce goods and services.

11. _____ capital refers to the money value of capital as represented by stocks and bonds.

12. Resources also are called _____ or _____ .
13. _____ are nonphysical products.
14. Economists believe human beings are _____ , not selfish.
15. What is economics?

_____

_____

_____

_____

Section 2: The Economic Approach

1. Analysis that does not impose the value judgments of one individual on the decisions of others is called _____ analysis.
2. _____ analysis involves imposing value judgments on the decisions of others.
3. Economists generally agree on the _____ aspects of economics.
4. List the five steps in the scientific method.

_____

_____

_____

_____

_____

5. The role of models and _____ is to reduce the complexity of a problem.
6. _____ means "other things being equal."
7. A theory, or _____ , is a simplification that is used to explain an event.
8. _____ is the study of economics at the level of the individual economic entity.
9. The _____ is the error of attributing what applies to one to the case of many.
10. The mistaken interpretation of _____ occurs when unrelated or coincidental events that occur at about the same time are believed to have a cause-and-effect relationship.
11. The outcome of positive analysis _____ as society's norms change.
12. The study of the economy as a whole is called _____ .

Thinking About and Applying Economics: The World Around You

I. The Relationship Between Speed Limits and Highway Deaths

In twenty-two of the thirty-eight states that chose to raise the speed limit on rural highways, highway deaths jumped 46 percent between May and July 1986. Former Transportation Committee Chairman James Howard attributed the increase in deaths to the higher speed limit. Can you think of any other reasons that highway deaths might have increased? If states that did not increase rural speed limits experienced a similar increase in highway deaths, what common mistake might Chairman Howard have made?

II. Scarce Parking in Wichita?

The following is an excerpt from the *Wichita Eagle:*

> It's become part of Wichita lore. Folks in these parts are nutty about parking.
> They want it free. They want it at the front door of wherever they're going. They refuse to look for a parking space anywhere for more than eight or 10 seconds. And they think the downtown Wichita parking situation is horrible.
> The fact is, there's plenty of parking in the city's core. About 20,000 people work downtown. There are almost 19,000 parking spaces. That nearly 1-to-1 ratio is better than other cities in the region such as Oklahoma City, and it's just as good as Topeka. And the average distance a person has to walk is about a block. That's better than similar-sized cities.

The editorial laments that people don't go downtown for activities because they think they'll have trouble parking and comments on a new report by the Metropolitan Area Planning Commission.

Relying on the information in the editorial, discuss whether parking spaces can be considered a scarce resource in downtown Wichita.

Copyright © Houghton Mifflin Company. All rights reserved.

III. Resource and Income Flows

Complete the figure below.

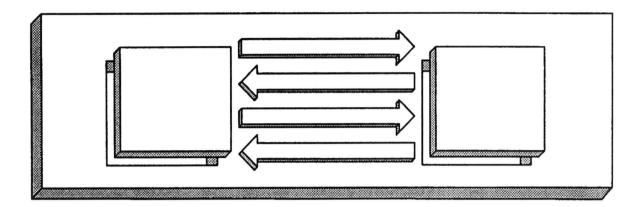

Chapter 1   Homework Problem

Name _____

A recent edition of the *Wall Street Journal* reported that some states were subsidizing Amtrak passenger trains so that state residents would have railroad transportation available.

The state of Oregon, however, had just decided to stop subsidizing a train between Eugene and Portland, Oregon, even though that meant the train would stop running. State Senator Greg Walden explained the decision this way: "Subsidizing rail passengers isn't as high a priority as kids' education and keeping criminals behind bars."

Using the concepts you learned in Chapter 1, explain the economic logic underlying Senator Walden's comments.

If your instructor assigns this problem, write your answer above, then tear out this page and hand it in.

Copyright © Houghton Mifflin Company. All rights reserved.

Answers

Quick-Check Quiz

Section 1: The Definition of Economics

1. d; 2. b; 3. d; 4. c; 5. e; 6. b; 7. c
If you missed any of these questions, you should go back and review Section 1 in Chapter 1.

Section 2: The Economic Approach

1. a; 2. e; 3. b; 4. c; 5. d; 6. a
If you missed any of these questions, you should go back and review Section 2 in Chapter 1.

Practice Questions and Problems

Section 1: The Definition of Economics

1. Scarcity
2. economic
3. free
4. bad
5. unlimited
6. Rational self-interest
7. land; rent
   labor; wages
   capital; interest
8. Land
9. Labor
10. Capital
11. Financial
12. factors of production; inputs
13. Services
14. self-interested
15. Economics is the study of how people choose to use their scarce resources to attempt to satisfy their unlimited wants.

Section 2: The Economic Approach

1. positive
2. Normative
3. positive
4. Recognize the problem.
   Make assumptions in order to cut away unnecessary detail.
   Develop a model of the problem.
   Make predictions.
   Test the model.
5. assumptions
6. *Ceteris paribus*
7. model

8. Microeconomics
9. fallacy of composition
10. association as causation
11. does not vary
12. macroeconomics

Thinking About and Applying Economics: The World Around You

I. The Relationship Between Speed Limits and Highway Deaths

Other factors that might have increased highway deaths include the following:

1. Has there been an increase in population? It seems reasonable to expect more accidents as congestion increases.
2. Are Americans buying more smaller cars? If so, auto deaths would be expected to increase because smaller cars provide less protection in a crash.
3. Has there been an increase in the number of people drinking (or otherwise impaired) and driving? If so, we would expect an increase in the number of traffic fatalities no matter what the speed limit was.

Perhaps you can think of other factors that might account for the increase in traffic fatalities that Howard attributed to the higher speed limit. If Howard had wrongly attributed the higher death toll to the higher speed limit, he would have been mistaking association for causation.

II. Scarce Parking in Wichita?

If there is not enough of an item to satisfy everyone who wants it at a zero price, then an item is scarce. If people want parking at the front door of wherever they are going and have to walk, on average, about a block, parking is scarce.

III. Resource and Income Flows

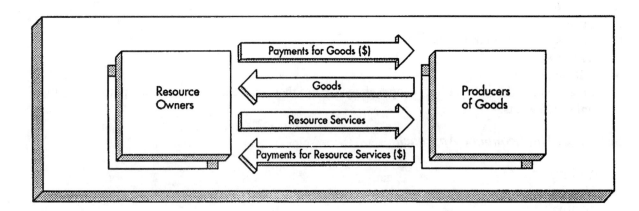

Appendix to Chapter 1

WORKING WITH GRAPHS

Summary

Most people are visually oriented: they are better able to understand things that they can "picture." The pictures that economists use to explain concepts are called *graphs*.

There are three commonly used types of graphs: the line graph, the bar graph, and the pie graph. The pie graph (or chart) is used to show the relative magnitude of the parts that make up a whole. Line graphs and bar graphs are used to show the relationship between two variables. One of the variables, the **independent variable,** has values that do not depend on the values of other variables. The values of **dependent variables** do depend on the values of other variables.

When two variables move in the same direction together, their relationship is called a **direct,** or **positive, relationship,** and the **slope** of the line or curve relating the two variables will be positive. When two variables move together but in opposite directions, their relationship is an **inverse, or negative, relationship,** and the slope of the line or curve relating the two variables will be negative. A curve **shifts** when, for each combination of variables measured on the horizontal and vertical axes, one of the variables changes by a certain amount while the other variable remains the same. Shifts occur when variables other than those on the axes are allowed to change.

The slope of a line is the ratio of the rise to the run. The slope of a straight line is the same at all points on the line. The slope of a curve that is not a straight line changes at every point on the curve. We can find the maximum or minimum point on a curve by finding where the slope of the curve is equal to zero. Where a slope goes from positive to zero to negative, a maximum occurs. Where a slope goes from negative to zero to positive, a minimum occurs.

Key Terms

independent variable   positive relationship   slope
dependent variable   inverse relationship
direct relationship   negative relationship

Practice Questions and Problems

1. The owner of a business that sells home heating oil has noticed that the amount of heating oil sold increases as the temperature outside decreases. Heating oil is the _____ (dependent, independent) variable. The relationship between the two variables is _____ (direct,

inverse), and the slope of the line will be _____ (positive, negative). Use the graph below to show the nature of the relationship between home heating oil sales and outside temperature. Be sure to label your axes.

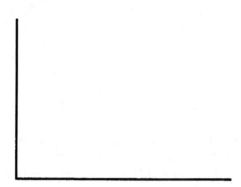

2. The slope of a straight-line curve is the same at all points. True or false?
3. The table below shows the relationship between the price of milk and the quantity of milk that dairy farmers are willing to offer for sale. This relationship is _____ (direct, inverse). The slope of the line will be _____ (positive, negative). Plot the curves on the graph below.

Price of Milk	Quantity of Milk Offered for Sale
$ .50	0
.75	2
1.00	4
1.25	6
1.50	8

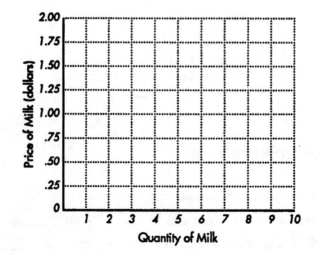

4. Consider the relationship between household spending (consumption) and national income on the graph below and answer the following questions.

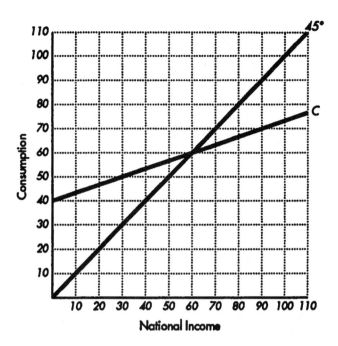

a. The relationship between consumption and income is _____ (direct, inverse).
b. What is the slope of the line? _____
   The intercept? _____
c. What is the equation for this line? _____
d. At what point does consumption equal income? _____

5. The graph below shows the percentages of income that the King family spends, pays in taxes, and saves. What kind of graph is this? _____

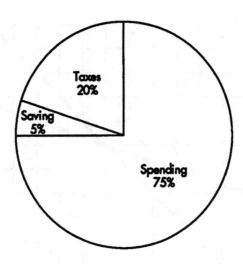

6. The table below shows the relationship between the quantity of airplanes built at a production plant in Wichita and the average cost per airplane. Make up a set of figures that shows that a minimum average cost occurs at 40,000 airplanes.

Quantity of Airplanes	Average Cost per Airplane
10,000	_____
20,000	_____
30,000	_____
40,000	_____
50,000	_____
60,000	_____
70,000	_____
80,000	_____

7. The demand for Mardi's Tacos in Hammondville is given by the equation $P = \$2.00 - .02Q$, where P is the price of tacos in dollars and Q is the quantity demanded of tacos. Plot the demand for Mardi's Tacos on the graph below.

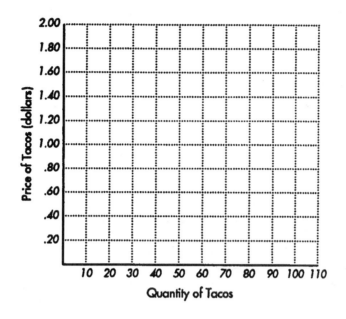

The relationship between price and quantity demanded is _____ (direct, inverse).

8. The supply for tacos in Hammondville is given by the equation $P = \$.40 + .005Q$, where P is the price of tacos in dollars and Q is the quantity supplied of tacos. Plot the supply of tacos on the graph below. Label the supply S.

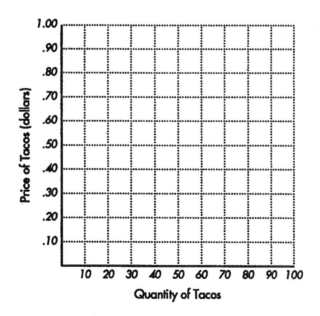

The relationship between price and quantity supplied is _____ (direct, inverse).

18 / Chapter 1

9. Several taco sellers in Hammondville have closed down, changing the equation for the supply of tacos to $P = \$.60 + .005Q$. Plot the new supply on the graph above and label the line S_1.

At each price, sellers will produce a _____ (larger, smaller) quantity than before.

Answers

1. dependent; inverse; negative

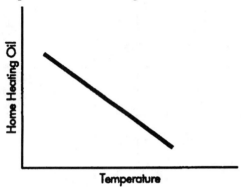

2. true
3. direct; positive

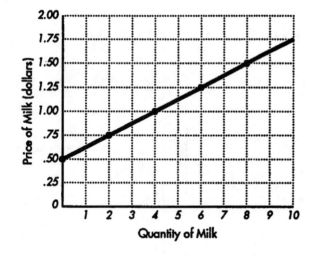

4. a. direct
   b. $\frac{1}{3}$; 40
   c. $C = 40 + \frac{1}{3}Y$
   d. 60
5. pie chart

6. There are many possible solutions. The numbers need to decrease until you reach the quantity 40,000 and increase thereafter. Here is one possible solution:

Quantity of Airplanes	Average Cost per Airplane
10,000	$40
20,000	30
30,000	20
40,000	10
50,000	20
60,000	30
70,000	40
80,000	50

7. inverse

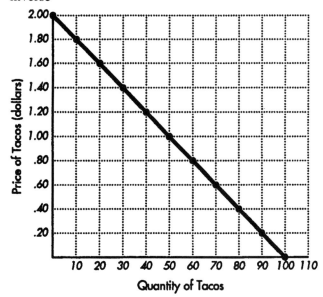

8. direct

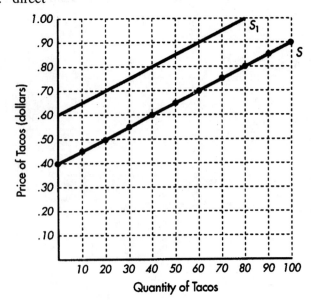

9. smaller

Chapter 2

CHOICE, OPPORTUNITY COSTS, AND SPECIALIZATION

FUNDAMENTAL QUESTIONS

1. What are opportunity costs? Are they part of the economic way of thinking?

   The **opportunity cost** of something is what you need to give up in order to get it. For example, if you would prefer to be sleeping now instead of studying economics, the opportunity cost of studying is the sleep you could be enjoying. Opportunity costs are a key element in the way economists look at the world.

2. What is a production possibilities curve?

   A **production possibilities curve** shows all the combinations of output that could be produced with a given set of resources, assuming that the resources are fully and efficiently used.

3. How are specialization and opportunity costs related?

   Resources tend to be specialized—that is, better at producing one kind of good or service than another. For example, suppose that Vickeryland can produce either guns or butter. If Vickeryland throws all its resources into producing guns, some resources will not be good at producing guns. If some cows are switched over from making guns to making butter, they will probably be much better at making butter than at making guns. Vickeryland will gain a lot of butter and lose very few guns. But as more and more butter is produced, eventually some resources that were very good at making guns will have to be switched into making butter. If these resources are very good at making guns and not so good at making butter, Vickeryland will give up lots of guns and gain very little butter. When you give up an increasing number of guns to get each additional unit of butter, the opportunity cost of each additional unit of butter increases. If resources were equally adaptable among uses, the opportunity cost of each additional unit of butter would remain constant. The **marginal opportunity cost** would be constant.

4. Why does specialization occur?

   It pays to specialize whenever opportunity costs are *different*. Two parties can specialize and then trade, which makes both parties better off. Even if one person or nation does something more efficiently than another in the production of a good or service, it does not mean that that person or nation should produce that good or service. Specialization occurs as a result of **comparative**, not absolute, **advantage**. Specialization according to comparative advantage minimizes opportunity costs.

5. What are the benefits of trade?

If both parties specialize according to comparative advantage, trading enables them to acquire more of the goods and services they want.

Key Terms

opportunity costs
tradeoff
marginal
marginal cost

marginal benefit
production possibilities curve
   (PPC)
marginal opportunity cost

comparative advantage

Quick-Check Quiz

Section 1: Opportunity Costs

1. Janine is an accountant who makes $30,000 a year. Robert is a college student who makes $8,000 a year. All other things being equal, who is more likely to stand in a long line to get a concert ticket?
   a. Janine, because her opportunity cost is lower
   b. Janine, because her opportunity cost is higher
   c. Robert, because his opportunity cost is lower
   d. Robert, because his opportunity cost is higher
   e. Janine, because she is better able to afford the cost of the ticket

2. Which of the following statements is false?
   a. At points inside the production possibilities curve, resources are not being fully or efficiently used.
   b. Points outside the production possibilities curve represent combinations that are not attainable with the current level of resources.
   c. If an individual is producing a combination on his or her production possibilities curve, in order to get more of one good, he or she must give up some of the other.
   d. As a nation obtains more resources, its production possibilities curve shifts outward.
   e. The "guns or butter" decision is a rare example of a costless choice.

3. At point A on a production possibilities curve, there are 50 tons of corn and 60 tons of wheat. At point B on the same curve, there are 40 tons of corn and 80 tons of wheat. If the farmer is currently at point A, the opportunity cost of moving to point B is
   a. 10 tons of corn.
   b. 20 tons of wheat.
   c. 1 ton of corn.
   d. 2 tons of wheat.
   e. 40 tons of corn.

4. President Johnson thought it was possible to spend more resources in Vietnam without giving up consumer goods at home. President Johnson must have believed that the
   a. American economy was operating at top efficiency.
   b. American economy was operating at a point inside its production possibilities curve.
   c. American economy was operating at a point on its production possibilities curve.
   d. American economy was operating at a point outside its production possibilities curve.
   e. production possibilities curve would shift in as the war progressed.

Use the table below to answer questions 5 through 8.

Combination	Clothing	Food
A	0	110
B	10	105
C	20	95
D	30	80
E	40	60
F	50	35
G	60	0

5. If the economy currently is producing at point B, the opportunity cost of 10 additional units of clothing is
   a. 25 units of food.
   b. 5 units of food.
   c. 10 units of food.
   d. 35 units of food.
   e. 3.5 units of food.

6. If the economy currently is producing at point F, the opportunity cost of 10 additional units of clothing is
   a. 25 units of food.
   b. 5 units of food.
   c. 10 units of food.
   d. 35 units of food.
   e. 3.5 units of food.

7. A combination of 20 units of clothing and 80 units of food is
   a. unattainable.
   b. inefficient.
   c. possible by giving up 15 units of food.
   d. possible if the economy obtains more resources.
   e. possible if an improvement in technology shifts the production possibilities curve inward.

8. A combination of 50 units of clothing and 70 units of food
   a. is inefficient.
   b. is obtainable by giving up 35 units of food.
   c. does not fully utilize resources.
   d. is unattainable.
   e. is possible if an improvement in technology shifts the production possibilities curve inward.

Section 2. Specialization and Trade

Use the table below to answer questions 1 through 4.

	Alpha		Beta	
Combination	Beef	Microchips	Beef	Microchips
A	0	200	0	300
B	25	150	25	225
C	50	100	50	150
D	75	50	75	75
E	100	0	100	0

1. The opportunity cost of a microchip in Alpha is _____ unit(s) of beef, and the opportunity cost of a microchip in Beta is _____ unit(s) of beef. The opportunity cost of a unit of beef is _____ unit(s) of microchips in Alpha and _____ unit(s) of microchips in Beta.
   a. 1/3; 1/2; 3; 2
   b. 2; 3; 1/2; 1/3
   c. 1/2; 1/3; 2; 3
   d. 3; 2; 1/3; 1/2
   e. 1/2; 3; 1/3; 2

2. Alpha has a comparative advantage in _____, and Beta has a comparative advantage in _____. Alpha should produce _____, and Beta should produce _____.
   a. beef; microchips; beef; microchips
   b. beef; microchips; microchips; beef
   c. microchips; beef; microchips; beef
   d. microchips; beef; beef; microchips
   e. There is no basis for specialization and trade between these two countries because Beta can produce just as much beef and more microchips than Alpha.

3. Which of the following statements is true?
   a. Alpha can produce more beef than Beta.
   b. Alpha can produce more microchips than Beta.
   c. Beta can produce more beef than Alpha.
   d. Beta can produce more microchips than Alpha.
   e. Alpha can produce both more beef and more microchips than Beta.

4. Which of the following statements is true?
   a. Individuals, firms, and nations specialize in the production of the good or service that has the highest opportunity cost.
   b. An individual, firm, or nation first must be able to produce more of a good or service before it can have a comparative advantage in the production of that good or service.
   c. Comparative advantage exists whenever one person, firm, or nation engaging in an activity incurs the same costs as some other individual, firm, or nation.
   d. An individual, firm, or nation specializes according to comparative advantage.
   e. An individual, firm, or nation should trade with parties that have the same opportunity costs for the goods and services produced.

Practice Questions and Problems

Section 1: Opportunity Costs

1. _____ are forgone opportunities or forgone benefits.
2. People purchase items and participate in activities that _____ (maximize, minimize) opportunity costs.
3. The opportunity cost of an activity is the _____-valued alternative that must be forgone.
4. A(n) _____ is a graph that illustrates the tradeoffs facing a society.
5. A point that lies _____ the production possibilities curve indicates that resources are not being fully or efficiently used.
6. Points outside the production possibilities curve represent combinations of goods and services that are _____.
7. A new semiconductor chip is designed that can deliver more computing power for less cost. As a result, the production possibilities curve will shift _____.
8. A society that prohibits certain groups of people from working (for example, women, children, and blacks) is producing at a point _____ its production possibilities curve.
9. It is possible to produce more of one good without giving up units of another good if a society is producing _____ its production possibilities curve.
10. It is not possible to produce more of one good without giving up units of another good if a society is producing _____ its production possibilities curve.
11. Opportunity cost is a(n) _____ (objective, subjective) concept.

12. Use the graph below to answer the following questions.

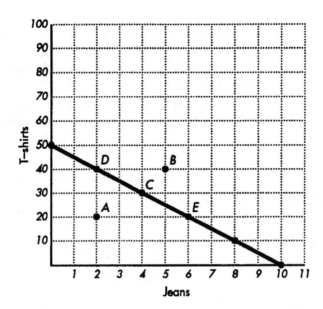

   a. Point A represents a combination of T-shirts and jeans that is _____.

   b. Point B represents a combination of T-shirts and jeans that is _____.

13. Mardi and Martin paid $20 each to see a new foreign film. Halfway through the film, Mardi got disgusted and wanted to leave. Martin insisted that they stay because they had paid $40 to see the film and he wanted to get his money's worth out of it. Can you offer them some economic insight to help them resolve the argument?

   _____
   _____
   _____
   _____

14. Roger Southby was almost finished with his accounting degree when he discovered the wonderful world of marketing. Roger would like to switch majors but does not want to waste the years of schooling he already has. What can you tell Roger to help him make his decision?

   _____
   _____
   _____
   _____

Section 2: Specialization and Trade

1. The _____ is the amount of one good or service that must be given up to obtain one additional unit of another good or service.

2. It is in your best interest to specialize where your opportunity costs are _____ (highest, constant, lowest).
3. A nation has a comparative advantage in those activities in which it has _____ (the highest, constant, the lowest) opportunity costs.
4. People specialize according to their _____ advantage.
5. If a country specializes in the production of goods and services in which it has a comparative advantage, it can trade with other countries and enjoy a combination of goods and services that lies _____ its production possibilities curve.
6. Use the table below to answer the following questions.

	Robinson Crusoe		Man Friday	
Combination	Coconuts	Fish	Coconuts	Fish
A	5	0	10	0
B	4	1	8	1
C	3	2	6	2
D	2	3	4	3
E	1	4	2	4
F	0	5	0	5

a. The marginal opportunity costs for Robinson Crusoe and Friday are _____ (increasing, constant, decreasing).
b. The marginal opportunity cost of a coconut is _____ fish for Robinson Crusoe and _____ fish for Friday.
c. The marginal opportunity cost of a fish is _____ coconut(s) for Robinson Crusoe and _____ coconut(s) for Friday.
d. Robinson Crusoe has a comparative advantage in _____, and Friday has a comparative advantage in _____.
e. Robinson Crusoe should specialize in producing _____, and Friday should specialize in producing _____.

f. Plot Robinson Crusoe's and Friday's production possibilities curves on the graphs below.

Friday's Production Possibilities Curve

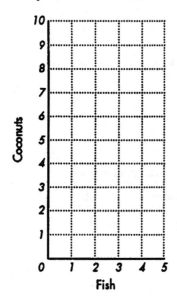

Robinson Crusoe's Production Possibilities Curve

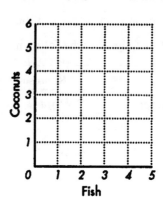

g. Without specialization, Robinson Crusoe would choose to produce 4 coconuts and 1 fish. Without specialization, Friday would choose to produce 4 coconuts and 3 fish.

Suppose they specialize according to comparative advantage and agree to trade in a ratio of 3 coconuts for 2 fish. Friday keeps 4 coconuts and trades _____ coconut(s) for _____ fish. Robinson Crusoe keeps 1 fish and trades _____ fish for _____ coconut(s).

With specialization and trade, Robinson Crusoe now has _____ coconut(s) and _____ fish. Label this point R on Crusoe's graph. Friday now has _____ coconuts and _____ fish. Label this point S on Friday's graph. Notice that both R and S are outside the original production possibilities curves, so specialization and trade enable both parties to have more fish and coconuts than they had before.

Robinson Crusoe's gain from trade is(are)_____; Friday's gain from trade is(are)_____.

7. Use the graph below to answer the following questions.

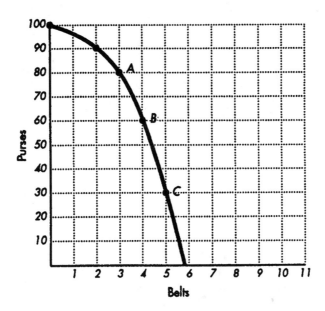

a. If an individual currently is producing the combination of purses and belts at point A, the marginal opportunity cost of 1 belt is _____ purse(s).

b. If an individual currently is producing the combination of purses and belts at Point B, the marginal opportunity cost of an additional belt is _____ purse(s).

c. The marginal opportunity cost is _____ (increasing, constant, decreasing).

d. If an individual currently is producing the combination of purses and belts at point B, the marginal opportunity cost of an additional purse is approximately _____ belt(s).

e. If an individual currently is producing the combination of purses and belts at point A, the marginal opportunity cost of an additional purse is approximately _____ belt(s).

8. Use the graph below to answer the following questions.

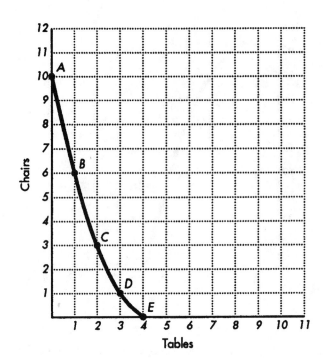

a. If an individual currently is producing the combination of chairs and tables at point A, the marginal opportunity cost of an additional table is _____ chair(s).

b. If an individual currently is producing the combination of chairs and tables at point B, the marginal opportunity cost of an additional table is _____ chair(s).

c. The marginal opportunity cost is _____ (increasing, constant, decreasing).

d. If an individual currently is producing the combination of chairs and tables at point C, the marginal opportunity cost of an additional chair is approximately _____ table(s).

e. If an individual currently is producing the combination of chairs and tables at point B, the marginal opportunity cost of an additional chair is approximately _____ table(s).

9. A straight-line production possibilities curve illustrates _____ (increasing, constant, decreasing) marginal opportunity costs.

10. A bowed-out production possibilities curve illustrates _____ (increasing, constant, decreasing) marginal opportunity costs.

11. A bowed-in production possibilities curve illustrates _____ (increasing, constant, decreasing) marginal opportunity costs.

12. Because resources tend to be specialized, the production possibilities curve is likely to be _____ (bowed in, bowed out, a straight line), indicating that marginal opportunity costs are _____ (increasing, decreasing, constant).

Thinking About and Applying Choice, Opportunity Costs, and Specialization

I. Opportunity Costs

Marc and Shelly Colby are a couple in their thirties with two children. Marc owns his own company and makes $150,000 a year, and Shelly has been responsible for raising their children. Now that the children are in school all day, Shelly is considering going back to school to finish her degree. She estimates that tuition will cost about $3,000. Marc likes carpentry and is thinking about going to a special school for a year to learn more about it. He estimates that the school will cost about $1,500. After they discuss it, they decide that Shelly should go back to school but that it costs too much for Marc to go to carpentry school. Explain.

II. More on Opportunity Costs

Mr. Safi and Mr. Nohr are neighbors. Mr. Safi makes $200 an hour as a consultant, while Mr. Nohr makes $10 an hour as an aerobics instructor. The men are complaining that the grass on their lawns has grown so fast due to recent rainy weather that it is hard to keep their lawns looking nice. Mr. Safi comments that he hires a neighbor's child to cut his grass "because it is too expensive for me to cut it myself." Explain Mr. Safi's comment.

Chapter 2   Homework Problems

Name _____

1. If you spent all evening next Friday studying economics, what would be your opportunity cost?

2. What do economists call a graph showing the different combinations of two products that a society can produce with given resources and technology?

3. Bob and Bill are woodcarvers. In a week of work, Bob can carve *either* one bird or two bookends. In a week of work, Bill can carve *either* two birds or six bookends.

   a. What is Bob's opportunity cost of making one bird?
   b. What is Bill's opportunity cost of making one bird?
   c. Does Bob or Bill have a comparative advantage in making birds? Why?

4. Bill is thinking about asking Bob to work with him in a woodcarving partnership. Since Bill can make more birds in a week than Bob can, and Bill can also make more bookends in a week than Bob can, why would Bill want to work with Bob?

5. The Longs and the Shorts are neighbors. Both husbands work full-time during the day, and both families have two small children. Mrs. Long stays at home during the day to care for her children, but Mrs. Short works full-time during the day and sends her children to day care. The Short family has a higher income, primarily because Mrs. Short works outside the home.

   a. There are two grocery stores near the Longs and the Shorts. One is a "no-frills" store that claims to have the lowest prices in town. The aisles are not marked, and specific items are hard to find. The other is a "superstore." Its prices are higher, but it is easy to find specific items, and the same store also offers dry cleaning, banking, photo developing, a pharmacy, and postal services. Which family is more likely to shop at the "no-frills" store? Use your economic reasoning to explain your answer.

   b. One family clips cents-off coupons from newspapers and magazines, watches for sales, and buys whatever brand is least expensive. The other family does not clip coupons and usually buys its favorite brands, whether on sale or not. Which family clips coupons and buys sale items? Explain why.

   c. Which family is more likely to buy milk and other small items at convenience stores? Why?

If your instructor assigns these problems, write your answers above, then tear out this page and hand it in.

Answers

Quick-Check Quiz

Section 1: Opportunity Costs

1. c; 2. e; 3. a; 4. b; 5. c; 6. d; 7. b; 8. d
If you missed any of these questions, you should go back and review Section 1 in Chapter 2.

Section 2: Specialization and Trade

1. c; 2. a; 3. d; 4. d
If you missed any of these questions, you should go back and review Section 2 in Chapter 2.

Practice Questions and Problems

Section 1: Opportunity Costs

1. Opportunity costs
2. minimize
3. highest
4. production possibilities curve (PPC)
5. inside
6. unattainable
7. outward
8. inside
9. inside
10. on
11. subjective
12. a. inefficient (does not fully utilize all resources)
    b. unattainable
13. Whether they stay or leave, they cannot get their $40 back. It is a *sunk cost* and should not enter the decision-making process. The relevant costs are the opportunity costs of staying versus the opportunity costs of leaving.
14. The years of schooling Roger already has are a *sunk cost*—he cannot get them back whether he continues as an accounting major or switches to marketing. These costs should have no effect on his decision to change majors because he cannot change what already has happened. The relevant costs are the opportunity costs of continuing his accounting major versus the opportunity costs of switching to marketing.

Section 2: Specialization and Trade

1. marginal opportunity cost
2. lowest
3. the lowest
4. comparative
5. outside
6. a. constant
   b. $1; \frac{1}{2}$

c. 1; 2
d. fish; coconuts
e. fish; coconuts
f.

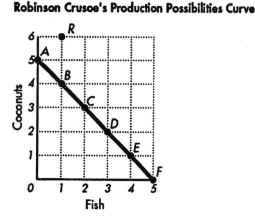

Robinson Crusoe's Production Possibilities Curve

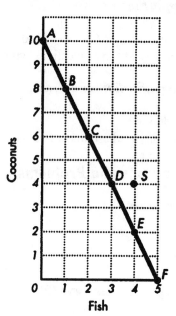

Friday's Production Possibilities Curve

g. 6; 4; 4; 6; 6; 1; 4; 4; 2 coconuts; 1 fish

7. a. 20
    b. 30 (To get an additional belt, we must move from *B* to *C*. At *B*, we had 60 purses and 4 belts. At *C*, we have 30 purses and 5 belts. We gave up 30 purses for 1 belt.)
    c. increasing
    d. 0.05 (We must move toward point *A* to get additional purses. Moving from *B* to *A*, we give up 1 belt for 20 purses. For 1 purse, we give up approximately $\frac{1}{20}$ or 0.05 belt.)
    e. 0.1 (We must move up the curve to get additional purses. At point *A* we have 80 purses and 3 belts. Moving up the curve, we have 90 purses and 2 belts. We gave up 1 belt for 10 purses. For 1 purse, we give up approximately $\frac{1}{10}$ or 0.1 belt. Notice that as we make more purses, the opportunity cost in terms of belts increases.)

8. a. 4
    b. 3 (To get more tables, we must move from *B* to *C*. At *B*, we had 6 chairs and 1 table. At *C*, we have 3 chairs and 2 tables. We gave up 3 chairs for 1 table.)
    c. decreasing
    d. $\frac{1}{3}$ (To get more chairs, we must move toward point *B*. At point *C* we had 2 tables and 3 chairs. At point *B* we have 1 table and 6 chairs. We gave up 1 table for 3 chairs. To get 1 chair, we give up approximately $\frac{1}{3}$ table.)
    e. $\frac{1}{4}$ (To get more chairs, we must move toward point *A*. At point *B* we had 1 table and 6 chairs. At point *A* we have no tables and 10 chairs. We gave up 1 table for 4 chairs. To get 1 chair, we give up approximately $\frac{1}{4}$ table.)

9. constant
10. increasing

11. decreasing
12. bowed out; increasing

Thinking About and Applying Choice, Opportunity Costs, and Specialization

I. Opportunity Costs

Tuition isn't the only cost. If Marc has to give up $150,000 a year to go to carpentry school for a year, he and Shelly may feel that the benefits from carpentry school are not worth $150,000. Carpentry school costs too much. Because Shelly is not working outside the home, her major cost is the leisure time she will have now that their children are in school. She may feel that the benefits of having her degree are worth giving up her leisure time.

II. More on Opportunity Costs

The opportunity cost for Mr. Safi to cut his grass is $200 an hour—what he would make in his next best use. It is better for him to spend his hour consulting and pay the neighbor's child to cut the grass (unless the neighbor's child charges $200 an hour!).

Chapter 3

MARKETS, DEMAND AND SUPPLY, AND THE PRICE SYSTEM

FUNDAMENTAL QUESTIONS

1. What is a market?

   A **market** is a place or service that allows buyers and sellers to exchange goods and services. A market may be a specific place or the exchange of a particular good or service at many different locations. Market transactions may involve the use of money or **barter.** In all markets, goods and services are exchanged and prices are determined.

2. What is demand?

   Demand is the quantity of a good or service that consumers are willing and able to buy at every possible price during a specific period of time, all other things being equal. People often confuse demand with quantity demanded. Demand refers to a list of prices and corresponding quantities. **Quantity demanded** is the amount of a good or service that people are willing and able to buy at *one* particular price. It is correct to say, "If the price of a hair dryer is $15, the *quantity demanded* is 20." It is not correct to say "If the price of a hair dryer is $15, the *demand* is 20."

   The **law of demand** states that as the price of a good decreases, people buy more (and vice versa). That's why stores have sales to get rid of merchandise they can't sell: they know that if they lower the price, people will buy more.

   When economists construct a **demand schedule,** they hold everything except the price of the good constant and determine the quantity consumers will buy at all the possible prices. However, things other than price affect how much of a good or service people are willing to buy. These other **determinants of demand** are income, tastes, prices of related goods or services, consumers' expectations, and number of buyers. When a good or service is sold in more than one country, the exchange rate is also a determinant of demand. When one of these determinants of demand changes, the whole demand schedule changes.

   Economists take seriously the adage "A picture is worth a thousand words," so they draw pictures of demand schedules. These pictures are called **demand curves.** Price is put on the vertical axis and quantity on the horizontal axis. Demand curves slope down from left to right. When one of the determinants of demand changes, the demand curve shifts to the left or the right. Increases in demand shift the curve to the right, and decreases in demand shift the curve to the left. A change in the price of a good or service does not shift the demand curve but instead is represented by a movement from one point to another along the same curve.

3. What is supply?

Supply is the quantity of a good or service that producers are willing and able to offer at each possible price during a specific period of time, all other things being equal. People often confuse supply with quantity supplied. Supply refers to a list of prices and corresponding quantities. **Quantity supplied** is the amount of a good or service offered for sale at *one* particular price. It is correct to say, "If the price of a hair dryer is $15, the *quantity supplied* will be 10." It is not correct to say, "If the price of a hair dryer is $15, the *supply* is 10."

The **law of supply** states that as the price of a good increases, producers will offer more for sale (and vice versa). That's why people offer a seller a higher price for the product when there is a shortage: they know the higher price will entice the producer to produce more.

When economists construct a **supply schedule,** they hold everything except the price of the good constant and determine the quantity producers will offer for sale at all the possible prices. However, things other than price affect how much of a good or service producers are willing to supply. These other **determinants of supply** are prices of resources, technology and **productivity,** expectations of producers, number of producers, and prices of related goods or services. When one of these determinants of supply changes, the whole supply schedule changes.

A picture of a supply schedule is called a **supply curve.** Again price goes on the vertical axis and quantity on the horizontal axis. Supply curves slope up from left to right. When one of the five determinants of supply changes, the supply curve shifts to the left or the right. Increases in supply shift the curve to the right; decreases in supply shift the curve to the left. A change in the price of a good or service does not shift the supply curve but instead is represented by a movement from one point to another along the same curve.

4. How is price determined by demand and supply?

The price of a good or service changes until the equilibrium price is reached. **Equilibrium** is the point at which the quantity demanded equals the quantity supplied at a particular price. At prices above the equilibrium price, the quantity supplied is greater than the quantity demanded, so a **surplus** develops. Sellers must lower their prices to get rid of the goods and services that accumulate. At prices below the equilibrium price, the quantity demanded is greater than the quantity supplied, and a **shortage** develops. Sellers see the goods and services quickly disappear and realize they could have asked a higher price. The price goes up until the shortage disappears. The price continues to adjust until the quantity demanded and the quantity supplied are equal.

5. What causes price to change?

Price may change when demand, supply, or both change. A change in demand causes price to change in the same direction: an increase in demand causes price to increase. A change in supply causes price to change in the opposite direction: an increase in supply causes price to decrease. If demand and supply both change, the direction of the change in price depends on the relative size of the changes in demand and supply. For example, if demand and supply both increase but the demand change is larger, price will increase: it will act as if the only change had been a change in demand. If demand and supply both increase but the supply change is larger, price will decrease: it will act as if the only change had been a change in supply.

6. What happens when price is not allowed to change with market forces?

When price is not allowed to change, the market can't reach equilibrium. If a price ceiling is set that is below the market equilibrium price, a shortage will exist and will stay in existence as long as the ceiling price is maintained. Similarly, if a price floor is set that is above the equilibrium price, a surplus will exist.

Key Terms

market
barter
double coincidence of wants
transaction costs
relative price
demand
quantity demanded
law of demand
determinants of demand

demand schedule
demand curve
substitute goods
complementary goods
exchange rate
supply
quantity supplied
law of supply
determinants of supply

supply schedule
supply curve
productivity
equilibrium
disequilibrium
surplus
shortage
price floor
price ceiling

Quick-Check Quiz

Section 1: Markets

1. A double coincidence of wants exists when
   a. A and B want the same good or service.
   b. A has what B wants.
   c. A has what B wants and B has what A wants.
   d. A has what B and C want.
   e. A has what C wants and B has what A wants.

2. Which of the following allocation schemes provides incentives for quantities of scarce goods to increase?
   a. first-come, first-served
   b. government scheme
   c. market system
   d. random allocation
   e. members of the clergy allocate the good on the basis of perceived need

3. In Mongoverna this year, apples cost $.50 each and oranges cost $.35 each. Suppose that next year, inflation runs rampant in Mongoverna. The price of apples increases to $1 each, and the price of oranges increases to $.70 each. Which of the following statements is true?
   a. The relative price of an apple has not changed.
   b. The relative price of an orange has changed.
   c. The absolute price of an apple has not changed.
   d. The absolute price of an orange has not changed.
   e. Both c and d are correct.

4. Which of the following statements is true?
   a. The transaction costs of finding a double coincidence of wants in order to barter are usually quite low.
   b. Money reduces transaction costs.
   c. People base economic decisions only on transaction costs.
   d. If all money prices doubled, relative prices would change.
   e. A double coincidence of wants is necessary to conduct money transactions.

Copyright © Houghton Mifflin Company. All rights reserved.

5. If the price of a T-shirt is $12 and the price of a pair of designer jeans is $66, the relative price of a pair of designer jeans is
   a. 5½ T-shirts.
   b. 2/11 T-shirt.
   c. 5½ jeans.
   d. 2/11 jean.
   e. $66.

Section 2: Demand

1. Which of the following would *not* cause a decrease in the demand for bananas?
   a. Reports surface that imported bananas are infected with a deadly virus.
   b. Consumers' incomes drop.
   c. The price of bananas rises.
   d. A deadly virus kills monkeys in zoos across the United States.
   e. Consumers expect the price of bananas to decrease in the future.

2. Which of the following is a determinant of demand?
   a. the number of sellers
   b. the exchange rate
   c. producers' expectations
   d. an increase in productivity
   e. a change in technology

3. Which of the following is *not* a determinant of demand?
   a. income
   b. tastes
   c. prices of resources
   d. prices of complements
   e. consumers' expectations about future prices

4. A pair of Reebok shoes costs $50 in the United States and £30 in the United Kingdom. Which of the following statements is true?
   a. $1 is equivalent to £.60.
   b. $1 is equivalent to £1.67.
   c. £1 is equivalent to $.60.
   d. Reebok shoes are more expensive in the United States.
   e. Reebok shoes are more expensive in the United Kingdom.

5. A decrease in quantity demanded could be caused by a(n)
   a. decrease in consumers' incomes.
   b. decrease in the price of a substitute good.
   c. increase in the price of a complementary good.
   d. decrease in the price of the good.
   e. increase in the price of the good.

Markets, Demand and Supply, and the Price System / 43

6. A recent Wichita State University study analyzed the effects of anticipated 6,000-plus layoffs at Boeing, a major Wichita employer. As a result of the anticipated layoffs,
   a. the demand for goods and services in Wichita will increase.
   b. the demand for goods and services in Wichita will decrease.
   c. the demand for Boeing airplanes will decrease.
   d. the demand for goods and services in Wichita will shift to the right.
   e. a and d are both correct.

7. The law of demand states that as the price of a good
   a. rises, the quantity demanded falls, *ceteris paribus*.
   b. rises, the quantity supplied falls, *ceteris paribus*.
   c. rises, the quantity demanded rises, *ceteris paribus*.
   d. rises, the quantity supplied rises, *ceteris paribus*.
   e. falls, the quantity demanded falls, *ceteris paribus*.

8. Which of the following would cause an increase in the demand for eggs?
   a. The price of eggs drops.
   b. The price of bacon rises.
   c. A government report indicates that eating eggs three times a week increases the chances of having a heart attack.
   d. A decrease in the cost of chicken feed makes eggs less costly to produce.
   e. None of the above would increase the demand for eggs.

9. If the price of barley, an ingredient in beer, increases,
   a. the demand for beer will increase.
   b. the demand for beer will not change.
   c. the demand for beer will decrease.
   d. the quantity of beer demanded will increase.
   e. a and d are both correct.

10. A freeze in Peru causes the price of coffee to skyrocket. Which of the following will happen?
    a. The demand for coffee will increase, and the demand for tea will increase.
    b. The demand for coffee will increase, and the quantity demanded of tea will increase.
    c. The quantity demanded of coffee will increase, and the demand for tea will increase.
    d. The quantity demanded of coffee will increase, and the quantity demanded of tea will increase.
    e. The quantity demanded of coffee will decrease, and the demand for tea will increase.

Section 3: Supply

1. According to the law of supply, as the price of a good or service
   a. rises, the quantity supplied decreases, *ceteris paribus*.
   b. rises, the quantity supplied increases, *ceteris paribus*.
   c. rises, the quantity demanded increases, *ceteris paribus*.
   d. rises, the quantity demanded decreases, *ceteris paribus*.
   e. falls, the quantity supplied increases, *ceteris paribus*.

2. Which of the following is *not* a determinant of supply?
   a. prices of resources
   b. technology and productivity
   c. prices of complements
   d. producers' expectations
   e. the number of producers

3. Japanese producers of a type of microchip offered such low prices that U.S. producers of the chip were driven out of business. As the number of producers decreased,
   a. the market supply of microchips increased—that is, the supply curve shifted to the right.
   b. the market supply of microchips increased—that is, the supply curve shifted to the left.
   c. the market supply of microchips decreased—that is, the supply curve shifted to the right.
   d. the market supply of microchips decreased—that is, the supply curve shifted to the left.
   e. there was no change in the supply of microchips (this event is represented by a movement from one point to another on the same supply curve).

4. Electronics firms can produce more than one type of good. Suppose that electronics firms are producing both military radios and microchips. A war breaks out, and the price of military radios skyrockets. The electronics firms throw more resources into making military radios and fewer resources into making microchips. Which of the statements below is true?
   a. The supply of microchips has decreased, and the quantity supplied of military radios has increased.
   b. The supply of microchips has decreased, and the supply of military radios has increased.
   c. The quantity supplied of microchips has decreased, and the supply of military radios has decreased.
   d. The quantity supplied of microchips has decreased, and the quantity supplied of military radios has decreased.
   e. There has been no change in the supply of microchips or in the supply of military radios.

5. Suppose that a change in technology makes car phones cheaper to produce. Which of the following will happen?
   a. The supply curve will shift to the left.
   b. The supply curve will shift to the right.
   c. The supply of car phones will increase.
   d. The supply of car phones will decrease.
   e. Both b and c are correct.

6. Which of the following is a determinant of supply?
   a. income
   b. tastes
   c. number of buyers
   d. the exchange rate
   e. the prices of resources

7. Suppose that automakers expect car prices to be lower in the future. What will happen now?
   a. Supply will increase.
   b. Supply will decrease.
   c. Supply will not change.
   d. Demand will increase.
   e. Demand will decrease.

8. Which of the following would *not* cause an increase in the supply of milk?
   a. an increase in the number of dairy farmers
   b. a change in technology that reduces the cost of milking cows
   c. a decrease in the price of cheese
   d. a decrease in the price of milk
   e. a decrease in the price of cow feed

9. Which of the following would *not* change the supply of beef?
   a. The U.S. government decides to give a subsidy to beef producers.
   b. An epidemic of cow flu renders many cattle unfit for slaughter.
   c. The price of fish increases.
   d. A new hormone makes cows fatter and they require less feed.
   e. Beef producers expect lower beef prices next year.

Section 4: Equilibrium: Putting Demand and Supply Together

1. If demand increases and supply does not change,
   a. equilibrium price and quantity increase.
   b. equilibrium price and quantity decrease.
   c. equilibrium price increases and equilibrium quantity decreases.
   d. equilibrium price decreases and equilibrium quantity increases.
   e. the demand curve shifts to the left.

2. If supply decreases and demand does not change,
   a. equilibrium price and quantity increase.
   b. equilibrium price and quantity decrease.
   c. equilibrium price increases and equilibrium quantity decreases.
   d. equilibrium price decreases and equilibrium quantity increases.
   e. the supply curve shifts to the right.

3. Prices above the equilibrium price cause a(n)
   a. shortage to develop and drive prices up.
   b. shortage to develop and drive prices down.
   c. surplus to develop and drive prices up.
   d. surplus to develop and drive prices down.
   e. increase in supply.

4. Prices below the equilibrium price cause a(n)
   a. shortage to develop and drive prices up.
   b. shortage to develop and drive prices down.
   c. surplus to develop and drive prices up.
   d. surplus to develop and drive prices down.
   e. increase in demand.

5. Utility regulators in some states are considering forcing operators of coal-fired generators to be responsible for cleaning up air and water pollution resulting from the generators. Utilities in these states currently do not pay the costs of cleanup. If this law goes into effect,
   a. demand for electricity will increase, and price and quantity will increase.
   b. demand for electricity will decrease, and price and quantity will decrease.
   c. the supply of electricity will decrease, and price and quantity will decrease.
   d. the supply of electricity will increase, price will decrease, and quantity will decrease.
   e. the supply of electricity will decrease, price will increase, and quantity will decrease.

6. Medical research from South Africa indicates that vitamin A may be useful in treating measles. If the research can be substantiated, the
   a. supply of vitamin A will increase, causing equilibrium price and quantity to increase.
   b. supply of vitamin A will increase, causing equilibrium price to fall and quantity to increase.
   c. demand for vitamin A will increase, causing equilibrium price and quantity to increase.
   d. demand for vitamin A will increase, causing equilibrium price to rise and quantity to fall.
   e. supply of vitamin A will increase, causing equilibrium price to rise and quantity to fall.

7. Since 1900, changes in technology have greatly reduced the costs of growing wheat. The population also has increased. If you know that the changes in technology had a greater effect than the increase in population, then since 1900 the
   a. price of wheat has increased and the quantity of wheat has decreased.
   b. price and quantity of wheat have increased.
   c. price and quantity of wheat have decreased.
   d. price of wheat has decreased and the quantity of wheat has increased.
   e. quantity of wheat has increased, and you haven't got the faintest idea what happened to the price.

8. Which of the following statements is false?
   a. Disequilibrium may persist in some markets because it is too costly to change prices rapidly.
   b. A ceiling price set higher than the equilibrium price will cause a shortage.
   c. Prices set by governments can be lower than equilibrium prices.
   d. Part of the cost of a restaurant meal is the opportunity cost of the time spent waiting for a table.
   e. All of the above are true.

Use the table below to answer questions 9 through 12.

Price	Quantity Demanded	Quantity Supplied
$0	24	0
1	20	2
2	16	4
3	12	6
4	8	8
5	4	10
6	0	12

9. The equilibrium price is
   a. $1.
   b. $2.
   c. $3.
   d. $4.
   e. $5.

10. The equilibrium quantity is
    a. 2.
    b. 4.
    c. 6.
    d. 8.
    e. 10.

11. If the price is $2, a _____ of _____ units will develop, causing the price to _____.
    a. shortage; 12; increase
    b. shortage; 12; decrease
    c. surplus; 12; increase
    d. surplus; 12; decrease
    e. surplus; 19; decrease

12. If the price is $5, a _____ of _____ units will develop, causing the price to _____.
    a. shortage; 6; increase
    b. shortage; 6; decrease
    c. surplus; 6; increase
    d. surplus; 6; decrease
    e. shortage; 12; increase

Use the graph below to answer questions 13 through 16.

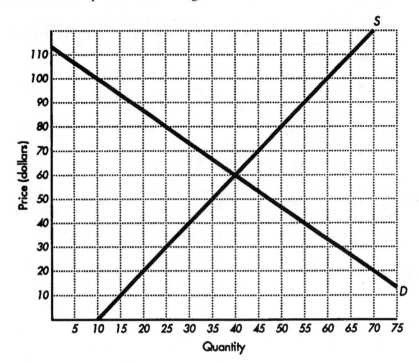

13. The equilibrium price is
    a. $20.
    b. $40.
    c. $60.
    d. $80.
    e. $100.

14. The equilibrium quantity is
    a. 25.
    b. 30.
    c. 35.
    d. 40.
    e. 45.

15. A price of $80 would cause a _____ of _____ units to develop, driving the price _____.
    a. shortage; 6; up
    b. shortage; 25; up
    c. surplus; 6; down
    d. surplus; 25; down
    e. surplus; 25; up

16. A price of $20 would result in a _____ of _____ units, driving the price _____.
    a. shortage; 10; up
    b. shortage; 50; up
    c. surplus; 10; down
    d. surplus; 50; down
    e. shortage; 50; down

Use the graph below to answer questions 17 through 20. The original supply curve is S_1, and the original demand curve is D_1.

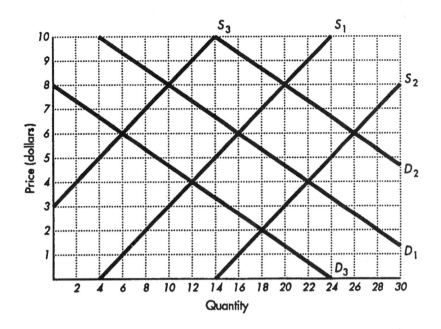

17. The original equilibrium price is _____, and the original equilibrium quantity is _____ units.
    a. $6; 6
    b. $4; 12
    c. $8; 20
    d. $6; 16
    e. $8; 20

18. An increase in the price of a resource causes _____ to shift to _____. The new equilibrium price is _____, and the new equilibrium quantity is _____ units.
    a. demand; D_2; $8; 20
    b. demand; D_3; $4; 12
    c. supply; S_2; $4; 22
    d. supply; S_3; $8; 10
    e. supply; S_3; $10; 14

19. Begin at the original equilibrium position at the intersection of D_1 and S_1. Now a decrease in the price of a complementary good causes _____ to shift to _____. The new equilibrium price is _____, and the new equilibrium quantity is _____ units.
    a. demand; D_2; $8; 20
    b. demand; D_3; $4; 12
    c. supply; S_2; $4; 22
    d. supply; S_3; $8; 10
    e. supply; S_3; $10; 14

20. Begin at the original equilibrium position at the intersection of D_1 and S_1. An increase in income occurs at the same time as a change in technology decreases the costs of production. The new equilibrium price will be _____, and the new equilibrium quantity will be _____ units.
    a. $6; 26
    b. $4; 22
    c. $8; 20
    d. $10; 14
    e. $6; 8

21. An increase in demand
    a. shifts the demand curve to the left.
    b. causes an increase in equilibrium price.
    c. causes a decrease in equilibrium price.
    d. causes a decrease in equilibrium quantity.
    e. does not affect equilibrium quantity.

22. When demand decreases,
    a. price and quantity increase.
    b. price and quantity decrease.
    c. price increases and quantity decreases.
    d. price decreases and quantity increases.
    e. supply decreases.

23. When supply decreases,
    a. the supply curve shifts to the right.
    b. equilibrium price and equilibrium quantity both increase.
    c. equilibrium price and equilibrium quantity both decrease.
    d. equilibrium price decreases and equilibrium quantity increases.
    e. equilibrium price increases and equilibrium quantity decreases.

Practice Questions and Problems

Section 1: Markets

1. A(n) _____ is a place or service that enables buyers and sellers to exchange goods and services.

2. The exchange of goods and services directly, without money, is called _____.

3. In a barter economy, trade cannot occur unless there is a(n) _____ of wants.

4. _____ prices are a measure of opportunity costs.

5. _____ occurs when an auto mechanic tunes up an accountant's car in exchange for the accountant's doing the mechanic's income taxes.

6. The costs involved in making a barter exchange are called _____ costs.

7. The price established when an exchange occurs is called the _____ price.
8. If all prices double, relative prices _____ (do, do not) change.

Section 2: Demand

1. _____ refers to the quantities of a well-defined commodity that consumers are willing and able to buy at every possible price during a given time period, *ceteris paribus*.
2. According to the law of demand, if you _____ your price, people will buy more, *ceteris paribus*.
3. List six determinants of demand.

   _____
   _____
   _____
   _____
   _____
   _____

4. Demand curves slope down because of the _____ relationship between price and _____.
5. Suppose that an increase in the price of Nohr Cola causes you to switch to Sooby Cola. You therefore buy less Nohr Cola. Sooby Cola is a(n) _____ for Nohr Cola.
6. The higher people's _____, the more goods they can purchase at any price.
7. A(n) _____ is a graph of a demand schedule.
8. _____ goods can be used in place of each other; these goods would not be consumed at the same time.
9. Goods that are used together are called _____ goods.
10. Dot, Diane, and Mardi are college students who share an apartment. Dot loves strawberries and buys them whenever they are available. Diane is a fair-weather strawberry eater: she only buys them if she thinks she is getting a good price. Mardi eats strawberries for their vitamin C content but isn't crazy about them. The table on the following page shows the individual demand schedules for Dot, Diane, and Mardi. Suppose that these three are the only consumers in the local market for strawberries. Add their individual demands to get the market demand schedule.

| | Quantity | | | |
Price per Quart	Dot	Diane	Mardi	Market
$0	6.00	4.00	2.00	_____
1	5.00	3.50	1.50	_____
2	4.00	3.00	1.00	_____
3	3.25	2.00	0.75	_____
4	2.00	1.50	0.50	_____
5	1.25	0.50	0.25	_____
6	0	0	0	_____

Plot the market demand for strawberries on the graph below.

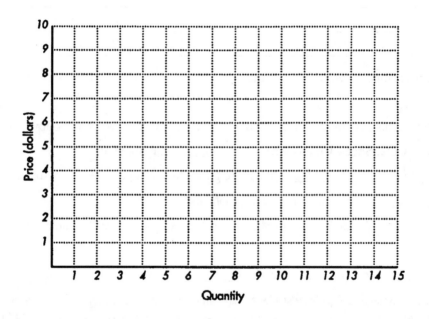

11. Suppose that the price of strawberries increases from $2 to $3 per quart. The increase in price would cause a decrease in the _____ (demand, quantity demanded) of strawberries. Show the effect of this change in the price of strawberries on the graph above.

12. Suppose that Dot reads in the paper that eating strawberries increases the health of females. As a group, Dot and her friends decide to buy twice as many strawberries as they did before at any price. Plot the new market demand curve in the graph above, and label it D_2. This change in tastes has caused a(n) _____ (increase, decrease) in _____ (demand, quantity demanded).

13. An increase in income _____ (increases, decreases) the _____ (demand, quantity demanded) for haircuts.

14. Many Americans have decreased their consumption of beef and switched to chicken in the belief that eating chicken instead of beef lowers cholesterol. This change in tastes has _____ (increased, decreased) the _____ (demand, quantity demanded) for beef and _____ (increased, decreased) the _____ (demand, quantity demanded) for chicken.

15. In the graph below, the price of good X increased, causing the demand for good Y to change from D_1 to D_2. The demand for good Y _____ (increased, decreased). X and Y are _____ (substitutes, complements).

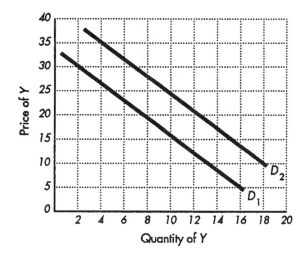

16. Mr. and Mrs. Gertsen are retiring next year and expect that their future income will be less than it is now. If D_1 is their current demand for bacon, show the effect of this expectation on the graph below. Label your new curve D_2. Demand for bacon has _____ (increased, decreased).

17. In the year 2000, one out of every five Americans will be over 65 years old. The demand for health-care facilities for the elderly will _____ (increase, not change, decrease).
18. A crisis in the Middle East causes people to expect the price of gasoline to increase in the future. The demand for gasoline today will _____ (increase, not change, decrease).
19. If the price of Pepsi increases, the demand for Coke and other substitutes will _____.

Section 3: Supply

1. _____ is the amount of a good or service that producers are willing and able to offer for sale at each possible price during a period of time, *ceteris paribus*.
2. According to the law of supply, as price _____, quantity supplied decreases.
3. A table or list of the prices and corresponding quantity supplied of a well-defined good or service is called a(n) _____.
4. A(n) _____ is a graph of a supply schedule.
5. Market supply curves have _____ slopes.
6. There are only two strawberry producers in the little town where Dot, Diane, and Mardi live. Their individual supply schedules are shown below. Add the individual supplies to get market supply, and then plot market supply (curve S_1) on the graph on the following page.

	Quantity Supplied		
Price per Quart	Farmer Dave	Farmer Ruth	Market
$0	2	2	_____
1	3	3	_____
2	4	4	_____
3	5	5	_____
4	6	6	_____
5	7	7	_____
6	8	8	_____

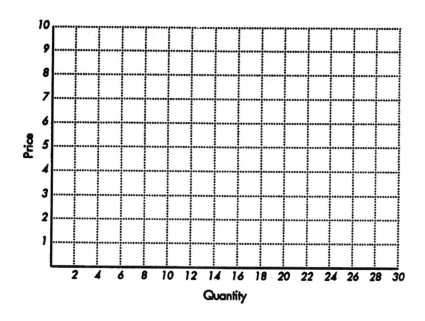

7. List the five determinants of supply.

_____
_____
_____
_____
_____

8. Suppose that a crisis in the Middle East cuts off the supply of oil from Saudi Arabia. If S_1 is the original market supply of oil, draw another supply curve, S_2, on the graph to show the effect of Saudi Arabia's departure from the market. The _____ (quantity supplied, supply) has _____ (increased, decreased).

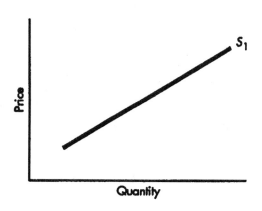

9. If the price of tomato sauce increases, the _____ (supply, quantity supplied) of pizza will _____ (increase, decrease).

10. _____ is the quantity of output produced per unit of resource.

11. A new process for producing microchips is discovered that will decrease the cost of production by 10 percent. The supply of microchips will _____ (increase, decrease, not change), which means the supply curve will _____ (shift to the right, shift to the left, not change).

12. A paper manufacturer can produce notebook paper or wedding invitations. If the price of wedding invitations skyrockets, we can expect the supply of _____ (notebook paper, wedding invitations) to _____ (increase, decrease).

13. A real-estate developer who specializes in two-bedroom homes believes that the incomes of young couples will decline in the future. We can expect the supply of this realtor's two-bedroom homes to _____ (increase, decrease).

14. Changes in quantity supplied are caused by changes in the _____ of the good.

Section 4: Equilibrium: Putting Demand and Supply Together

1. The point at which the quantity demanded equals the quantity supplied at a particular price is known as the point of _____.

2. Whenever the price is greater than the equilibrium price, a(n) _____ arises.

3. A(n) _____ arises when the quantity demanded is greater than the quantity supplied at a particular price.

4. Shortages lead to _____ (increases, decreases) in price and quantity supplied and _____ (increases, decreases) in quantity demanded.

5. Surpluses lead to _____ (increases, decreases) in price and quantity supplied and _____ (increases, decreases) in quantity demanded.

6. The only goods that are not scarce are _____ goods.

7. As long as supply does not change, a change in equilibrium price and quantity is in the _____ (same, opposite) direction as a change in demand.

8. Balloon manufacturers are nervous about a children's movement that may affect their product. The children are lobbying state legislatures to ban launchings of more than ten balloons at a time, citing the danger that balloons can pose to wildlife. If the children are successful, we can expect the _____ (demand for, supply of) balloons to _____ (increase, decrease), causing the equilibrium price to _____ and the equilibrium quantity to _____.

9. If design changes in the construction of milk cartons cause the cost of production to decrease, we can expect the _____ (demand for, supply of) cartons to _____ (increase, decrease), the equilibrium price to _____, and the equilibrium quantity to _____.

10. A decrease in supply leads to a(n) _____ in price and a(n) _____ in quantity.
11. Remember Dot, Diane, and Mardi and the strawberry farmers Dave and Ruth? The local market for strawberries (before Dot read about the effects of strawberries on women's health) is reproduced in the graph below. The original demand is D_1 and the original supply S. The equilibrium price is _____, and the equilibrium quantity is _____.

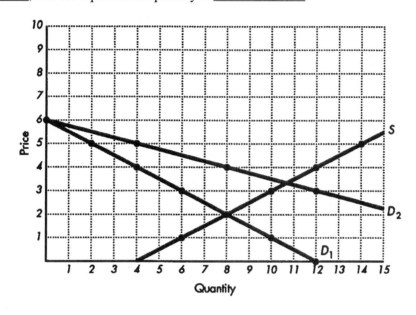

After Dot read the article on strawberries and health, the market demand curve shifted to D_2. The new equilibrium price is _____, and the new equilibrium quantity is _____. There was also a change in _____ (supply, quantity supplied).

12. _____ occurs when the quantity demanded and the quantity supplied are not equal.
13. The graph below shows the market for corn. The equilibrium price is _____, and the equilibrium quantity is _____.

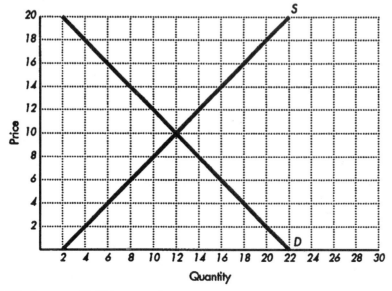

58 / Chapter 3

If the price of corn is $14, the quantity demanded will be _____, and the quantity supplied will be _____. A(n) _____ of _____ units will develop, causing the price and quantity supplied to _____ and the quantity demanded to _____.

If the price is $4, the quantity demanded will be _____, and the quantity supplied will be _____. A(n) _____ of _____ units will develop, causing the price and quantity supplied to _____ and the quantity demanded to _____.

14. List three reasons why there can be excess supply or demand in a market.

_____
_____
_____

Thinking About and Applying Markets, Demand and Supply, and the Price System

I. Changes in Demand

Indicate whether there is an increase or decrease in demand, an increase or decrease in quantity demanded, or no effect on demand. The market of interest is in italic.

1. *TV sets.* The number of producers of TV sets decreases.   _____
2. *Radios.* The price of radios goes up.   _____
3. *Cassette recorders.* The price of cassette recorders falls.   _____
4. *Coffee.* The price of tea falls.   _____

II. Changes in Supply

Indicate whether the supply curve would shift to the left or right in the following situations. If there is no effect, say so.

	Right	Left	No Effect
1. The number of producers of the product decreases.	____	____	____
2. Consumers expect higher prices in the future.	____	____	____
3. The price of the product goes up.	____	____	____
4. The cost of an input decreases.	____	____	____
5. Consumers' incomes fall.	____	____	____
6. A change in technology reduces the costs of producing the product.	____	____	____
7. A tariff is placed on the product.	____	____	____

	Right	Left	No Effect
8. The price of a substitute in production increases.	_____	_____	_____
9. A tax on the product is increased.	_____	_____	_____
10. The price of the product falls.	_____	_____	_____

III. Distinguishing Changes in Demand from Changes in Supply

It is important that you be able to distinguish between factors that affect demand and factors that affect supply. Place a *D* next to items that are determinants of demand and an *S* next to items that affect supply.

_____ 1. producers' expectations

_____ 2. income

_____ 3. exchange rates

_____ 4. changes in technology

_____ 5. prices of substitutes in production

_____ 6. prices of related goods

_____ 7. number of sellers

_____ 8. tastes

_____ 9. prices of complements

_____ 10. consumers' expectations

_____ 11. number of buyers

_____ 12. changes in productivity

_____ 13. prices of resources

_____ 14. prices of substitutes in consumption

IV. The Market for Battery-Operated Dancing Flowers

For each event below, indicate whether it affects the demand or supply of battery-operated dancing flowers and the direction (increase or decrease) of the change. Also indicate what will happen to equilibrium price and quantity. Remember, the determinants of demand are income, tastes, prices of related goods or services, consumers' expectations, number of buyers, and exchange rates. The determinants of supply are prices of resources, changes in technology or productivity, producers' expectations, number of producers, and prices of related goods or services (goods that are substitutes in production).

1. There is a change in tastes toward battery-operated dancing gorillas.
2. The price of plastic falls.
3. A technological breakthrough makes it cheaper to produce plastic flowers.
4. Consumers' incomes rise.
5. The price of battery-operated dancing gorillas rises.
6. The price of plastic flowers skyrockets.

7. A fire destroys a major production facility for dancing flowers.
8. Consumers expect lower prices for dancing flowers in the future.

	Demand	Supply	Price	Quantity
1.	_____	_____	_____	_____
2.	_____	_____	_____	_____
3.	_____	_____	_____	_____
4.	_____	_____	_____	_____
5.	_____	_____	_____	_____
6.	_____	_____	_____	_____
7.	_____	_____	_____	_____
8.	_____	_____	_____	_____

V. Drinking and Cancer

The *Wichita Eagle* reported the results of a study that suggest that the anticancer benefit of eating lots of fruits and vegetables is lost if you wash them down with more than two drinks of alcohol.

As a result of this study, the _____ (demand, supply) for alcoholic drinks will _____ (increase, not change, decrease). The equilibrium price will _____ (increase, not change, decrease), and the equilibrium quantity will _____ (increase, not change, decrease).

Assume the market for alcoholic drinks was in equilibrium before the study, as shown below. Illustrate the effects of the research linking the loss of anticancer benefits with alcohol. Be sure your graph matches your answers above.

VI. Simultaneous Shifts in Demand and Supply: A Shortcut Approach

What do you do if events occur that shift both demand and supply at the same time? If you know the relative magnitudes of the shifts in demand and supply, you can predict both the equilibrium price and the equilibrium quantity. If you do not know the relative magnitudes of the shifts, you will be able to predict either equilibrium price or equilibrium quantity, but not both. Let's look at a quick way to do this.

Suppose demand and supply both increase. Look at what happens to price and quantity when you consider *only* an increase in demand:

	D↑
Price	↑
Quantity	↑

Now add what happens to price and quantity when you consider *only* an increase in supply:

	D↑	S↑
Price	↑	↓
Quantity	↑	↑

When you look at the changes *together*, it's easy to see that the quantity increases but that the effect on price is uncertain. If the demand change is larger than the supply change, price increases. If the supply change is larger than the demand change, price decreases.

Let's try it again. Suppose demand increases and supply decreases. First look at what happens to price and quantity when you consider *only* an increase in demand:

	D↑
Price	↑
Quantity	↑

Now add what happens to price and quantity when you consider *only* a decrease in supply:

	D↑	S↓
Price	↑	↑
Quantity	↑	↓

When you look at the changes together, can you see that the price increases but that the effect on quantity is uncertain? If the demand change is larger than the supply change, quantity increases. If the supply change is larger than the demand change, quantity decreases.

62 / Chapter 3

1. In the chart below, indicate a decrease in demand coupled with an increase in supply, then predict in what direction price and quantity will change.

	D	S
Price		
Quantity		

P _____ , Q _____

2. Now try a decrease in demand coupled with a decrease in supply, then predict in what direction price and quantity will change.

	D	S
Price		
Quantity		

P _____ , Q _____

Now let's try some more concrete examples.

3. We are analyzing the market for home computers. We foresee three main events coming up that will affect this market:

   a. Consumers' incomes are likely to increase.

   b. There will be an increase in the number of buyers as more schoolchildren become familiar with home computers in the classroom.

   c. We expect improvements in technology that will decrease the costs of production.

Use the chart below to determine what will happen to the equilibrium price and equilibrium quantity of home computers.

	D	S
Price		
Quantity		

P _____ , Q _____

4. Suppose the cost of turkey food increases at the same time the price of chicken increases. What will happen to the market for turkey? Defend your answer with this chart.

	D	S
Price		
Quantity		

P _____ , Q _____

VII. Wooden Bats Versus Metal Bats

The supply of wooden bats is shown as S_w on the graph below. It has a steeper slope than the supply of metal bats, S_m, reflecting the fact that it is easier to produce additional metal bats than additional wooden bats.

1. Assume D_m is the demand for metal bats. Suppose baseball purists are willing to pay more for a "sweet crack" sound than for a dull metallic "ping" when they connect with a fastball. Draw a demand curve for wooden bats and label it D_w.

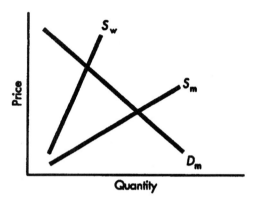

2. What are the consequences for the relative prices of wooden and metal bats?

_____
_____
_____
_____

VIII. For the Algebraically Inclined

1. The Market Demand for Commodity X
   The market for commodity X has three consumers: Gene, Darren, and Todd. The schedules below show each consumer's demand for commodity X.

Gene		Darren		Todd	
P	Q	P	Q	P	Q
$6	0	$6	0	$6	0
5	2	5	1	5	3
4	4	4	2	4	6
3	6	3	4	3	8
2	8	2	6	2	10
1	10	1	8	1	12

a. Derive and plot the market demand for X on the graph below. Label the curve D_1. The market supply curve is $Q = 3P + 18$. Plot market supply (curve S) on the graph.

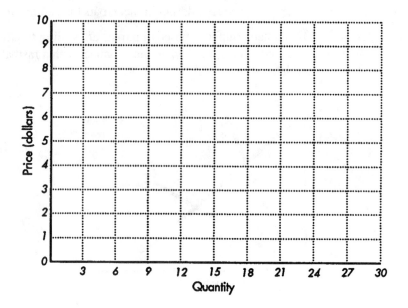

b. The equilibrium price is _____. The equilibrium quantity is _____ units.

2. The Market Demand for Commodity Y

The market for commodity Y has three consumers: Andreas, Katinka, and Sophia. The schedules below show each consumer's demand for commodity Y.

Andreas		Katinka		Sophia	
P	Q	P	Q	P	Q
$10	0	$10	0	$10	0
9	2	9	2	9	0
8	4	8	3	8	1
7	6	7	4	7	2
6	8	6	5	6	3
5	10	5	6	5	4
4	12	4	7	4	5
3	14	3	8	3	6
2	16	2	9	2	7
1	18	1	10	1	8
0	20	0	11	0	9

a. Derive and plot the market demand curve for Y on the graph below. Label the curve D_1. The market supply curve is $Q = 2P - 2$. Plot market supply (curve S) on the graph.

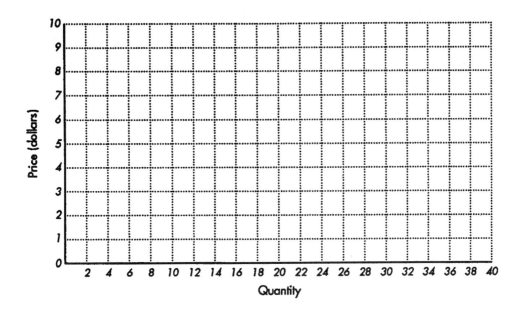

b. The equilibrium price is _____. The equilibrium quantity is _____ units.

c. Now suppose the price of Z increases, shifting market demand to $Q = 34 - 4P$. Plot and label the new curve D_2.

d. The new equilibrium price is _____. The new equilibrium quantity is _____.

e. Z and Y are _____ (complements, substitutes).

3. Market Equilibrium

   a. The equation for demand is $Q = -20P + 110$. Plot demand (curve D) on the graph below. The equation for supply is $Q = 20P - 10$. Plot supply (curve S).

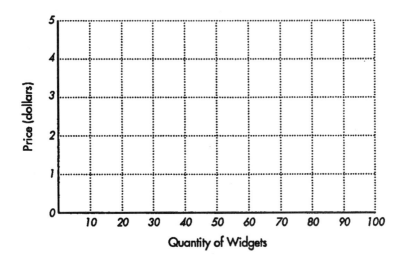

b. The equilibrium price is _____. The equilibrium quantity is _____ units.
c. A price ceiling of $2 will cause _____ (a shortage, a surplus, no change in equilibrium).
d. A price floor of $4 will cause _____ (a shortage, a surplus, no change in equilibrium).
e. A price ceiling of $4 will cause _____ (a shortage, a surplus, no change in equilibrium).
f. A price floor of $2 will cause _____ (a shortage, a surplus, no change in equilibrium).

4. Surpluses and Shortages

   a. The market supply equation is $Q = P - 4$. Plot market supply on the graph below. Label it S. The market demand equation is $Q = 12 - P$. Plot market demand. Label it D_1.

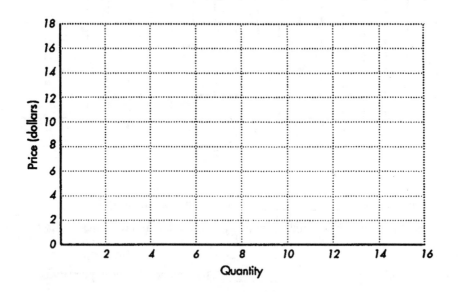

   b. The equilibrium price is _____. The equilibrium quantity is _____ units.
   c. If the price was $10, a _____ (surplus, shortage) of _____ units would develop, driving the price _____ (up, down).
   d. If the price was $6, a _____ (surplus, shortage) of _____ units would develop, driving the price _____ (up, down).
   e. Now suppose consumers' incomes increase, shifting market demand to $Q = 16 - P$. Plot the new demand curve. Label it D_2.
   f. The new equilibrium price is _____, and the new equilibrium quantity is _____ units.

Chapter 3   Homework Problems

Name _____

1. State the law of demand and the law of supply.

2. List the six determinants of demand.

3. Explain the difference between a change in demand and a change in quantity demanded.

4. List the five determinants of supply.

5. Recently, the *Wall Street Journal* ran a story entitled "Man's New Best Friend: The Scaly Iguana." According to the article, iguanas have become very popular pets in some parts of the United States, with sales rising from 28,000 per year in 1986 to over 500,000 per year now. The movie *Jurassic Park* is cited as a reason for the new popularity of iguanas.

   a. Assuming that the supply of iguanas hasn't changed since 1986, sketch a graph showing what happened in the market for iguanas that explains the increase in sales.

   b. Of the six demand determinants, which one best explains the change in the market for iguanas?

   c. As iguanas became more popular, what do you think happened to the price of iguanas?

If your instructor assigns these problems, write your answers above, then tear out this page and hand it in.

Answers

Quick-Check Quiz

Section 1: Markets

1. c; 2. c; 3. a; 4. b; 5. a
   If you missed any of these questions, you should go back and review Section 1 in Chapter 3.

Section 2: Demand

1. c (A change in the price of a good causes movement along the curve—a change in quantity demanded—not a change in demand.); 2. b; 3. c; 4. a; 5. e (Items a, b, and c are determinants of demand and cause the demand curve to shift. Item d causes an *increase* in quantity demanded.); 6. b; 7. a; 8. e (Item a causes an increase in quantity demanded. Items b and c cause decreases in demand. Item d affects the *supply* of eggs.); 9. b; 10. e (The demand for coffee tells us the quantity demanded when the price changes, so it does not shift when price changes: you move from one price to another on the same curve. Coffee and tea are substitutes in consumption. When the price of coffee rises, people buy less coffee and substitute tea. They buy more tea at every price, so the demand for tea increases.)
   If you missed any of these questions, you should go back and review Section 2 in Chapter 3.

Section 3: Supply

1. b; 2. c; 3. d; 4. a (The supply of military radios tells us the quantity of military radios supplied when the price of radios changes. Supply doesn't change when the price changes: you simply move from one price to another on the same curve. Because microchips and military radios are substitutes in production, when the price of military radios increases, the supply of microchips decreases.); 5. e; 6. e; 7. a; 8. d (A change in the price of a good causes a change in quantity supplied, not a change in supply. Cheese and milk are substitutes in production, so if the price of cheese decreases, the supply of milk increases.); 9. c
   If you missed any of these questions, you should go back and review Section 3 in Chapter 3.

Section 4: Equilibrium: Putting Demand and Supply Together

1. a; 2. c; 3. d; 4. a; 5. e; 6. c; 7. d (Item e would be correct if you did not know that the supply change was greater than the demand change.); 8. b; 9. d; 10. d; 11. a; 12. d; 13. c; 14. d; 15. d; 16. b; 17. d; 18. d; 19. a; 20. a; 21. b; 22. b; 23. e
   If you missed any of these questions, you should go back and review Section 4 in Chapter 3.

Practice Questions and Problems

Section 1: Markets

1. market
2. barter
3. double coincidence
4. Relative
5. Barter
6. transaction

7. relative
8. do not

Section 2: Demand

1. Demand
2. lower
3. income
   tastes
   prices of related goods or services
   consumers' expectations
   number of buyers
   the exchange rate
4. inverse; quantity
5. substitute good
6. income
7. demand curve
8. Substitute
9. complementary
10. _____

Price per Quart	Market
$0	12
1	10
2	8
3	6
4	4
5	2
6	0

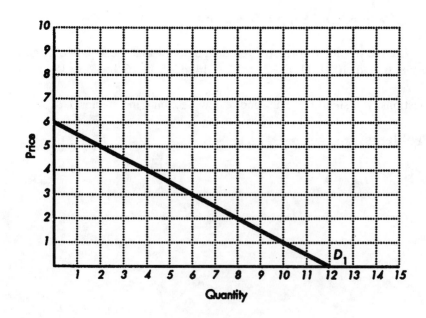

11. quantity demanded

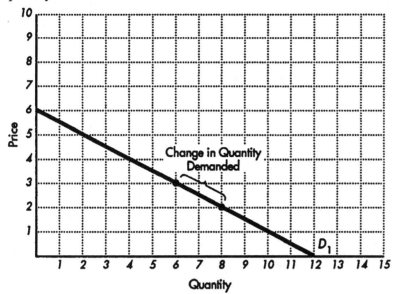

12. increase; demand

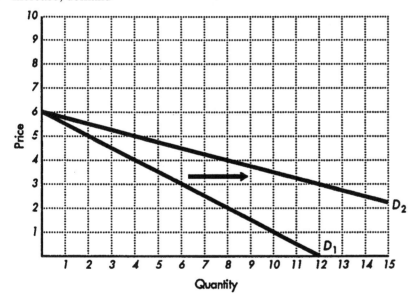

13. increases; demand
14. decreased; demand; increased; demand
15. increased; substitutes
16. decreased

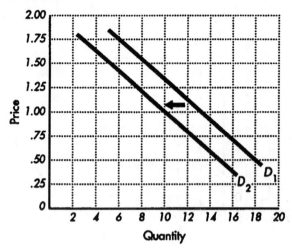

17. increase
18. increase
19. increase

Section 3: Supply

1. Supply
2. decreases
3. supply schedule
4. supply curve
5. positive
6.

Price per Quart	Market
$0	4
1	6
2	8
3	10
4	12
5	14
6	16

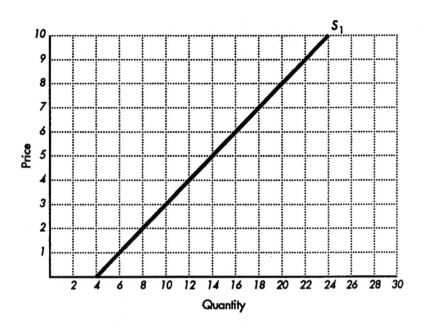

7. prices of resources
   technology and productivity
   expectations of producers
   number of producers
   prices of related goods or services
8. supply; decreased

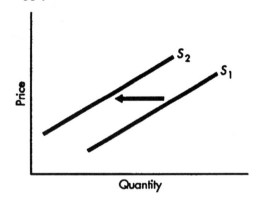

9. supply; decrease
10. Productivity
11. increase; shift to the right
12. notebook paper; decrease
13. increase (The real-estate developer will try to offer as many homes for sale *now*, before incomes drop and the prices of houses drop.)
14. price

Section 4: Equilibrium: Putting Demand and Supply Together

1. equilibrium
2. surplus
3. shortage
4. increases; decreases
5. decreases; increases
6. free
7. same
8. demand for; decrease; decrease; decrease
9. supply of; increase; decrease; increase
10. increase; decrease
11. $2; 8; 3⅓; 10⅔ (The last two values are eyeballed from the graph.); quantity supplied
12. Disequilibrium
13. $10; 12; 8; 16; surplus; 8; decrease; increase; 18; 6; shortage; 12; increase; decrease
14. Government intervention affects prices (price ceilings or floors).
    Price changes can be slow.
    Buyers and sellers may not want price changes.

Thinking About and Applying Markets, Demand and Supply, and the Price System

I. Changes in Demand

1. No effect on demand. The decrease in supply causes the price to increase, which ultimately will decrease the quantity demanded.
2. No effect on demand. This movement along the demand curve decreases the quantity demanded.
3. No effect on demand. This movement along the demand curve increases the quantity demanded.
4. The demand for coffee decreases (because some people will switch to tea). The quantity demanded decreases.

II. Changes in Supply

1. Left
2. No effect (Consumers' expectations affect demand.)
3. No effect (This is a movement along the supply curve.)
4. Right
5. No effect (This affects demand.)
6. Right
7. Left (A tariff increases producers' costs.)
8. Left (Producers move out of this product and produce the substitute instead.)
9. Left (Taxes increase producers' costs.)
10. No effect (This is a movement along the curve.)

III. Distinguishing Changes in Demand from Changes in Supply

1. S
2. D
3. D
4. S
5. S

Markets, Demand and Supply, and the Price System / 75

6. D, S
7. S
8. D
9. D
10. D
11. D
12. S
13. S
14. D

IV. The Market for Battery-Operated Dancing Flowers

	Demand	Supply	Price	Quantity
1.	decrease	no change	decrease	decrease
2.	no change	increase	decrease	increase
3.	no change	increase	decrease	increase
4.	increase	no change	increase	increase
5.	increase	no change	increase	increase
6.	no change	decrease	increase	decrease
7.	no change	decrease	increase	decrease
8.	decrease	no change	decrease	decrease

V. Drinking and Cancer

demand; decrease; decrease; decrease

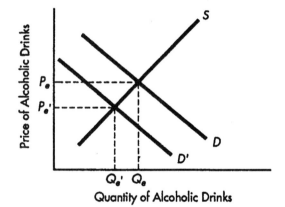

VI. Simultaneous Shifts in Demand and Supply: A Shortcut Approach

1.

	D↓	S↑
Price	↓	↓
Quantity	↓	↑

Price will surely decrease, but the effect on quantity is uncertain. If the demand change is larger than the supply change, quantity will decrease. If the supply change is larger than the demand change, quantity will increase.

2.

	D↓	S↓
Price	↓	↑
Quantity	↓	↓

Quantity will surely decrease, but the effect on price is uncertain. If the demand change is larger than the supply change, price will decrease. If the supply change is larger than the demand change, price will increase.

3. An increase in consumers' incomes is one of the six determinants of demand, so this factor will cause demand to increase. Likewise, an increase in the number of buyers will increase demand. Improvements in technology are one of the five determinants of supply. Because these improvements lower costs, supply will increase. We therefore are looking at an increase in demand coupled with an increase in supply. Our chart looks like this:

	D↑	S↑
Price	↑	↓
Quantity	↑	↑

The quantity of home computers will surely increase, but whether the price rises or falls depends on whether the demand shifts outweigh the supply shift. If the shifts in demand overwhelm the shift in supply, prices will increase. If the supply change is larger than the demand change, prices will decrease.

4.

	D↑	S↓
Price	↑	↑
Quantity	↑	↓

Turkey food is an input for turkey, so if the cost of turkey food increases, the supply of turkey will decrease. Chicken and turkey are substitutes. If the price of chicken increases, consumers will switch to turkey, and the demand for turkey will increase. The price of turkey will surely increase, but whether the quantity increases or decreases depends on which shift (supply or demand) is greater.

VII. Wooden Bats Versus Metal Bats

1.

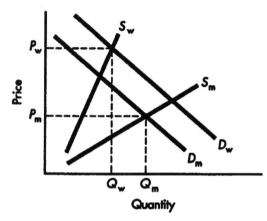

2. If baseball purists prefer wooden bats to metal bats, the demand for wooden bats (D_w) will be to the right of the demand for metal bats (D_m). The price of wooden bats will be higher than the price of metal bats.

VIII. For the Algebraically Inclined

1. The Market Demand for Commodity X
   a. _____

Market Demand	
P	Q
$6	0
5	6
4	12
3	18
2	24
1	30

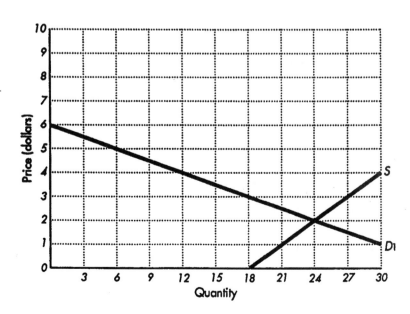

b. $2; 24

2. The Market Demand for Commodity Y
   a. _____

Market Demand	
P	Q
$10	0
9	4
8	8
7	12
6	16
5	20
4	24
3	28
2	32
1	36
0	40

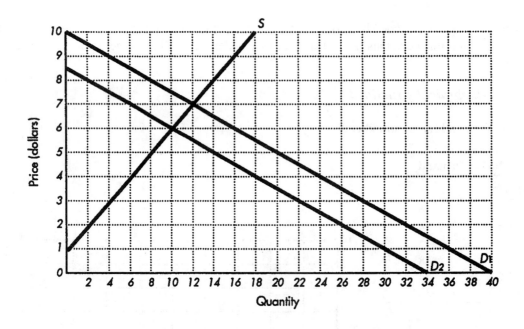

   b. $7; 12
   c. See graph.
   d. $6; 10
   e. complements (When the price of Z increases, consumers buy less of Z. Because the demand for Y decreased when less of Z was bought, Y and Z are complements.)

3. Market Equilibrium
   a.
   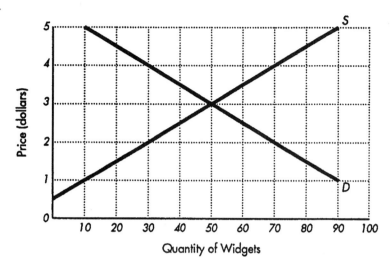

   b. $3; 50
   c. a shortage (of 40 units)
   d. a surplus (of 40 units)
   e. no change in equilibrium
   f. no change in equilibrium

4. Surpluses and Shortages
   a.
   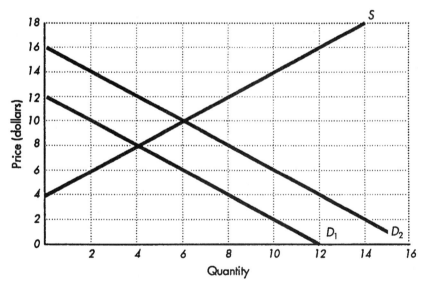

   b. $8; 4
   c. surplus; 4; down
   d. shortage; 4; up
   e. See a.
   f. $10; 6

Chapter 4

THE MARKET SYSTEM AND THE PRIVATE SECTOR

FUNDAMENTAL QUESTIONS

1. In a market system, who decides what goods and services are produced and how they are produced, and who obtains the goods and services that are produced?

    In a market system, consumers decide what goods and services are produced by means of their purchases. If consumers want more of a good or service and are willing to pay for it, demand increases and the price of the good or service increases. Higher profits then attract new producers to the industry. If consumers want less of an item, demand decreases and the price of the item decreases. Resources are then attracted away from the industry.

    The search for profits dictates how goods and services are produced. Firms must use the least-cost combination of resources or be driven out of business.

    Income and prices determine who gets what. Income is determined by ownership of resources: those who own highly valued resources get more income. Output then is allocated to whoever is willing to pay the price.

2. What is a household, and what is household income and spending?

    A **household** consists of one or more persons who occupy a unit of housing. Household spending is called **consumption** and is the largest component of total spending in the economy.

3. What is a business firm, and what is business spending?

    A **business firm** is a business organization controlled by a single management. Business firms can be organized as **sole proprietorships, partnerships,** or **corporations.** Business spending by firms is called **investment** and consists of expenditures of capital goods that are used in producing goods and services.

4. How does the international sector affect the economy?

    The nations of the world can be divided into two categories: industrial countries and developing countries. The economies of industrial nations are highly interdependent. As business conditions change in one country, business firms shift resources among countries so that economic conditions in one country spread to other countries.

    The international trade of the United States occurs primarily with the industrial countries, especially Canada and Japan. **Exports** are products the United States sells to foreign countries. **Imports** are products it buys from other countries.

5. How do the three private sectors—households, businesses, and the international sector—interact in the economy?

Households own the **factors of production** and sell them to firms in return for income. Business firms combine the factors of production into goods and services and sell them to households and the international sector in exchange for revenue. The international sector buys and sells goods and services to business firms. The **circular flow diagram** illustrates these relationships.

Key Terms

consumer sovereignty
private sector
public sector
household
consumption
business firm

sole proprietorship
partnership
corporation
multinational business
investment
imports

exports
trade surplus
trade deficit
net exports
financial intermediaries
circular flow diagram

Quick-Check Quiz

Section 1: The Market System

1. In a market system, _____ decide what is produced.
   a. producers
   b. consumers
   c. politicians
   d. government authorities
   e. central planning boards

2. Many fitness educators are advocating step exercise as a way to improve cardiovascular fitness. Special boxes are used by participants, who step up and down, from side to side, and so on. If these boxes catch on, the _____ them will _____, their price will _____, and _____ boxes will be produced.
   a. demand for; increase; increase; more
   b. supply of; increase; increase; more
   c. supply of; increase; decrease; more
   d. demand for; increase; decrease; more
   e. supply of; increase; decrease; fewer

3. Assume that land costs $1 per unit, labor costs $3 per unit, and capital costs $2 per unit. All of the following combinations of resources produce 35 units of good X. How should good X be produced?
   a. 3 units of land, 4 units of labor, and 2 units of capital
   b. 2 units of land, 1 unit of labor, and 2 units of capital
   c. 5 units of land, 1 unit of labor, and 2 units of capital
   d. 1 unit of land, 2 units of labor, and 3 units of capital
   e. 2 units of land, 2 units of labor, and 3 units of capital

Section 2: Households

1. Householders _____ years old make up the largest number of households.
   a. 15 to 24
   b. 25 to 34
   c. 35 to 44
   d. 45 to 54
   e. 55 to 64

2. Householders _____ years old have the largest median annual income.
   a. 15 to 24
   b. 25 to 34
   c. 35 to 44
   d. 45 to 54
   e. 55 to 64

3. The largest percentage of households consist of _____ person(s).
   a. one
   b. two
   c. three
   d. four
   e. five

4. Household spending, or consumption, is the _____ component of total spending in the economy.
   a. largest
   b. second largest
   c. third largest
   d. fourth largest
   e. smallest

Section 3: Business Firms

1. In _____ the owner of the business is responsible for all the debts incurred by the business and may have to pay those debts from his or her personal wealth.
   a. sole proprietorships
   b. partnerships
   c. corporations
   d. sole proprietorships and partnerships
   e. sole proprietorships, partnerships, and corporations

2. _____ are the most common form of business organization, but _____ account for the largest share of total revenues.
   a. Sole proprietorships; partnerships
   b. Sole proprietorships; corporations
   c. Partnerships; corporations
   d. Corporations; sole proprietorships
   e. Partnerships; sole proprietorships

3. *Investment* as used in the text is
   a. a financial transaction, like buying bonds or stock.
   b. business spending on capital goods.
   c. equal to about one half of household spending.
   d. a relatively stable form of spending.
   e. All of the above describe *investment*.

Section 4: The International Sector

1. The United States tends to import primary products such as agricultural produce and minerals from _____ countries.
   a. low-income
   b. medium-income
   c. high-income
   d. industrial
   e. developing

2. About one-third of U.S. imports and more than a third of U.S. exports came from trade between the United States and
   a. the United Kingdom and Germany.
   b. Eastern Europe.
   c. Canada and Japan.
   d. oil exporters.
   e. developing countries.

3. A trade surplus occurs when
   a. net exports are positive.
   b. net exports are negative.
   c. a country buys more from other countries than it sells to other countries.
   d. imports exceed exports.
   e. industrial countries sell to developing countries.

4. Low-income countries are concentrated heavily in
   a. Central America.
   b. South America.
   c. North America.
   d. Africa and Asia.
   e. western Europe.

5. Which of the following statements is false?
   a. Imports are products that a country buys from another country.
   b. Exports are products that a country sells to another country.
   c. Net exports equal exports minus imports.
   d. Net exports equal imports minus exports.
   e. A trade surplus is the same as positive net exports.

Section 5: Linking the Sectors

1. Which of the following statements is false?
   a. Households sell the factors of production in exchange for money payments.
   b. Firms buy the factors of production from households.
   c. The value of output must equal the value of income.
   d. The value of input must equal the value of household income.
   e. Money that is saved by households reenters the economy in the form of investment spending.

2. _____ own the factors of production.
   a. Corporations
   b. Partnerships
   c. The international sector
   d. State and local governments
   e. Households

Practice Questions and Problems

Section 1: The Market System

1. The _____ system is an economic system in which supply and demand determine what goods and services are produced and the prices at which they are sold.

2. To clarify the operation of the national economy, economists usually group individual buyers and sellers into three sectors: _____ , _____ , and _____ .

3. _____ is the authority of consumers to determine, by means of their purchases, what is produced.

4. Resources tend to flow from _____-valued uses to _____-valued uses as firms seek to make a profit.

5. When consumers' tastes change in favor of a good, _____ (demand, supply) _____ (increases, decreases) and the _____ (higher, lower) price attracts new firms to the production of that good.

6. When consumers' tastes change away from a good, _____ (demand, supply) _____ (increases, decreases) and the _____ (higher, lower) price causes firms to reduce production of that good.

7. In a market system, _____ dictate what is produced by means of their purchases of goods and services.

Section 2: Households

1. A(n) _____ consists of one or more persons who occupy a unit of housing.
2. Household spending is called _____ .
3. Householders between _____ and _____ years old have the largest median incomes.
4. A household is most likely to consist of _____ persons.

Section 3: Business Firms

1. A(n) _____ is a business organization controlled by a single management.
2. A(n) _____ is a business owned by one person.
3. A(n) _____ is a business owned by two or more individuals who share both the profits of the business and the responsibility for the firm's losses.
4. A(n) _____ is a legal entity owned by shareholders whose liability for the firm's losses is limited to the value of the stock they own.
5. A(n) _____ business is a firm that owns and operates producing units in foreign countries.
6. In the United States, the most common form of business organization is the _____ .
7. _____ is the expenditure by business firms for capital goods.
8. _____ account for the largest percentage of business revenue.

Section 4: The International Sector

1. The _____ is an international organization that makes loans to developing countries.
2. Low-income economies are heavily concentrated in _____ and _____ .
3. Products that a country buys from another country are called _____ .
4. Products that a country sells to another country are called _____ .
5. The United States trades the most with two countries, _____ and _____ .
6. A trade _____ exists when exports exceed imports.
7. A trade _____ exists when imports exceed exports.
8. _____ equal exports minus imports.
9. _____ net exports signal a trade surplus; _____ net exports signal a trade deficit.

Section 5: Linking the Sectors

1. List the three factors of production.

   _____

   _____

   _____

2. _____ own the factors of production.

3. The _____ is a model showing the flow of output and income from one sector of the economy to another.

Thinking About and Applying the Market System and the Private Sector

I. The Demand for Services in the Travel Industry

Consider the economic incentives for travel firms to add services. These services add costs to the expenses of the firm but may also increase demand. If the demand shift is greater than the supply shift, it pays the firm to add the service. If the supply shift is greater than the demand shift, it does not pay the firm to add the service.

1. The graph below represents the demand for hotel rooms without daily delivery of newspapers. Plot new demand and supply curves (D_2 and S_2) that show the effects of providing daily newspapers. Construct your curves to make it profitable for hotels to provide the newspapers.

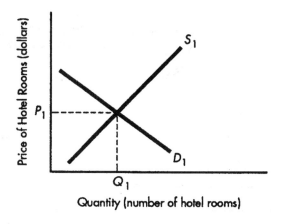

2. What happens to the price of hotel rooms?

   _____

   _____

II. The Circular Flow Diagram

Use the diagram below to see if you understand how the three sectors of the economy are linked together. In the blanks below, fill in the appropriate labels. Money flows are represented by broken lines. Flows of physical goods and services are represented by solid lines.

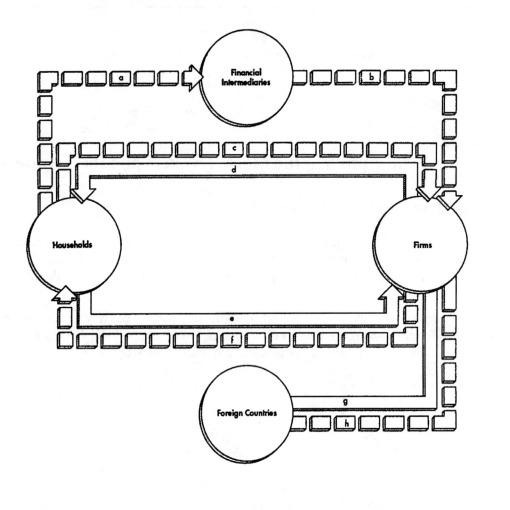

a. _____ e. _____
b. _____ f. _____
c. _____ g. _____
d. _____ h. _____

Chapter 4   Homework Problems

Name _____

1. In a market economy, who owns the factors of production, and who pays for their use?

2. How do economists define the term *household?*

3. What two countries are the largest trading partners of the United States?

4. In the 1970s, parrots were very popular pets in the United States. In the 1990s, iguanas became very popular.
    a. What would you predict happened to the prices and quantities of iguanas and parrots sold between the 1970s and 1990s?

    b. What economic principle describes *why* markets react to changes in people's tastes for pets?

5. Suppose you were an English merchant in the 1600s, trying to start a business shipping cargoes of raw materials to England from the newly established English colonies around the world and shipping finished goods back from England to the colonies. The business will be risky; many cargo ships sink due to storms or navigation hazards.

   You need to raise money from many investors to start the business. Think about the differences between partnerships and corporations and explain why setting up the business as a corporation would make it much easier to attract investors to your business.

If your instructor assigns these problems, write your answers above, then tear out this page and hand it in.

Answers

Quick-Check Quiz

Section 1: The Market System

1. b; 2. a; 3. b

If you missed any of these questions, you should go back and review Section 1 in Chapter 4.

Section 2: Households

1. c; 2. d; 3. b; 4. a

If you missed any of these questions, you should go back and review Section 2 in Chapter 4.

Section 3: Business Firms

1. d; 2. b; 3. b

If you missed any of these questions, you should go back and review Section 3 in Chapter 4.

Section 4: The International Sector

1. e; 2. c; 3. a; 4. d; 5. d

If you missed any of these questions, you should go back and review Section 4 in Chapter 4.

Section 5: Linking the Sectors

1. d; 2. e

If you missed either of these questions, you should go back and review Section 5 in Chapter 4.

Practice Questions and Problems

Section 1: The Market System

1. market
2. households; business firms; the international sector
3. Consumer sovereignty
4. lower, higher
5. demand; increases; higher
6. demand; decreases; lower
7. consumers

Section 2: Households

1. household
2. consumption
3. 45; 54
4. two

Section 3: Business Firms

1. business firm
2. sole proprietorship
3. partnership
4. corporation
5. multinational
6. sole proprietorship
7. Investment
8. Corporations

Section 4: The International Sector

1. World Bank
2. Africa; Asia
3. imports
4. exports
5. Canada; Japan
6. surplus
7. deficit
8. Net exports
9. Positive; negative

Section 5: Linking the Sectors

1. land
   labor
   capital
2. Households
3. circular flow diagram

Thinking About and Applying the Market System and the Private Sector

I. The Demand for Services in the Travel Industry

1. If your graph is correct, the demand shift (to the right) is greater than the supply shift (to the left). If the new equilibrium price and quantity are greater than the original equilibrium price and quantity, you've plotted the curves correctly.

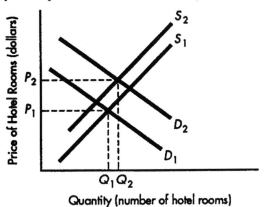

2. The price of hotel rooms increases.

II. The Circular Flow Diagram

a. saving
b. investment
c. payments for goods and services
d. goods and services
e. resource services
f. payments for resource services
g. net exports
h. payments for net exports

Chapter 5

THE PUBLIC SECTOR

FUNDAMENTAL QUESTIONS

1. How does the government interact with the other sectors of the economy?

   Households sell resources to the government—which uses those resources to produce government services—in return for income. Business firms sell the goods and services they produce to the government for revenue. Taxes are the income the government receives from households and firms. In reality, the government may interact directly with foreign consumers and businesses, but most government activity with the international sector occurs when the government uses business firms as intermediaries.

2. What is the economic role of government?

   One outcome of the market system is **economic efficiency**—that is, no one can be made better off without making someone else worse off. However, economic efficiency can be limited by **market imperfections, externalities, public goods, monopolies,** and **business cycles.** The economic role of government is to reduce economic inefficiencies by controlling these factors.

3. Why is the public sector such a large part of a market economy?

   There are two explanations for the role of government in the market economy. One view suggests that government intervenes in the economy only to correct market failures. Another argument suggests that government actions result from the rent-seeking behaviors of the individuals who make up the government. That is, voters and politicians use the power of government to transfer benefits to themselves from others.

4. What does the government do?

   The economic role of government can be divided into two categories: microeconomic policy and macroeconomic policy. Microeconomic policy deals with providing public goods, correcting externalities, and promoting competition. Macroeconomic policy is divided into two categories: fiscal policy and monetary policy. **Monetary policy** is directed toward control of money and credit, and **fiscal policy** is directed toward government spending and taxation.

5. How do the sizes of public sectors in various countries compare?

   The United States and Canada are representative of market systems which rely on the decisions of individuals and in which the public sector is relatively small. Nations like Cuba rely on a planning board or central committee and have large public sectors. The economics of France, the United Kingdom, Germany, Japan, and Sweden lie in between.

Copyright © Houghton Mifflin Company. All rights reserved.

Key Terms

economic efficiency
technical efficiency
market imperfection
externalities
public goods
private property right

free ride
monopoly
business cycles
rent seeking
public choice
monetary policy

Federal Reserve
fiscal policy
transfer payments
budget surplus
budget deficit
centrally planned economy

Quick-Check Quiz

Section 1: The Circular Flow

1. The text assumes that the government sector does not interact directly with
   a. households.
   b. business firms.
   c. foreign countries.
   d. foreign countries and business firms.
   e. households and the international sector.

2. Which of the following statements is false?
   a. The government employs the factors of production to produce government services.
   b. Money flows from the government to households.
   c. The value of private production equals the value of household income.
   d. The total value of output in the economy equals the total income received.
   e. In a sense, the household sector purchases goods and services from the government.

Section 2: The Role of Government in the Market System

1. *Economic efficiency* refers to
   a. the combination of inputs that results in the lowest cost.
   b. a situation in which no one can be made better off without making someone else worse off.
   c. the role of central planning boards in determining what goods and services should be produced.
   d. the role of government in providing public goods.
   e. the role of government in imposing taxes on those goods and services that produce negative externalities.

2. Which of the following is an example of a market externality problem?
   a. Lana hates her new haircut.
   b. Stan's new car turns out to be a clunker.
   c. Jan's neighbor blasts her out of bed with his new stereo at 4:00 A.M.
   d. Dan's new sweater falls apart the first time he washes it.
   e. Tim buys expensive basketball shoes that hurt his feet.

3. Which of the following does *not* involve negative externalities?
   a. cigarette smoke in a crowded restaurant
   b. acid rain
   c. Amazon rain forests, which help neutralize the effects of air pollution
   d. a blaring stereo
   e. the use of a highway by an additional vehicle

4. A lighthouse is an example of a
   a. negative externality.
   b. positive externality.
   c. public good.
   d. commonly owned good.
   e. private property right.

5. If negative externalities are involved in the production or consumption of a good, _____ of the good is produced or consumed. The government should _____ to encourage producers to produce _____ of the good.
   a. too little; grant subsidies; more
   b. too little; impose taxes; less
   c. too much; impose taxes; more
   d. too much; impose taxes; less
   e. too much; grant subsidies; less

6. Which of the following statements is false?
   a. It is not possible to exclude people from the benefits of public goods.
   b. Education is an example of a good with positive externalities.
   c. People have an incentive to try for a free ride when goods are public goods.
   d. If a good has positive externalities, too little of the good is produced.
   e. The price system ensures that the appropriate amount of public goods is produced.

7. The market system does *not* work efficiently when
   a. the market price reflects the full costs and benefits of producing and consuming a particular good or service.
   b. the least-cost combinations of resources are used.
   c. the benefits derived from consuming a particular good or service are available only to the consumer who buys the good or service.
   d. private property rights exist.
   e. market imperfections exist.

8. Public choice economists believe that
   a. people who do not like a market outcome use the government to change the outcome.
   b. the government intervenes only to correct market inefficiencies.
   c. rent-seeking activities increase economic efficiency.
   d. resources devoted to enacting the transfer of benefits are productive.
   e. redistributing income increases economic efficiency.

9. Which of the following is *not* a public good?
   a. police protection
   b. national defense
   c. streetlights
   d. cable television
   e. education

Section 3: Overview of the United States Government

1. Combined government spending on goods and services is larger than _____ but smaller than _____ .
   a. consumption; net exports
   b. consumption; investment
   c. net exports; investment
   d. investment; net exports
   e. investment; consumption

2. A budget deficit
   a. exists when federal revenues exceed federal spending.
   b. last occurred in the United States in 1969.
   c. occurs when federal spending exceeds federal revenues.
   d. has no effect on consumption and investment.
   e. has no effect on economic relationships with other countries.

3. Which of the following is *not* a microeconomic function of government?
   a. provision of public goods
   b. control of money and credit
   c. correction of externalities
   d. promotion of competition
   e. minimizing the free-rider problem

4. Which of the following is a macroeconomic function of government?
   a. redistribution of income
   b. promotion of competition
   c. determining the level of government spending and taxation
   d. provision of public goods
   e. correction of externalities

5. The _____ is (are) responsible for fiscal policy, and the _____ is (are) responsible for monetary policy.
   a. Federal Reserve; Congress
   b. Federal Reserve; Congress and the president
   c. Congress; Federal Reserve
   d. Congress and the president; Federal Reserve
   e. Congress; Federal Reserve and the president

Section 4: Government in Other Economies

1. Which of the following has an economy that is primarily centrally planned?
   a. United Kingdom
   b. Japan
   c. Cuba
   d. Germany
   e. Canada

2. In _____ , government spending (as a percentage of total output) was lower than that of Japan in 1997.
   a. the United States
   b. Sweden
   c. France
   d. Germany

Practice Questions and Problems

Section 1: The Circular Flow

1. Government in the United States exists at the _____ , _____ , and _____ levels.
2. The household sector obtains government goods and services primarily by _____ .
3. The _____ illustrates how the main sectors of the economy fit together.

Section 2: The Role of Government in the Market System

1. _____ efficiency is the combination of inputs that results in the lowest cost.
2. _____ efficiency is the point at which no one in society can be made better off without making someone else worse off.
3. A small company continues to use an old mimeograph machine even though a new personal copier would cut the company's copying costs by 50 percent. This is an example of _____ inefficiency.
4. An African American repeatedly is passed over for promotion because of race. This is an example of _____ inefficiency.
5. Situations in which the least-cost combination of resources is not used or in which a resource is not used where it has its highest value are called _____ .
6. _____ are the costs or benefits of a market activity borne by someone who is not a party to the market transaction.

7. When negative externalities exist, the market price _____ (overstates, understates) the full cost of the activity.
8. _____ are goods whose consumption benefits more than the person who purchased the good.
9. The limitation of ownership to an individual is called a(n) _____.
10. A producer or consumer who enjoys the benefits of a good without having to pay for it is getting a(n) _____.
11. Common ownership of a resource results in _____ (overutilization, underutilization).
12. Market imperfections may result from _____ or inaccurate information.
13. Once streetlights exist, people who have not paid for them cannot be excluded from their benefits. Streetlights are _____ goods.
14. A situation in which there is only one producer of a good is called a(n) _____.
15. Fluctuations in the economy are called _____.
16. The use of resources to transfer income from one sector of the economy to another is called _____.
17. Monopolies may produce _____ (more, less) of a good in order to be able to charge a higher price.
18. _____ theory says that the government may be brought into the market system whenever someone or some group can benefit, even if efficiency is not served.

Section 3: Overview of the United States Government

1. List three microeconomic functions of government.
   _____
   _____
   _____
2. The macroeconomic functions of government are _____ and _____ policies.
3. The _____ is the central bank of the United States.
4. Monetary policy is directed toward control of _____ and _____.
5. Fiscal policy is directed toward _____ and _____.
6. Monetary policy is the responsibility of the _____.
7. Fiscal policy is the responsibility of the _____.
8. The _____ usually initiates major policy changes.
9. If federal government spending is less than tax revenue, a budget _____ exists.
10. If federal government spending is greater than tax revenue, a budget _____ exists.

Section 4: Government in Other Economies

1. A(n) _____ is an economy in which the government determines what goods and services are produced and the prices at which they are sold.

2. Match the country with the description of its economy.

   France   United Kingdom
   Cuba   Germany
   Japan   Sweden

   a. a capitalist economy in which the government plays an important role through its influence on industrial families _____

   b. a market economy in the production of goods and services in which the government accounts for nearly 45 percent of total purchases _____

   c. a country in which the public sector owns few businesses but intervenes a great deal to foster social programs _____

   d. a country whose economy is primarily centrally planned _____

   e. a European country in which public-sector spending was about 40 percent of total output _____

   f. a market economy in which a national economic plan has been used to influence resource allocation _____

3. A market economy relies on _____ and _____ to solve economic problems. In a centrally planned economy, the _____ decides what is produced, how it is produced, and who gets what.

Thinking About and Applying the Public Sector

I. The Circular Flow Diagram

Use the diagram below to see if you understand how the four sectors of the economy are linked together. In the blanks below, fill in the appropriate labels. Money flows are represented by broken lines. Flows of physical goods and services are represented by solid lines.

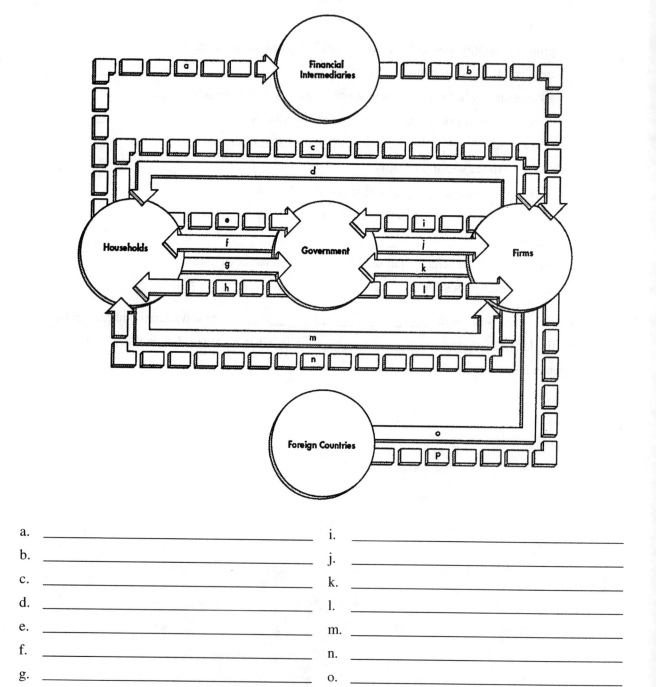

a. _____
b. _____
c. _____
d. _____
e. _____
f. _____
g. _____
h. _____
i. _____
j. _____
k. _____
l. _____
m. _____
n. _____
o. _____
p. _____

II. Government Response to Externalities

1. The graph below shows the demand and supply of an industry's product. This industry currently spews pollution into the air but bears no costs for its actions. If the industry is made responsible for the cleanup, show the effect on the market for this firm's product.

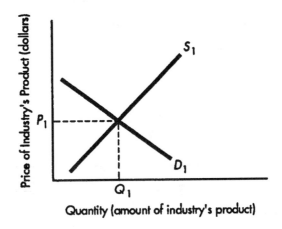

2. How could the government make this cost internal to the firm? What would this do to the price of the firm's output?

_____
_____
_____
_____

III. Justifying the Nutrition Labeling and Education Act

The Nutrition Labeling and Education Act requires food manufacturers to disclose what is in their products in a uniform manner. The idea of the act is to allow consumers to compare the nutritional values of dissimilar products.

Consider the role of the public sector as explained in the text, and provide the economic rationale for the Nutrition Labeling and Education Act.

_____
_____
_____
_____

IV. Extending Regulation

A few years ago, the *Wall Street Journal* ran the following headline: "Clinton's Team Moves to Extend Regulation in Variety of Industries." Consider the role of the public sector as explained in the text, and provide the economic rationale for the following actions:

1. "Major airlines have been put on notice that the government is scrutinizing their pricing practices."

2. "Strict quality-control rules will be imposed on the seafood industry, and more inspectors will be sent into meat and poultry plants to curb a rise in food-borne illness."

3. "The prescription-drug industry may get slapped with price controls."

Chapter 5 Homework Problems

Name _____

1. What is included in the U.S. government's microeconomic policy?

2. What is included in macroeconomic fiscal policy? In the United States, who makes decisions regarding fiscal policy?

3. What is included in macroeconomic monetary policy? In the United States, who makes decisions regarding monetary policy?

4. Last year, the government of an island nation spent $100,000 to build a lighthouse on a dangerous rock 10 miles from the nation's main harbor. Before the lighthouse was built, an average of 25 ships a year ran onto the rock, causing the loss of several millions of dollars every year. During the year the lighthouse has been in operation, no ships have run onto the rock. Why didn't a private company build the lighthouse before, since the benefits are so much more than the costs?

5. The "Economic Insight" box in this chapter describes the problem of overfishing of halibut around Alaska, and how the U.S. government created ownership rights to fish caught in that area as a way to limit the number of fish caught.

   In a market economy, resources that nobody owns, like fish in the ocean or clean air, tend to become overused. Think about the way that halibut fishing permits created ownership rights and an economically efficient market, and describe how a market for air pollution permits could be an economically efficient way to limit the amount of pollution.

Answers

Quick-Check Quiz

Section 1: The Circular Flow

1. c; 2. c
If you missed either of these questions, you should go back and review Section 1 in Chapter 5.

Section 2: The Role of Government in the Market System

1. b; 2. c; 3. c; 4. c; 5. d; 6. e; 7. e; 8. a; 9. d
If you missed any of these questions, you should go back and review Section 2 in Chapter 5.

Section 3: Overview of the United States Government

1. e; 2. c; 3. b; 4. c; 5. d
If you missed any of these questions, you should go back and review Section 3 in Chapter 5.

Section 4: Government in Other Economies

1. c; 2. a
If you missed either of these questions, you should go back and review Section 4 in Chapter 5.

Practice Questions and Problems

Section 1: The Circular Flow

1. federal; state; local
2. paying taxes
3. circular flow diagram

Section 2: The Role of Government in the Market System

1. Technical
2. Economic
3. technical
4. economic
5. market imperfections
6. Externalities
7. understates
8. Goods with positive externalities, or public goods,
9. private property right
10. free ride
11. overutilization
12. incomplete
13. public
14. monopoly
15. business cycles

16. rent seeking
17. less
18. Public choice

Section 3: Overview of the United States Government

1. provision of public goods
   correction of externalities
   promotion of competition
2. fiscal; monetary
3. Federal Reserve
4. money; credit
5. government spending; taxation
6. Federal Reserve
7. Congress and the president
8. president
9. surplus
10. deficit

Section 4: Government in Other Economies

1. centrally planned economy
2. a. Japan
   b. Sweden
   c. Germany
   d. Cuba
   e. United Kingdom
   f. France
3. individual actions; prices; government

Thinking About and Applying the Public Sector

I. The Circular Flow Diagram

a. saving
b. investment
c. payments for goods and services
d. goods and services
e. taxes
f. government services
g. resource services
h. payments for resource services
i. taxes
j. government services
k. goods and services
l. payments for goods and services
m. resource services
n. payments for resource services

o. net exports
p. payments for net exports

II. Government Response to Externalities

1. If the industry is forced to pay for the cleanup, costs will rise, shifting the supply curve to the left (curve S_2). The price of the firm's output will rise, and the quantity produced will fall.

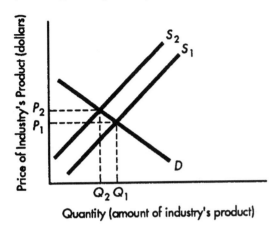

2. The government could achieve this effect by imposing a tax on the industry or by setting quotas on its output. The price would increase.

III. Justifying the Nutrition Labeling and Education Act

When information is not perfect, market imperfections can result. This means that least-cost combinations of resources may not be used or that resources may not be used where they have the highest value. The Nutrition Labeling and Education Act is an attempt to give consumers accurate and complete information.

IV. Extending Regulation

1. The government plans to do this to promote competition, which in turn should encourage technical and economic efficiency.
2. Because consumers lack complete information regarding the safety of seafood, meat, and poultry products, firms do not bear the full cost of improper practices.
3. The government is considering price controls to promote competition. Also, lower drug costs have positive externalities.

Sample Test Chapters 1–5
(*Economics* Chapters 1–5)

1. A good economic model is one that
   a. relies on assumptions that mirror reality.
   b. incorporates knowledge agreed on by all economists.
   c. is limited to predictive statements.
   d. explains or predicts well.
   e. describes reality as closely as possible.

2. One of the key assumptions in economics is that
   a. people make choices that maximize their own self-interest.
   b. resources are limited only because income is distributed unequally.
   c. people focus on those activities in which their opportunity costs are highest.
   d. individual wants are homogeneous.
   e. the government dictates individual consumer behavior.

3. "The United States government must ensure that jobs are provided for the entire labor force." This is an example of a
   a. "what is" statement.
   b. fallacy of composition.
   c. positive statement.
   d. normative statement.
   e. *ceteris paribus* statement.

4. In economics, individuals must make choices because resources
   a. and wants are unlimited.
   b. are scarce and wants are unlimited.
   c. are unlimited and wants are limited.
   d. are unlimited and wants are uniform.
   e. are scarce and wants are limited.

5. A bowed-out production possibilities curve shows
   a. that the marginal opportunity costs of producing a good are constant.
   b. that the incremental costs of a first good are constant as we produce successively larger increments of a second good.
   c. the increasing difficulty or cost of moving resources from one activity to another.
   d. that it is possible to produce more of both goods with available resources.
   e. that the incremental costs of a first good fall as we produce successively larger increments of a second good.

Use the figure below to answer questions 6 and 7.

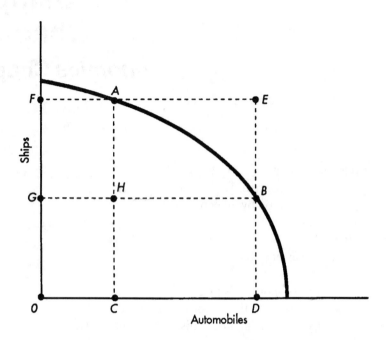

6. The combination of 0–C automobiles and 0–F ships
   a. implies that economic resources are not fully employed.
   b. is not attainable given society's available pool of resources.
   c. suggests that opportunity costs are constant.
   d. is a more efficient output combination than the one at point B.
   e. is one maximum output that can be produced under full employment of available resources.

7. Which of the following statements about point E is true?
   a. It represents a combination of automobiles and ships that underutilizes resources.
   b. It requires an outward shift of the current production possibilities curve to be attainable.
   c. It requires an inward shift of the current production possibilities curve to be attainable.
   d. It represents the maximum amount of automobiles and ships that can be produced with available resources.
   e. It implies that 0–D automobiles can be produced only if 0–F ships are forgone.

Suppose that Mike can produce either 10 surfboards or 2 bicycles per day. Tim, on the other hand, can produce either 12 surfboards or 3 bicycles per day. Use this information to answer questions 8 and 9.

8. The opportunity cost of producing one surfboard is
   a. $\frac{1}{5}$ bicycle for Mike and $\frac{1}{4}$ bicycle for Tim.
   b. $\frac{1}{4}$ bicycle for Mike and $\frac{1}{5}$ bicycle for Tim.
   c. 5 bicycles for Mike and 4 bicycles for Tim.
   d. $\frac{1}{5}$ bicycle for Mike and 4 bicycles for Tim.
   e. 5 bicycles for Mike and $\frac{1}{4}$ bicycle for Tim.

9. From the information above we can conclude that
   a. Mike has a comparative advantage in producing bicycles.
   b. Tim and Mike incur the same opportunity cost in producing surfboards.
   c. Tim has a comparative advantage in producing bicycles.
   d. Mike has a comparative advantage in producing both surfboards and bicycles.
   e. Tim incurs a lower opportunity cost in producing surfboards than does Mike.

10. When we specialize in production activities in which we are most efficient and trade for those goods and services in which other individuals are more efficient, we are applying the principle of
    a. declining opportunity costs.
    b. comparative advantage.
    c. market externalities.
    d. consumer sovereignty.
    e. unlimited wants.

11. A barter system
    a. involves the exchange of goods for money.
    b. exists only when there is no trade.
    c. has fewer transaction costs than does a monetary system.
    d. is an ancient trading system that was eliminated in the Middle Ages.
    e. relies on a double coincidence of wants.

12. The term *price* in the context of individual trade always refers to the
    a. money, or absolute, price of a good.
    b. relative price of a good.
    c. average price of all goods and services in the economy.
    d. transaction costs associated with finding a double coincidence of wants.
    e. value of a good in terms of gold.

13. Changes along the demand curve for a good are changes in
    a. demand caused by changes in the price of the good.
    b. the quantity demanded caused by changes in income.
    c. the quantity demanded caused by changes in the price of the good.
    d. the quantity supplied caused by changes in the price of the good.
    e. demand caused by changes in the price of a complement.

14. The market demand curve can be derived by
    a. adding all individual demand curves horizontally.
    b. adding all individual demand curves vertically.
    c. subtracting all individual demand curves from all individual supply curves.
    d. subtracting all individual demand curves vertically.
    e. picking the midpoint of all individual demand curves.

15. Assume that the market for good Y is initially in equilibrium. If everything else is held constant, an increase in demand for good Y will result in a(n)
    a. decrease in the equilibrium price for good Y.
    b. decrease in the equilibrium quantity demanded of good Y.
    c. increase in the equilibrium quantity of good Y.
    d. decrease in the price of complementary goods.
    e. increase in the supply of good Y.

Use the figure below to answer questions 16 and 17.

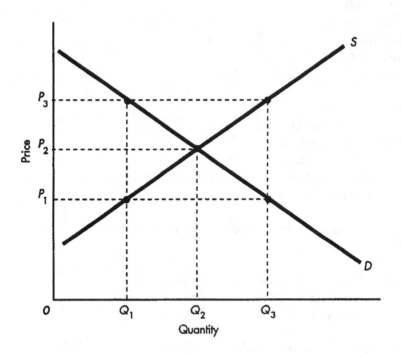

16. An increase in price from P_2 to P_3 would result in a
    a. surplus of $Q_3 - Q_1$ units.
    b. surplus of $Q_1 - 0$ units.
    c. shortage of $Q_3 - Q_1$ units.
    d. shortage of $Q_2 - 0$ units.
    e. surplus of $Q_3 - 0$ units.

17. If price is currently at P_1, over time it will
    a. increase to P_3 because firms will raise prices until they earn a profit.
    b. increase to P_2 because the shortage will put upward pressure on price.
    c. stay at P_1 unless the government imposes a price ceiling.
    d. drop to zero because the shortage will put downward pressure on price.
    e. result in a surplus equal to $Q_3 - Q_1$ units.

18. A leftward shift of the demand curve for a good would most likely be caused by
    a. a reduction in resource costs.
    b. technological improvements.
    c. a decrease in the number of producers.
    d. optimistic profit expectations.
    e. a decrease in the price of a substitute good.

19. Consumer sovereignty refers to the idea that
    a. consumers determine where goods and services are produced.
    b. consumers determine what goods and services are produced.
    c. business firms dictate for whom goods and services are produced.
    d. government dictates the production and sale of certain goods and services.
    e. consumers determine how to deal with inflation.

20. In the circular flow diagram,
    a. the value of national output always exceeds national income.
    b. business firms supply factors of production in exchange for the goods and services provided by households.
    c. financial services are supplied only to business firms.
    d. negative net exports imply a net inflow of foreign goods and services into the home country.
    e. business revenues constitute payment for resource services provided by households.

21. Which of the following is *not* a factor of production?
    a. a risk-taking, innovative architect who starts her own business
    b. $1,000,000 of financial capital provided to PolyGram Record Company
    c. a robot used to speed up production of computer microchips
    d. the acquisition of 50 acres of farmland to be used for cultivating wheat
    e. the entrance of 1,500 people with new Ph.D.s in economics into the labor force

22. Externalities are the
    a. costs of the factors of production.
    b. costs associated with public goods.
    c. efficiency losses associated with a monopoly.
    d. costs or benefits of a transaction that are borne by someone not directly involved in the transaction.
    e. social costs associated with business cycles.

23. What is a key problem associated with public goods?
    a. Public goods can be produced in unlimited quantities.
    b. Public goods are subject to external costs.
    c. It is difficult to exclude individuals from free consumption of public goods.
    d. Frequent government intervention in production processes causes an underallocation of public goods.
    e. Public goods are deemed "economic bads" and so require tax subsidies to be consumed by individuals.

24. Public choice theory
   a. seeks to understand the dynamics of an economic system in which market participants have perfect information.
   b. argues that government intervention in the marketplace tends to benefit small special-interest groups at the expense of a majority of the population.
   c. supports a strong role for government in the economy, to minimize the harmful social effects of market imperfections.
   d. claims that free-riding is not really a problem associated with public goods.
   e. seeks to make monetary and fiscal policies subject to the public's approval.

25. Which of the following is *not* one of the economic responsibilities of government?
   a. manipulating the nation's money supply
   b. promoting fair business practices
   c. subsidizing goods that provide external benefits to society
   d. minimizing the social costs associated with business cycles
   e. providing resources to businesses

Answers to Sample Test

1. d (Chapter 1, Section 2.b; *Economics* Chapter 1)
2. a (Chapter 1, Section 1.c; *Economics* Chapter 1)
3. d (Chapter 1, Section 2.a; *Economics* Chapter 1)
4. b (Chapter 1, Section 1.b; *Economics* Chapter 1)
5. c (Chapter 2, Section 2.a; *Economics* Chapter 2)
6. e (Chapter 2, Section 1.c; *Economics* Chapter 2)
7. b (Chapter 2, Section 1.c; *Economics* Chapter 2)
8. a (Chapter 2, Section 2.b; *Economics* Chapter 2)
9. c (Chapter 2, Section 2.c; *Economics* Chapter 2)
10. b (Chapter 2, Section 2.c; *Economics* Chapter 2)
11. e (Chapter 3, Section 1.b; *Economics* Chapter 3)
12. b (Chapter 3, Section 1.c; *Economics* Chapter 3)
13. c (Chapter 3, Section 2.e; *Economics* Chapter 3)
14. a (Chapter 3, Section 2.d; *Economics* Chapter 3)
15. c (Chapter 3, Section 4.b; *Economics* Chapter 3)
16. a (Chapter 3, Section 4.a; *Economics* Chapter 3)
17. b (Chapter 3, Section 4.a; *Economics* Chapter 3)
18. e (Chapter 3, Section 2.e; *Economics* Chapter 3)
19. b (Chapter 4, Section 1.a; *Economics* Chapter 4)
20. d (Chapter 4, Section 5.b; *Economics* Chapter 4)
21. b (Chapter 4, Section 1.b; *Economics* Chapter 4)
22. d (Chapter 5, Section 2.c; *Economics* Chapter 5)
23. c (Chapter 5, Section 2.d; *Economics* Chapter 5)
24. b (Chapter 5, Section 2.g; *Economics* Chapter 5)
25. e (Chapter 5, Section 3; *Economics* Chapter 5)

Chapter 6

NATIONAL INCOME ACCOUNTING

FUNDAMENTAL QUESTIONS

1. How is the total output of an economy measured?

   Suppose you read an article in the financial section of today's newspaper in which the president argues that the Federal Reserve should lower interest rates because of recent slow growth in the economy. How did the president know that the economy was growing slowly?

   We want to be able to compare the condition of the economy across different points in time and also against the economies of other countries. How can we tell whether the economy is better or worse than before? If we are producing more goods and services than before, the economy is growing. In order to combine dissimilar items like apples and oranges, economists use the market value of goods and services. The **gross domestic product (GDP)** is the market value of all final goods and services produced in a year in a country. We use final goods and services to avoid double-counting. If a tire is to be sold directly to a consumer, the value of the tire is included in the GDP. But if the tire is sold as part of an automobile, its value is already included in the value of the automobile, so we do not count it separately.

2. Who produces the nation's goods and services?

   Economists divide domestic producers into three categories: households, businesses, and the government. Business firms produce the largest part of the U.S. GDP.

3. Who purchases the goods and services produced?

   The groups that purchase the GDP are households, businesses, government, and the international sector. Household spending is called *consumption;* business spending is called *investment; government spending* is spending by the government for goods and services; and spending by the international component is called *net exports*. In the United States, households are the largest purchasers of goods and services. A shorthand way of expressing the GDP as the sum of expenditures is $GDP = C + I + G + X$.

4. Who receives the income from the production of goods and services?

   Income is received by the factors of production, which economists divide into three categories: real property, labor, and capital. The payment to real property is called *rent,* the payment to labor is called *wages,* and the payment to capital is called *interest. Profits* are the sum of corporate profits plus profits from sole proprietorships and partnerships. Two income categories that are not payments to the factors of production are included in the GDP: **capital consumption allowance** and **indirect business taxes**. For GDP as output to be equal to GDP as income, we must include all the expenses producers incur in the production of output. A shorthand way to write GDP as income is GDP = wages + interest + rent + profit − net factor income from abroad + capital consumption allowance + indirect business taxes. (We subtract net factor income from abroad since U.S. GDP refers only to income earned within U.S. borders.)

5. What is the difference between nominal and real GDP?

Nominal GDP measures output in terms of its current dollar value. A rise in nominal GDP can be from an increase in physical goods and services, a rise in prices, or both. **Real GDP** measures output in constant prices. Real GDP can only increase if the production of physical goods and services increases. Real GDP is thus a better indicator of economic activity than nominal GDP.

6. What is a price index?

A **price index** measures the level of average prices and shows how prices, on average, have changed. If a pair of running shoes costs $75 this year, then 10 pairs of running shoes have a market value of $750. If the same shoes cost $80 next year, then 10 pairs have a market value of $800. The nominal value has increased, but we still have only 10 pairs of running shoes. A price index adjusts nominal values for price changes.

Key Terms

national income accounting
gross domestic product (GDP)
intermediate good
value added
inventory
capital consumption allowance
depreciation
indirect business tax
gross national product (GNP)

net national product (NNP)
gross investment
net investment
national income (NI)
personal income (PI)
transfer payment
disposable personal income (DPI)
nominal GDP

real GDP
price index
base year
chain-type real GDP
GDP price index
consumer price index (CPI)
cost of living adjustment (COLA)
producer price index (PPI)

Quick-Check Quiz

Section 1: Measures of Output and Income

1. Gross domestic product is
   a. the market value of all goods and services produced in the United States in a year.
   b. the market value of all final goods and services produced in a year.
   c. the market value of all final goods and services produced in a year within a country's borders.
   d. the market value of all final goods and services sold in a year.
   e. the total number of final goods and services produced in a year by domestic resources.

2. GDP *as expenditures* can be expressed as
   a. $C + I + G + X$.
   b. wages + interest + rent + profits − net factor income from abroad + capital consumption allowance + indirect business taxes.
   c. the sum of the values added at each stage of production.
   d. NI + indirect business taxes.
   e. NI + capital consumption allowance.

3. Which of the following is incorrect?
   a. PI = DPI − personal taxes
   b. GDP = GNP − net factor income from abroad
   c. DPI = PI − personal taxes
   d. NI = NNP − indirect business taxes
   e. NNP = GNP − capital consumption allowance

4. Unplanned inventory
   a. is a cushion above expected sales.
   b. is gross investment − capital consumption allowance.
   c. is the difference between the value of the output and the value of the intermediate goods used in the production of that output.
   d. is unsold goods that the firm had expected to be able to sell when it placed the order.
   e. is the market value of the goods and services produced by a firm in one year.

5. The largest component of total expenditures is
   a. consumption.
   b. investment.
   c. government spending.
   d. net exports.
   e. rent.

6. To get disposable personal income from GNP, we must subtract all of the following except
   a. indirect business taxes.
   b. net factor income from abroad.
   c. capital consumption allowance.
   d. income earned but not received.
   e. personal taxes.

7. To get NNP from GNP, we subtract
   a. capital consumption allowance.
   b. net factor income from abroad.
   c. capital consumption allowance and indirect business taxes.
   d. capital consumption allowance, indirect business taxes, and personal taxes.
   e. capital consumption allowance, indirect business taxes, net transfer payments, and personal taxes.

8. National income equals
   a. GNP – capital consumption allowance.
   b. GNP – net factor income from abroad.
   c. GNP – capital consumption allowance – indirect business taxes.
   d. NNP – indirect business taxes.
   e. Both c and d above are correct.

9. Which of the following is a transfer payment?
   a. profits that are retained by corporations rather than paid out to stockholders
   b. social security benefits
   c. FICA taxes
   d. estimated in-kind wages
   e. barter and cash transactions in the underground economy

10. Which of the following is counted in the GDP?
    a. the value of homemaker services
    b. estimated illegal drug transactions
    c. the value of oil used in the production of gasoline
    d. estimated in-kind wages
    e. the sale of a used automatic dishwasher

Section 2: Nominal and Real Measures

1. Nominal GDP
   a. is real GDP divided by the price level.
   b. measures output in constant prices.
   c. decreases when the price level increases.
   d. measures output in terms of its current dollar value.
   e. is real GDP divided by the consumer price index.

2. In calculating chain-type real GDP growth, economists first calculate growth rates using both beginning and ending year prices, then find real GDP growth by
   a. adding the two growth rates together.
   b. using the larger of the two growth rates.
   c. finding the difference between the two growth rates.
   d. finding the arithmetic mean of the two growth rates.
   e. finding the geometric mean of the two growth rates.

3. The producer price index (PPI)
   a. is the price index given by the ratio of nominal GDP to real GDP.
   b. measures the average price of consumer goods and services that a typical household purchases.
   c. measures average prices received by producers.
   d. was originally known as the COLA.
   e. is used to get real GDP from nominal GDP.

4. The real GDP
   a. is calculated by multiplying the GDP price index by nominal GDP.
   b. measures the average level of prices in the economy and shows, on average, how prices have changed.
   c. measures output in constant prices.
   d. is calculated by dividing nominal GDP by the CPI.
   e. is calculated by dividing nominal GDP by the PPI.

5. A price index equal to 90 in a given year
   a. indicates that prices were lower than prices in the base year.
   b. indicates that the year in question was a year previous to the base year.
   c. indicates that prices were 10 percent higher than prices in the base year.
   d. is inaccurate—price indexes cannot be lower than 100.
   e. indicates that real GDP was lower than GDP in the base year.

6. Social security payments are tied to the
   a. GDP price index.
   b. CPI.
   c. PPI.
   d. wholesale price index.
   e. nominal GDP.

Section 3: Flows of Income and Expenditures

1. Total expenditures on final goods and services
   a. equal NNP.
   b. equal the total value of goods and services produced.
   c. equal total income from selling goods and services.
   d. All of the above are correct.
   e. Only b and c are correct.

Practice Questions and Problems

Section 1: Measures of Output and Income

1. Gross domestic product is the _____ value of all _____ goods and services produced in a year within a country's borders.

2. _____ are goods that are used in the production of a final product.

3. _____ is the difference between the value of output and the value of the intermediate goods used in the production of that output.

4. _____ is a firm's stock of unsold goods.

5. The estimated value of capital goods used up or worn out in a year plus the value of accidental damage to capital goods is called _____ , or depreciation.

6. Excise taxes and sales taxes are forms of _____ .
7. List the three factors of production and the name of the payments each factor receives. What additional four items must be figured in to find gross domestic product?

_____

_____

_____

8. GNP minus net factor income from abroad yields _____ .
9. A lei maker buys flowers from a nursery for $125. She makes 50 leis from the flowers and sells each lei for $3.99. What is the value added for the lei maker? _____
10. A Kansas farmer sells wheat to a craftsperson to make into decorative ornaments. The farmer sells his wheat to the craftsperson for $300. The craftsperson adds labor, valued at $200, and some ribbons, valued at $50, and produces 110 ornaments. What is the final market value of each ornament? _____
11. Unplanned inventory _____ (is, is not) included in the GDP.
12. Government spending on goods and services _____ (is, is not) the largest component of GDP as expenditures.
13. Write the formulas for the following:

    Gross domestic product as expenditures (GDP) _____

    Gross domestic product as income (GDP) _____

    Gross national product (GNP) _____

    Net national product (NNP) _____

    National income (NI) _____

    Personal income (PI) _____

    Disposable personal income (DPI) _____

14. Use the information below to calculate GDP, GNP, NNP, and NI. All figures are in billions of dollars.

Capital consumption allowance	328	Wages and salaries	1,803
Corporate profits	124	Personal taxes	398
Rents	6	Indirect business taxes	273
Interest	264	Proprietor's income	248
Net factor income from abroad	43		

    GDP _____ GNP _____ NNP _____ NI _____

Section 2: Nominal and Real Measures

1. The table below shows nominal GDP and the GDP price index for 3 years. Use this information to calculate the real GDP and to answer the following questions.

Year	Nominal GDP	GDP Price Index	Real GDP
1	206	98	_____
2	216	100	_____
3	228	115	_____

   a. Which year is the base year? _____
   b. Prices in year 3 were _____ (higher, lower) than prices in the base year.
   c. During year 3, nominal GDP _____ (increased, did not change, decreased) and real GDP _____ (increased, did not change, decreased).

2. You have been asked to calculate chain-type real GDP growth from year 1 to year 2 for an economy that produces three products: cereal, beef, and doughnuts. You have been given the following data:

	Product	Quantity	Price
Year 1	Cereal	1,000	$1.00
	Beef	700	$2.00
	Doughnuts	600	$0.50
Year 2	Cereal	1,400	$1.10
	Beef	900	$2.50
	Doughnuts	500	$0.75

   a. What is the constant-dollar real GDP growth rate from year 1 to year 2, using year 1 as the base year? _____
   b. What is the constant-dollar real GDP growth rate from year 1 to year 2, using year 2 as the base year? _____
   c. What is the chain-type real GDP growth rate from year 1 to year 2? _____

3. An increase in the _____ index can indicate a coming change in the CPI.

4. Why isn't nominal GDP a good measure of the strength or weakness of the economy? What measure would be better?

   _____
   _____
   _____
   _____

5. If the price index in the current year is 212, then prices have _____ (increased, not changed, decreased) by _____ percent from the base year.

Section 3: Flows of Income and Expenditures

1. Fill in the diagram below with the terms listed below. Dollar flows are represented by broken lines. The flow of physical goods and services is represented by solid lines.

   investment
   payments for goods and services
   taxes
   resource services
   net exports

   saving
   goods and services
   government services
   payments for resource services
   payments for net exports

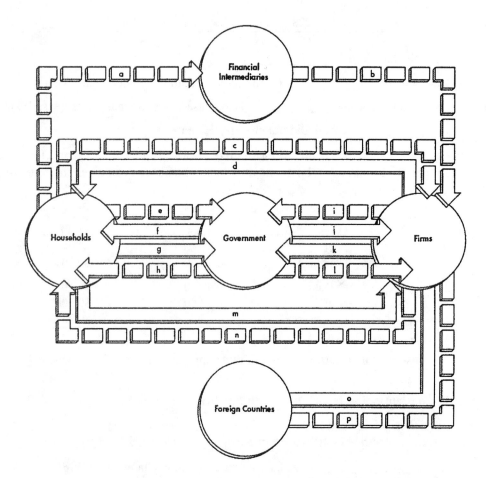

Thinking About and Applying National Income Accounting

I. Difficulties in Measuring GDP

GDP is used to measure economic performance and to determine whether the overall standard of living is improving or declining. But does GDP really measure the total output of the economy? Decide if each item listed below is counted as part of GDP. If the item is *not* counted but is productive activity, indicate whether its omission overstates or understates GDP.

1. cocaine sold by Colombians to U.S. consumers
2. your parents' service to the family doing housework

3. a college textbook published this year
4. the fee for your cat's yearly rabies vaccine
5. intermediate goods
6. $10 paid for a 3-year-old infant car seat purchased at a garage sale
7. your teacher's salary this year
8. this year's rental income from an office building
9. the services of a homeowner painting his or her own house
10. pollution produced as a result of steel production

II. The Expenditures Approach for Calculating GDP

1. Use the information below to calculate GDP, GNP, NNP, NI, PI, and DPI. All figures are in billions of dollars.

Net factor income from abroad	112
Income earned but not received	110
Personal taxes	198
Government purchases of goods and services	396
Capital consumption allowance	684
Personal consumption expenditures	1,326
Imports	800
Gross private domestic investment	296
Income received but not earned	225
Exports	670
Indirect business taxes	515

   GDP _____ GNP _____ NNP _____

   NI _____ PI _____ DPI _____

III. Understanding Price Indexes

Suppose the economy of Strandasville produces only four goods: trolls, pizza, desk chairs, and sweaters. The table below shows the dollar value of output for three different years.

Year	Number of Trolls	Price per Troll	Number of Pizzas	Price per Pizza
1	1,000	$5	8,000	$6.00
2	1,000	$6	8,000	$6.60
3	4,000	$7	10,000	$6.80

Year	Number of Desk Chairs	Price per Chair	Number of Sweaters	Price per Sweater
1	3,000	$20	5,000	$20
2	3,000	$25	5,000	$18
3	3,500	$25	4,900	$15

1. Calculate the total dollar value of output for year 1, year 2, and year 3.

2. The dollar value of output in year 2 is higher than the dollar value of output in year 1
   a. entirely because of price changes.
   b. entirely because of output changes.
   c. because of both price and output changes.

3. The dollar value of output in year 3 is higher than the dollar value of output in year 1
   a. entirely because of price changes.
   b. entirely because of output changes.
   c. because of both price and output changes.

IV. Reconciling GDP as Income and GDP as Expenditures

Martin Rabblerouser is trying to calculate the GDP for an obscure Latin American country, but has gotten his accounts all mixed up. Use the information below to calculate

1. GDP as expenditures _____

2. GDP as income _____

Income received but not earned	133
Net factor income from abroad	50
Personal consumption expenditures	2,466
Rent	−15
Capital consumption allowance	396
Imports	25
Indirect business taxes	331
Personal taxes	452
Income earned but not received	45
Government spending	691
Wages	2,200
Gross investment	457
Profits	454
Interest	284
Exports	11

   Your answers to (1) and (2) should match.

3. Now use your answer from (1) and (2) and the information above to calculate GNP, NNP, NI, PI, and DPI.

   GNP _____ NNP _____ NI _____ PI _____

   DPI _____

Chapter 6 Homework Problems

Name _____

1. What does GDP stand for, and what does it measure?

2. Express GDP as the sum of expenditures in the economy.

3. Express GDP as the sum of incomes in the economy.

4. In 1999, the nominal GDP of the hypothetical country of Dimmenland was 1.02 billion dimmens; 1999 is also the base year for calculating the GDP price index. In 2000, the nominal GDP of Dimmenland grew to 1.08 billion dimmens. The GDP price index for 2000 was 105.
   a. What was the real GDP for Dimmenland in 1999 and 2000?

   b. Did the people of Dimmenland have a larger economy in 1999 or in 2000?

5. You have been hired by the government as an economic statistician and given the job of calculating the CPI (the *chili* price index, not the consumer price index). According to the government's official recipe, the ingredients for a batch of chili are:

3 pounds of hamburger

2 pounds of tomatoes

.5 pounds of onions

The base year for calculating the CPI is 1991. The prices of the ingredients for chili are determined by an extensive nationwide survey. The current and 1991 prices for the ingredients are:

Hamburger: $1.20 per pound in 1991; $1.15 per pound currently

Tomatoes: $1.50 per pound in 1991; $1.75 per pound currently

Onions: $.20 per pound in 1991; $.30 per pound currently

Calculate the cost of a batch of chili in 1991 and currently, and express the current price as a price index with 1991 as the base year.

If your instructor assigns these problems, write your answers above, then tear out this page and hand it in.

Answers

Quick-Check Quiz

Section 1: Measures of Output and Income

1. c; 2. a; 3. a; 4. d; 5. a; 6. b; 7. a; 8. e; 9. b; 10. d
If you missed any of these questions, you should go back and review Section 1 of Chapter 6.

Section 2: Nominal and Real Measures

1. d; 2. e; 3. c; 4. c; 5. a; 6. b
If you missed any of these questions, you should go back and review Section 2 of Chapter 6.

Section 3: Flows of Income and Expenditures

1. e
If you missed this question, you should go back and review Section 3 of Chapter 6.

Practice Questions and Problems

Section 1: Measures of Output and Income

1. market; final
2. Intermediate goods
3. Value added
4. Inventory
5. capital consumption allowance
6. indirect business taxes
7. real property   rent
   labor   wages
   capital   interest
   To get GDP, you must add profits, capital consumption allowance, and indirect business taxes and subtract net factor income from abroad.
8. gross domestic product
9. $74.50 (The lei maker gets $3.99 for each of her 50 leis, for a total of $199.50. Since her cost for the flowers was $125, her value added is $199.50 − $125 = $74.50.)
10. $5 (The total of the values added is $300 + $200 + $50 = $550. The 110 ornaments are worth $550, or $5 each.)
11. is
12. is not—Consumption is the largest expenditure component.
13. GDP (as expenditures) = $C + I + G + X$
    GDP (as income) = wages + rent + interest + profits − net factor income from abroad + indirect business taxes + capital consumption allowance
    GNP = GDP + net factor income from abroad
    NNP = GNP − capital consumption allowance

NI = NNP − indirect business taxes
PI = NI + income received but not earned − income earned but not received
DPI = PI − personal taxes

14. GDP = wages + rent + interest + profits (corporate profits + proprietor's income) − net factor income from abroad + indirect business taxes + capital consumption allowance = 1,803 + 6 + 264 + (124 + 248) − 43 + 328 + 273 = 3,003
GNP = GDP + net factor income from abroad = 3,003 + 43 = 3,046
NNP = GNP − capital consumption allowance = 3,046 − 328 = 2,718
NI = NNP − indirect business taxes = 2,718 − 273 = 2,445

Section 2: Nominal and Real Measures

1.

Year	Real GDP
1	206/98 × 100 = 210.20
2	216 (this is the base year)
3	228/115 × 100 = 198.26

   a. Year 2. You can tell because the price index is 100 for that year.
   b. higher
   c. increased; decreased

2. a. 5.6%
   (Expenditures in year 2 using year 1 prices)/(Expenditures in year 1 using year 1 prices) − 1 =

   $$\frac{(1{,}400 \text{ cereal} \times \$1.00) + (600 \text{ beef} \times \$2.00) + (500 \text{ doughnuts} \times \$0.50)}{(1{,}000 \text{ cereal} \times \$1.00) + (700 \text{ beef} \times \$2.00) + (600 \text{ doughnuts} \times \$0.50)} - 1 =$$

   $$\frac{\$2{,}850}{\$2{,}700} - 1 = 1.056 - 1 = .056 \text{ or } 5.6\%$$

   b. 3.5%
   (Expenditures in year 2 using year 2 prices)/(Expenditures in year 1 using year 2 prices) − 1 =

   $$\frac{(1{,}400 \text{ cereal} \times \$1.10) + (600 \text{ beef} \times \$2.50) + (500 \text{ doughnuts} \times \$0.75)}{(1{,}000 \text{ cereal} \times \$1.10) + (700 \text{ beef} \times \$2.50) + (600 \text{ doughnuts} \times \$0.75)} - 1 =$$

   $$\frac{\$3{,}415}{\$3{,}300} - 1 = 1.035 - 1 = .035 \text{ or } 3.5\%$$

   c. 4.5%
   Square root of (expenditures ratio with year 1 base × expenditures ratio with year 2 base) − 1 = square root of (1.056 × 1.035) − 1 = square root of 1.093 − 1 = 1.045 − 1 = .045 or 4.5%

3. producer price
4. Increases in nominal GDP can come about from a rise in prices, an increase in output, or both. To know if the economy is performing better than before, we need to know if output has increased. Real GDP is a better measure, since it rises only when output has increased.
5. increased; 112

Section 3: Flows of Income and Expenditures

line a—saving
line b—investment
line c—payments for goods and services
line d—goods and services
line e—taxes
line f—government services
line g—resource services
line h—payments for resource services
line i—taxes
line j—government services
line k—goods and services
line l—payments for goods and services
line m—resource services
line n—payments for resource services
line o—net exports
line p—payments for net exports

Thinking About and Applying National Income Accounting

I. *Difficulties in Measuring GDP*

1. The Colombians' sale of cocaine to U.S. consumers is an illegal activity and therefore not represented in the GDP. If the resources used to produce cocaine are domestically owned and production occurred this year, then this activity should be included in the GDP. Its omission would understate the GDP.
2. This activity does not involve a market transaction and therefore is not included in the GDP. It is productive activity, however, and its omission understates the GDP.
3. A college textbook published this year would be included in the GDP.
4. The fee for your cat's yearly rabies vaccine would be included in the GDP.
5. Intermediate goods are not counted in the GDP. To do so would be double-counting.
6. A 3-year-old car seat was not produced this year. It is not and should not be counted in the GDP.
7. Your teacher's salary this year is for productive activity and is included in the GDP.
8. This year's rental income from an office building represents productive activity—the use of the space over a period of time. It is included in the GDP.
9. The services of a homeowner painting his or her own house would not be included in the GDP, since no market transaction is involved. However, it does represent productive activity and should be included. GDP is understated by its omission.
10. Some economists feel that the production of "bads" such as pollution should be included in GDP if we are to get a true picture of economic well-being. Production of "bads" such as pollution is not currently included in GDP. Inclusion of "bads" would lower the GDP.

II. *The Expenditures Approach for Calculating GDP*

1. GDP = $C + I + G + X$ = 1,326 + 296 + 396 + (670 − 800) = 1,888
   GNP = GDP + net factor income from abroad = 1,888 + 112 = 2,000
   NNP = GNP − capital consumption allowance = 2,000 − 684 = 1,316
   NI = NNP − indirect business taxes = 1,316 − 515 = 801

PI = NI − income earned but not received + income received but not earned = 801 − 110 + 225 = 916
DPI = PI − personal taxes = 916 − 198 = 718

III. Understanding Price Indexes

1. The dollar value of output for year 1 is 1,000(5) + 8,000(6) + 3,000(20) + 5,000(20) = 213,000. For year 2 the value is 1,000(6) + 8,000(6.6) + 3,000(25) + 5,000(18) = 223,800. For year 3 the value is 4,000(7) + 10,000(6.8) + 3,500(25) + 4,900(15) = 257,000.
2. a
3. c

IV. Reconciling GDP as Income and GDP as Expenditures

1. GDP (as expenditures) = C + I + G + X
   = 2,466 + 457 + 691 + (11 − 25) = 3,600
2. GDP (as income) = wages + rent + interest + profits − net factor income from abroad
       + indirect business taxes + capital consumption allowance
   = 2,200 + (−15) + 284 + 454 − 50 + 331 + 396 = 3,600
3. GNP = GDP + net factor income from abroad = 3,600 + 50 = 3,650
   NNP = GNP − capital consumption allowance = 3,650 − 396 = 3,254
   NI = NNP − indirect business taxes = 3,254 − 331 = 2,923
   PI = NI + income received but not earned − income earned but not received
      = 2,923 + 133 − 45 = 3,011
   DPI = PI − personal taxes = 3,011 − 452 = 2,559

Chapter 7

AN INTRODUCTION TO THE FOREIGN EXCHANGE MARKET AND THE BALANCE OF PAYMENTS

FUNDAMENTAL QUESTIONS

1. How do individuals of one nation trade money with individuals of another nation?

   People trade one currency for another in **foreign exchange markets.** It is not necessary for large traders to go to a specific place to conduct such transactions. They call a bank that deals in foreign currency and ask the bank to convert some of their dollars to the currency they want. The amount of foreign currency exchanged for dollars depends on the **exchange rate**—the price of one country's money in terms of another.

2. How do changes in exchange rates affect international trade?

   If the dollar appreciates against a foreign currency, you will get more of that currency per dollar. If the dollar depreciates against a foreign currency, you will get less of that currency per dollar. If a country's currency appreciates in value, international demand for its products falls, all other things being equal. This is because that country's goods become more expensive in terms of other currencies. If a country's currency depreciates, the prices of its goods and services in terms of other countries' currencies fall and international demand for its products increases.

3. How do nations record their transactions with the rest of the world?

   The record of a nation's transactions with the rest of the world is called its **balance of payments.** The balance of payments is divided into two categories: the **current account** and the **capital account.** The current account is the sum of the balances for merchandise, services, investment income, and unilateral transfers. The capital account records the transactions necessary to move these into and out of the country. The net balance in the balance of payments must be zero, so a **deficit** (or surplus) in the current account must be offset by a **surplus** (or deficit) in the capital account. A country becomes a larger net debtor (or smaller net creditor) if it shows a deficit in its current account (or surplus in its capital account).

Key Terms

foreign exchange
foreign exchange market
exchange rate
balance of payments

double-entry bookkeeping
current account
surplus
deficit

balance of trade
capital account

Quick-Check Quiz

Section 1: The Foreign Exchange Market

1. The foreign exchange market, like the New York Stock Exchange, is located in a specific building in New York City. (true or false?) _____

2. Most foreign exchange transactions involve the movement of currency. (true or false?) _____

3. As a country's currency depreciates, international demand for its products _____ (rises, falls), all other things being equal.

4. If one U.S. dollar sells for 90.00 yen, then the price of the Japanese yen in terms of dollars is
   a. $.01111.
   b. $.1111.
   c. $1.1111.
   d. $90.00.
   e. $.90.

5. Suppose that a cassette recorder costs 226.44 Norwegian krone and that the current exchange rate between the U.S. dollar and the Norwegian krone is $.1590. What is the price of the cassette recorder in U.S. dollars?
   a. $1,424.15
   b. $36.00
   c. $181.15
   d. $283.05
   e. $212.99

6. Suppose that the exchange rate between the U.S. dollar and the Australian dollar is $.7985 (1AUD = $.7985). If the exchange rate tomorrow is $.7975, then the Australian dollar has _____ against the U.S. dollar. Australian goods will be _____ in the United States.
   a. appreciated; more expensive
   b. appreciated; less expensive
   c. depreciated; more expensive
   d. depreciated; less expensive
   e. depreciated; the same price as before

7. If a Malaysian ringgit is equivalent to $.2632 U.S. dollars, then $1 is equal to _____ , and an opal ring costing 950 ringgits would have a U.S. dollar value of _____ .
   a. 3.80; 3,609.42
   b. 3.80; 250.04
   c. .26; 3,609.42
   d. .26; 250.04
   e. 1; 950

8. If the U.S. dollar drops to .9222 euros from .9374 euros, then
   a. the dollar has appreciated against the euro, and the prices of German cars will increase in the United States.
   b. the dollar has appreciated against the euro, and the prices of German cars will decrease in the United States.
   c. the dollar has depreciated against the euro, and the prices of German cars will increase in the United States.
   d. the dollar has depreciated against the euro, and the prices of German cars will decrease in the United States.
   e. the dollar has depreciated against the euro, and the prices of American cars will increase in Germany.

9. The great majority of transactions in the foreign exchange market involve
   a. foreign coins.
   b. foreign paper money.
   c. bank deposits denominated in foreign currency.
   d. foreign currency.
   e. items b and c above.

Section 2: The Balance of Payments

1. Which of the following is *not* included in the current account?
   a. merchandise balances
   b. service balances
   c. unilateral transfer accounts
   d. purchases of stocks and bonds
   e. All of the above are included in the current account.

2. If a Japanese investor bought the Epic Center office building in Wichita, Kansas, the transaction would be recorded as a _____ in the _____ account.
   a. credit; current
   b. debit; current
   c. credit; investment income
   d. credit; capital
   e. debit; capital

3. Since 1985, the United States has had a _____ (deficit, surplus) in its current account.

4. Trade involving financial assets and international investment is recorded in the _____ account.
   a. current
   b. merchandise
   c. capital
   d. services
   e. investment income

5. If export goods exceed import goods, the (merchandise, services, unilateral transfers) account will show a (deficit, surplus).
   a. merchandise; deficit
   b. merchandise; surplus
   c. services; deficit
   d. services; surplus
   e. unilateral transfers; surplus

6. Which account contains all of the activities involving goods and services?
   a. merchandise
   b. services
   c. unilateral transfers
   d. current
   e. capital

7. In the terminology of the balance of payments, *capital* refers to all of the following except
   a. bank deposits.
   b. purchases of stocks.
   c. purchases of bonds.
   d. loans.
   e. purchases of equipment.

8. A country with a deficit in its current account
   a. exports more goods and services than it imports.
   b. is running a deficit in its capital account.
   c. is a net lender to the rest of the world.
   d. is a net borrower from the rest of the world.
   e. is running a surplus in its merchandise account.

9. The net balance in the balance of payments
   a. is positive if a country is a net creditor to the rest of the world.
   b. is negative if a country imports more goods and services than it exports.
   c. is negative if the country is a net debtor to the rest of the world.
   d. is positive if a country exports more goods and services than it imports.
   e. must be zero.

10. The United States
    a. has always run a surplus in its merchandise account.
    b. typically runs a surplus in its unilateral transfers account.
    c. typically runs a deficit in its services account.
    d. was an international creditor from the end of World War I until the mid-1980s.
    e. had large capital account deficits in the 1980s.

Practice Questions and Problems

Section 1: The Foreign Exchange Market

1. _____ is another expression for foreign money.
2. A global market in which people trade one currency for another is called a(n) _____.
3. A(n) _____ is the price of one country's money in terms of another.
4. A rise in the value of a currency is called _____, and a decrease in the value of a currency is called _____.
5. What is the price of one U.S. dollar given the following exchange rates?
    a. 1 Canadian dollar = $.86610 _____
    b. 1 Swiss franc = $.70597 _____
    c. 1 euro = $.9222 _____
    d. 1 Japanese yen = $.00677 _____
    e. 1 British pound = $1.8155 _____
6. A 35-mm camera manufactured in the United States costs $150. Using the exchange rates listed in the table below, what would the camera cost in each of the following countries?

Country	U.S. Dollar Equivalent	Currency per U.S. Dollar
Britain (pound)	1.4559	.6869
Canada (dollar)	.6610	1.5129
Mexico (peso)	.1033	9.678
Pakistan (rupee)	.0463	21.61
Philippines (peso)	.04413	22.66

   a. Britain _____
   b. Canada _____
   c. Mexico _____
   d. Pakistan _____
   e. Philippines _____

7. Suppose the dollar ended at 1.4165 Swiss francs today, well above yesterday's 1.4045 francs.
   a. The dollar has _____ (appreciated, depreciated) against the franc.
   b. Swiss goods are now _____ (more expensive, cheaper) in the United States.
   c. As a result of the change in exchange rates, U.S. exports to Switzerland will _____ (increase, decrease), all other things being equal.

8. You read in the paper that the euro is expected to depreciate against the dollar. Therefore, the price of a Finnish sweater sold in the United States will _____ (increase, decrease) and the price of U.S. blue jeans sold in Finland will _____ (increase, decrease).

Section 2: The Balance of Payments

1. The _____ is a record of a country's trade in goods, services, and financial assets with the rest of the world.

2. _____ record activities that bring payments into a country, and _____ record activities that involve payments to the rest of the world.

3. _____ means that for every transaction there is a credit entry and a debit entry.

4. When exports exceed imports, the merchandise account shows a _____.

5. The balance on the _____ account is frequently referred to as the balance of trade.

6. A net _____ owes more to the rest of the world than it is owed.

7. The sum of the balances in the merchandise, services, investment income, and unilateral transfers accounts is called the _____ account.

8. Use the table below to calculate the current account, capital account, and statistical discrepancy for the mythical country of Dimmenland.

Account	Credit	Debit	Net Balance
Merchandise	412.68	212.89	199.79
Services	142.52	108.37	34.15
Investment income	114.24	91.12	23.12
Unilateral transfers			−100.32
Current account			_____
Capital account	170.36	322.36	_____
Statistical discrepancy			_____

9. Refer to problem 8. Dimmenland is running a _____ (deficit, surplus) in its current account and a _____ (deficit, surplus) in its capital account. Dimmenland is becoming a greater net _____ (debtor, creditor) to the rest of the world.

10. Net exports is the sum of the merchandise and services balances. Refer to problem 8. Calculate Dimmenland's net exports. If consumption = $2,490, investment = $58.48, and government spending = $540.12, what is Dimmenland's GDP? _____

11. A government-tolerated alternative to the official exchange market is called a _____ market rather than a black market.

Thinking About and Applying the Foreign Exchange Market and the Balance of Payments

I. The Balance of Payments as an Indicator

A surplus in the merchandise account means that a nation is exporting more goods than it is importing. This is often interpreted as a sign that a nation's producers can produce at a lower cost than their foreign counterparts. A trade deficit may indicate that a nation's producers are less efficient than their foreign counterparts.

In 1993, the U.S. Department of Commerce announced that the United States was a debtor nation. Can you explain why many analysts viewed the U.S. balance of payments accounts with concern?

_____
_____
_____
_____

II. The Balance of Payments and Exchange Rates

If U.S. residents lend and invest less in foreign countries than foreigners lend and invest in the United States, the capital account will be in surplus. If U.S. purchases of foreign stocks and bonds exceed foreign purchases of U.S. stocks and bonds, then more funds are leaving the country than entering it, and the capital account will be in deficit. Pretend that you are willing to sell your stereo system to a French resident. Would you prefer to be paid in U.S. dollars or euro? Since you can't easily spend euros in this country, you would prefer to be paid in U.S. dollars. So if the French buy more U.S. goods and services, they will need dollars to pay for them and the dollar will appreciate against the euro. Similarly, if U.S. investors demand more French bonds and stocks, the euro will appreciate.

In view of what you have read about U.S. and foreign lending, what impact will a capital account surplus have on a domestic currency? If U.S. federal budget deficits continue, what will be the impact on the dollar?

_____
_____
_____
_____

III. Black Markets in Foreign Exchange

1. Consider the market for dollars in terms of the borg, the domestic currency of Dimmenland. The government of Dimmenland has set an artificially low official exchange rate of 5 borgs per U.S. dollar.

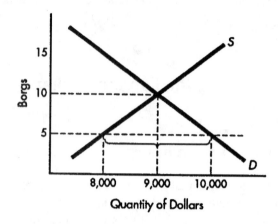

The demand for dollars is D, and the supply is S. The free market price is 10 borgs, but the government has set an artificial exchange rate of 5 borgs per dollar. At this low rate, only 8,000 dollars will be supplied, but 10,000 will be demanded. A shortage develops, spawning a black market. How high will the black market price be bid up?

_____
_____
_____
_____

2. In August 1982, the Mexican government banned the sale of U.S. dollars by Mexican banks. The exchange rate went from 69.5 pesos per dollar to 120.0 pesos per dollar. Use the graph below to illustrate how the black market developed.

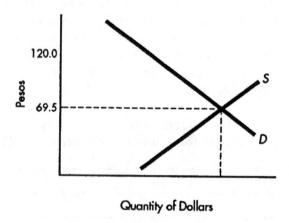

IV. The Current Account

Martin Rabblerouser has gotten his accounts all jumbled again. Please place these accounts under their proper heading.

travel and tourism
unilateral transfers
royalties

merchandise
insurance premiums
transportation costs

investment income
services

Current Account

1. _____
2. _____
3. _____
   a. _____
   b. _____
   c. _____
   d. _____
4. _____

V. Japan's Trade Surplus

Recently, the *Wall Street Journal* reported that U.S. and Japanese negotiators would meet in Washington to discuss a "framework accord" aimed at opening Japanese markets. "Mr. Bentsen [Treasury Secretary] and other U.S. officials increasingly blame Japan for much of what ails the world's economy. Mr. Bentsen said Japan's huge trade surplus hurts world growth and he continued his call on Japan to step up government spending or cut taxes to strengthen its economy. . . ."

From what you know about the balance of payments, is Mr. Bentsen referring to a surplus in Japan's current account or in its capital account? Is Japan a net lender to or a net borrower from the rest of the world?

_____
_____
_____
_____

Chapter 7   Homework Problems

Name _____

1. If you hear the following on the evening news: "In foreign exchange markets today, the dollar appreciated compared to the euro," what happened?

2. If you hear the following on the evening news: "In foreign exchange markets today, the dollar depreciated compared to the Japanese yen," what happened?

3. If you hear the following on the evening news: "Last month, the U.S. balance of trade ran a $50 billion deficit," what happened?

4. What is the difference between the balance of trade and the balance on current account?

5. Suppose the exchange rate between the U.S. dollar and the euro changed from 1.5 euros per dollar to 2.0 euros per dollar.
   a. Did the dollar appreciate or depreciate, relative to the mark?

   b. Did the euro appreciate or depreciate, relative to the dollar?

   c. Suppose you are a wheat farmer in the United States, where your wheat sells for $4.00 per bushel. When the exchange rate changed, what happened to the price that a German buyer had to pay in euros for your wheat? Will German buyers want to buy more or less wheat after the exchange rate changed than they bought before?

   d. Suppose you are a car dealer in the United States selling BMWs made in Germany. The German price for your best-selling model BMW is 60,000 euros. When the exchange rate changed, what happened to the price that you have to pay in dollars for the BMW? As an importer, will you be better off or worse off as a result of the exchange rate change?

If you instructor assigns these problems, write your answers above, then tear out this page and hand it in.

Answers

Quick-Check Quiz

Section 1: The Foreign Exchange Market

1. false; 2. false; 3. rises; 4. a; 5. b; 6. d; 7. b; 8. c; 9. c
If you missed any of these questions, you should go back and review Section 1 of Chapter 7.

Section 2: The Balance of Payments

1. d; 2. d; 3. deficit; 4. c; 5. b; 6. d; 7. e; 8. d; 9. e; 10. d
If you missed any of these questions, you should go back and review Section 2 of Chapter 7.

Practice Questions and Problems

Section 1: The Foreign Exchange Market

1. Foreign exchange
2. foreign exchange market
3. exchange rate
4. appreciation; depreciation
5. a. 1/.86610 = CAD1.154601
   b. 1/.70597 = CHF1.4164907
   c. 1/.9222 = EUR1.844
   d. 1/.00677 = JPY147.71048
   e. 1/1.8155 = GBP.5508124
6. a. $150 × GBP.6869/ = GBP103.04
   b. $150 × CAD1.5129 = CAD226.94
   c. $150 × MXP9.678 = MXP1,451.70
   d. $150 × RS21.61/$ = RS3,241.5
   e. $150 × 22.66 pesos/$ = 3,399 pesos
7. a. appreciated
   b. cheaper
   c. decrease
8. decrease; increase

Section 2: The Balance of Payments

1. balance of payments
2. Credits; debits
3. Double-entry bookkeeping
4. surplus
5. merchandise
6. debtor
7. current

8. Current account = merchandise balance + services balances + investment income + unilateral transfers = 199.79 + 34.15 + 23.12 − 100.32 = 156.74
   Capital account = capital credits − capital debits = 170.36 − 322.36 = − 152
   Current account + capital account + statistical discrepancy = 0
   156.74 + − 152 + statistical discrepancy = 0
   Statistical discrepancy = 4.74
9. surplus; deficit; creditor
10. Net exports = merchandise balance + services balance = 199.79 + 34.15 = 233.94
    GDP = $C + I + G + X$ = 2,490 + 58.48 + 540.12 + 233.94 = 3,322.54
11. parallel

Thinking About and Applying the Foreign Exchange Market and the Balance of Payments

I. The Balance of Payments as an Indicator

A merchandise deficit such as the United States had in 1993 may indicate that domestic producers have higher costs than their foreign competitors. Many analysts viewed the 1993 current account deficit as a sign that U.S. manufacturers had lost their competitive edge.

II. The Balance of Payments and Exchange Rates

A capital account surplus means that there are more foreign purchases of U.S. stocks and bonds than U.S. purchases of foreign stocks and bonds. Foreign purchasers therefore need to acquire U.S. dollars, so the dollar will appreciate. U.S. federal budget deficits may signal higher domestic interest rates. Foreign investors will be attracted to the high U.S. interest rates, and the dollar will appreciate.

III. Black Markets in Foreign Exchange

1. The demand curve indicates that consumers will be willing to pay 15 borgs per dollar for 8,000 dollars. As the black market exchange rate rises above the official rate, however, more dollars will be supplied so that the exchange rate is less than 15.
2.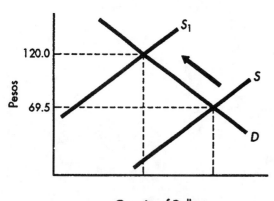

A decrease in the number of suppliers shifts the supply curve to the left and increases the price of the dollar.

IV. The Current Account

Current Account
1. merchandise
2. unilateral transfers
3. services
    a. travel and tourism
    b. royalties
    c. insurance premiums
    d. transportation costs
4. investment income

V. *Japan's Trade Surplus*

Mr. Bentsen refers to a surplus in Japan's current account, meaning that Japan exported more goods and services than it imported. Japan is a net lender to the rest of the world.

Chapter 8

UNEMPLOYMENT AND INFLATION

FUNDAMENTAL QUESTIONS

1. What is a business cycle?

   Business cycles are recurring patterns of ups and downs in real GDP. A typical cycle has four stages: expansion, peak, contraction, and trough. During an economic expansion (boom), output, employment, incomes, and prices all rise. A peak is reached, after which economic activity declines. During the contraction (**recession**) phase, output, employment, and income all drop. If the contraction is severe enough, prices may also decline. The trough marks the end of a contraction and the beginning of a new expansion.

2. How is the unemployment rate defined and measured?

   The **unemployment rate** is the percentage of the labor force that is not working. Economists do not include the entire population in the labor force: it is of little consequence, for example, that a newborn baby is unemployed. To be in the U.S. labor force, an individual must be working or actively seeking work.

   Some types of unemployment have more impact on the economy than others. *Frictional unemployment* occurs when previously employed workers change jobs or new workers seek their first jobs. *Seasonal unemployment* is a product of regular, recurring changes in the hiring needs of certain industries. Both these types of unemployment tend to be short-term. *Structural unemployment*, on the other hand, results from fundamental changes in the structure of the economy, and can be long-term. Structurally unemployed persons can't find *any* job they can do. Likewise, *cyclically unemployed* persons who are out of work because the economy is in a recession may be unemployed for a long time.

3. What is the cost of unemployed resources?

   The cost of unemployed resources is lost output. **Potential real GDP** is the level of output that can be produced if all nonlabor resources are fully utilized and unemployment is at its natural rate—that is, if the economy is producing the level of output it can realistically produce. To measure lost output, one subtracts the actual real GDP from potential real GDP. The resulting figure indicates the *GDP gap*—the cost of unemployed resources.

   Economists do not advocate a zero unemployment rate. Some unemployment is necessary so that workers may be channeled to their most productive employment as their skills change. Economists use the term **natural rate of unemployment** to describe the unemployment rate that would exist in the absence of cyclical unemployment. It describes the labor market when the economy is producing what it realistically can produce. Estimates of the natural rate of unemployment vary from 4 percent to around 7 percent.

4. What is inflation?

Inflation is a sustained rise in the average level of prices. This does not mean that *all* prices will rise. Some may rise and some may fall, but inflation occurs when the *average* level of prices rises.

5. Why is inflation a problem?

Inflation is not a problem if prices and incomes rise at the same rate. But if incomes rise more slowly than prices, households will not be able to buy as many goods and services as they did before. Unanticipated inflation redistributes income away from those who receive fixed incomes toward those who make fixed expenditures. Suppose that your mother agrees to lend you $1,000 for school and that prices unexpectedly double between the time you receive the money and the time you repay your mother. Your mother has lost half of her purchasing power: the $1,000 that you paid back can only buy what $500 bought at the time she lent you the money. Your mother, like other creditors, has lost purchasing power to inflation.

Key Terms

business cycle
recession
depression
leading indicator
coincident indicator

lagging indicator
unemployment rate
discouraged workers
underemployment
potential real GDP

natural rate of unemployment
inflation
nominal interest rate
real interest rate
hyperinflation

Quick-Check Quiz

Section 1: Business Cycles

1. All of the following are leading economic indicators except
   a. the average workweek.
   b. unemployment claims.
   c. new plant and equipment orders.
   d. the prime interest rate.
   e. stock prices.

2. All of the following change at the same time real output changes except
   a. labor cost per unit of output.
   b. personal income.
   c. payroll employment.
   d. industrial production.
   e. manufacturing and trade sales.

3. Which of the following does *not* change its value until after the value of real GDP has changed?
   a. outstanding commercial loans
   b. the prime interest rate
   c. the labor cost per unit of output
   d. unemployment duration
   e. All of the above are lagging indicators.

4. In correct sequence, the four stages of the business cycle are
   a. peak, boom, expansion, and contraction.
   b. peak, contraction, trough, and expansion.
   c. recession, expansion, peak, and boom.
   d. contraction, trough, expansion, and boom.
   e. recession, contraction, peak, and boom.

5. Which of the following statements is true?
   a. Leading indicators are infallible predictors of future changes in real GDP.
   b. Business fluctuations are called business cycles because they tend to follow regular and predictable patterns.
   c. Real GDP has risen over the long term.
   d. According to the NBER, there have been eight recessions since 1929.
   e. The average time workers are unemployed is a coincident indicator.

6. Which of the following statements is false?
   a. The average workweek is a leading indicator.
   b. The inventories to sales ratio is a lagging indicator.
   c. Manufacturing and trade sales are a coincident indicator.
   d. The money supply is a coincident indicator.
   e. Delivery times of goods are a leading indicator.

Section 2: Unemployment

1. To arrive at the number in the U.S. labor force, we subtract all of the following from the number of all U.S. residents except
   a. residents under 16 years old.
   b. institutionalized adults.
   c. adults who are not looking for work.
   d. unemployed adults.
   e. All of the above must be subtracted from the number of U.S. residents to arrive at the number in the labor force.

2. Which of the following cause(s) the unemployment rate to be overstated?
   a. discouraged workers
   b. underground economic activities
   c. part-time employment
   d. underemployment
   e. students who are not looking for work

3. A graduating college basketball star who has one month off before reporting to his new NBA team is an example of
   a. frictional unemployment.
   b. structural unemployment.
   c. cyclical unemployment.
   d. technological unemployment.
   e. a rich, employed person.

4. Unemployed migrant workers are examples of
   a. frictional unemployment.
   b. seasonal unemployment.
   c. structural unemployment.
   d. discouraged workers.
   e. cyclical unemployment.

5. A person who finds that her skills are no longer needed because she has been replaced by a machine is an example of
   a. frictional unemployment.
   b. seasonal unemployment.
   c. cyclical unemployment.
   d. search unemployment.
   e. structural unemployment.

6. A steelworker who has been laid off during a recession is an example of
   a. frictional unemployment.
   b. seasonal unemployment.
   c. cyclical unemployment.
   d. search unemployment.
   e. structural unemployment.

7. Job training and counseling are policy measures used to fight primarily
   a. frictional unemployment.
   b. seasonal unemployment.
   c. cyclical unemployment.
   d. structural unemployment.
   e. both a and d.

8. Which of the following statements is false?
   a. The GDP gap widens during recessions and narrows during expansions.
   b. The influx of women and baby boomers into the labor force has increased the natural rate of unemployment in recent decades.
   c. Men have higher unemployment rates than women because women move out of the labor force to have children.
   d. Teenagers have the highest unemployment rates in the economy.
   e. Nonwhites have higher unemployment rates than whites.

Section 3: Inflation

1. If a college professor's income has increased by 3 percent at the same time that prices have risen by 5 percent, the professor's real income has
   a. decreased by 2 percent.
   b. increased by 2 percent.
   c. increased by 7 percent.
   d. decreased by 7 percent.
   e. not changed.

2. Which of the following groups benefits from unanticipated inflation?
   a. creditors
   b. retirees on fixed incomes
   c. debtors
   d. workers whose salaries are tied to the CPI
   e. suppliers who have contracted to supply a fixed amount of their product for a fixed price

3. Which of the following could be a cause of demand-pull inflation?
   a. war in the Middle East, which can increase oil prices
   b. drought in the Midwest, which can cause crop failures
   c. suppliers who increase their profit margins by raising prices faster than their costs increase
   d. increased government spending in the absence of increased taxes
   e. labor unions, which can force wage increases that are not justified by increases in productivity

4. Which of the following statements is true?
   a. The higher the price level, the higher the purchasing power of money.
   b. Demand-pull inflation can be a result of increased production costs.
   c. High rates of inflation are generally caused by rapid growth of the money supply.
   d. Unexpectedly high inflation redistributes income away from those who make fixed dollar payments toward those who receive fixed dollar payments.
   e. The real interest rate increases as the rate of inflation increases.

5. A lender who does not expect any change in the price level is willing to make a mortgage loan at a 10 percent rate of interest. If that same lender anticipates a future inflation rate of 5 percent, she will charge the borrower
   a. 5 percent interest.
   b. 10 percent interest.
   c. 15 percent interest.
   d. 2 percent interest.
   e. ½ percent interest.

Practice Questions and Problems

Section 1: Business Cycles

1. The recurring pattern of real GDP rising and then falling is called a(n) _____ .
2. When real GDP is growing, the economy is in the _____ phase, or boom period, of the business cycle.
3. The _____ marks the end of a contraction and the start of a new business cycle.
4. The _____ marks the end of the expansion phase of a business cycle.
5. Real GDP falls during the contraction, or _____ , phase of the business cycle.
6. The _____ has the responsibility of officially dating recessions in the United States.
7. A(n) _____ is a prolonged period of severe economic contraction.
8. _____ change before real GDP changes.
9. _____ are economic variables that tend to change at the same time real output changes.
10. Variables that do not change their value until after the value of real GDP has changed are called _____ .

Section 2: Unemployment

1. The _____ is the percentage of the labor force that is not working.
2. _____ have given up looking for work because they believe that no one will hire them.
3. The employment of workers in tasks that do not fully utilize their productive potential is called _____ .
4. _____ unemployment is a product of business-cycle fluctuations.
5. _____ unemployment is a product of regular, recurring changes in the hiring needs of certain industries over the months or seasons of the year.
6. _____ unemployment is a product of short-term movements of workers between jobs and of first-time job seekers.
7. _____ unemployment is a product of technological change and other changes in the structure of the economy.
8. The level of output produced when nonlabor resources are fully utilized and unemployment is at its natural rate is called _____ .
9. The _____ is the unemployment rate that would exist in the absence of cyclical unemployment.
10. Potential real GDP minus actual real GDP equals the _____ .
11. The existence of _____ and _____ causes the official unemployment rate in the United States to be understated.

12. The existence of the underground economy causes the official unemployment rate in the United States to be _____ .
13. Economists measure the cost of unemployment in terms of _____ .

Section 3: Inflation

1. _____ is a sustained rise in the average level of prices.
2. The higher the price level, the _____ the purchasing power of the dollar.
3. The observed rate of interest in the market is called the _____ rate of interest.
4. The nominal interest rate minus the rate of inflation equals the _____ interest rate.
5. Unexpectedly high inflation hurts _____ and benefits _____ because it lowers real interest rates.
6. _____ inflation is the result of increased spending that is not offset by increases in the supply of goods and services.
7. Increases in prices caused by increases in production costs characterize _____ inflation.
8. A very high rate of inflation is called a(n) _____ .
9. _____-push pressures are created by suppliers who want to increase their profit margins by raising prices faster than their costs increase.
10. _____-push pressures are created by labor unions and workers who are able to increase their wages faster than their productivity.

Thinking About and Applying Unemployment and Inflation

I. Economic Indicators

A clumsy economist has dropped his basket of the following economic indicators, and now they are all jumbled together. Try to use economic reasoning to sort them out in the table that follows.

Labor cost per unit of output
Money supply
Stock prices
Prime interest rate
Payroll employment
Average workweek
Outstanding commercial loans
New plant and equipment orders
Unemployment duration
Unemployment claims

Manufacturing and trade sales
New building permits
Personal income
Consumer credit to personal income ratio
Manufacturers' new orders
Inventories to sales ratio
Delivery time of goods
Industrial production
Consumer expectations
Inflation rate for services

Leading Indicators	Coincident Indicators	Lagging Indicators
_____	_____	_____
_____	_____	_____
_____	_____	_____
_____		_____
_____		_____
_____		_____
_____		
_____		

II. Unemployment Rates and Discouraged Workers

1. The tiny country of Lanastan has a civilian labor force of 40,000, of whom 38,000 are employed. There are _____ unemployed persons in Lanastan, and the unemployment rate is _____ percent.

2. Five hundred of the unemployed people become discouraged and quit looking for a job. Now the official unemployment rate in Lanastan is _____ percent. These discouraged workers have _____ the unemployment rate.

III. Inflation and the Elderly

Thanks to the late congressman Claude Pepper, most of us immediately think of elderly people living on fixed incomes when we think of people who are hurt by unexpected inflation. Social security payments are now indexed to the CPI, but elderly people still say they are hurt by unexpected inflation: the inflation adjustment does not cover the rising prices of things they must buy. What do elderly people buy that is inadequately represented by the CPI?

IV. In or Out of the Labor Force?

The Department of Labor defines the labor force as all U.S. residents minus residents under 16 years old minus institutionalized adults minus adults who are not looking for work. A person is seeking work if he or she is available to work, has looked for work in the past four weeks, is waiting for a recall after being laid off, or is starting a job within 30 days.

Place an "X" next to those who would be considered part of the labor force.

_____ Björn Dimmen is a Norwegian citizen who is looking for a job in the United States. He plans to move to the United States to marry his American sweetheart.

_____ Carl Wolcutt is a retired police chief who has recently been offered a position as head of his state's policy academy. Mr. Wolcutt is happily raising beagles and has turned down the job.

_____ Blake Stephans has just been laid off from his quality-control job at Boeing. He is waiting for a recall, but the company has just announced it will lay off even more workers.

_____ Thomas Buttking is a recent college graduate who quit his part-time job but is taking the summer off before searching for a "real" job.

_____ Joe Shocker, a pitcher on Wichita State University's baseball team, has been selected in the first round of the draft and expects to join the Mets after he finishes playing in the College World Series. In the meantime he will enjoy the sights and sounds of beautiful downtown Omaha.

V. Illustrating the Business Cycle

The horizontal axis measures time and the vertical axis measures economic activity. Label the points on the diagram with the appropriate phases of the business cycle.

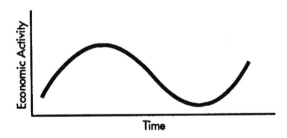

VI. Economic Reporting

Assume you are a reporter for the *Wall Street Journal*. Respond to the following developments. You should bear in mind whether the indicator in question leads, lags, or moves with the economy.

1. The Commerce Department has just released its index of leading indicators, which rose only 0.1 percent in April after dropping 1 percent the previous month. What can you tell your readers about the probable growth of the economy?

2. The Commerce Department reported that new plant and equipment orders were flat in April, after a 3.7 percent decline in March. What does this news imply about the economy?

3. Manufacturers' new orders rose in April, up 4.8 percent from March.

4. The Commerce Department originally reported that the economy grew at a 1.8 percent annual rate in the first quarter. What measure was released? The figures were revised after the U.S. trade deficit increased sharply in March. Would your estimate of economic growth be revised upward or downward as a result of the trade figures?

Chapter 8   Homework Problems

Name _____

1. What criteria does a person have to meet before being counted as part of the U.S. labor force?

2. List and define the four categories of unemployment used by economists.

3. Newspaper stories today provide the economic data listed below, giving the changes in economic statistics over the last month. Use your knowledge of economic indicators to figure out where in the business cycle the economy most likely is today. Explain your conclusion.

   Money supply is up.   Unemployment duration is increasing.
   Industrial production is unchanged.   Personal income is unchanged.
   Stock prices are up.   New building permits are up.

4. Suppose you were a farmer back in the 1890s. You took out a mortage loan to buy your farm, and you have to pay $100 every month for the next twenty years to pay off the mortgage loan. Candidate B for U.S. president advocates an economic policy that will cause significant inflation in the future, while Candidate M advocates policies that will lead to stable or falling prices.

   a. Based on your own economic self-interest, which candidate would you vote for, and why?

   b. Based on economic self-interest, which candidate would your banker vote for, and why?

5. A politician was recently heard making the following argument:

   Unemployment is a tragedy, both for the unemployed people and for the U.S. economy. We need to use government policies to create more jobs until the number of unemployed people is down to zero. No one should ever be unemployed.

   Use economic reasoning to explain why economists would disagree with the goal of zero unemployment.

If your instructor assigns these problems, write your answers above, then tear out this page and hand it in.

Answers

Quick-Check Quiz

Section 1: Business Cycles

1. d; 2. a; 3. e; 4. b; 5. c; 6. d
If you missed any of these questions, you should go back and review Section 1 of Chapter 8.

Section 2: Unemployment

1. d; 2. b; 3. a; 4. b; 5. e; 6. c; 7. e; 8. c
If you missed any of these questions, you should go back and review Section 2 of Chapter 8.

Section 3: Inflation

1. a; 2. c; 3. d; 4. c; 5. c
If you missed any of these questions, you should go back and review Section 3 of Chapter 8.

Practice Questions and Problems

Section 1: Business Cycles

1. business cycle
2. expansion
3. trough
4. peak
5. recession
6. NBER (National Bureau of Economic Research)
7. depression
8. Leading indicators
9. Coincident indicators
10. lagging indicators

Section 2: Unemployment

1. unemployment rate
2. Discouraged workers
3. underemployment
4. Cyclical
5. Seasonal
6. Frictional (or search)
7. Structural
8. potential real GDP
9. natural rate of unemployment
10. GDP gap
11. discouraged workers; underemployment
12. overstated
13. lost output (or the GDP gap)

Copyright © Houghton Mifflin Company. All rights reserved.

Section 3: Inflation

1. Inflation
2. lower
3. nominal
4. real
5. creditors; debtors
6. Demand-pull
7. cost-push
8. hyperinflation
9. Profit
10. Wage

Thinking About and Applying Unemployment and Inflation

I. Economic Indicators

Leading Indicators
Money supply
Stock prices
Average workweek
New plant and equipment orders
Unemployment claims
New building permits
Manufacturers' new orders
Delivery time of goods
Consumer expectations

Coincident Indicators
Payroll employment
Manufacturing and trade sales
Personal income
Industrial production

Lagging Indicators
Labor cost per unit of output
Prime interest rate
Outstanding commercial loans
Unemployment duration
Consumer credit to personal income ratio
Inventories to sales ratio
Inflation rate for services

II. Unemployment Rates and Discouraged Workers

1. 2,000; 5
   To find the number of unemployed persons, we subtract the number employed from the number in the labor force: 40,000 – 38,000 = 2,000. The unemployment rate is the number unemployed divided by the labor force: 2,000/40,000 = .05, or 5 percent.
2. 3.8; understated
   If 500 unemployed people drop out of the labor force, the labor force becomes 40,000 – 500 = 39,500. We still have 38,000 employed, so the number of "unemployed" people is 39,500 – 38,000 = 1,500. The official unemployment rate becomes 1,500/39,500 = .0379746, or about 3.8 percent. Thus the existence of discouraged workers understates the true unemployment rate.

III. Inflation and the Elderly

Elderly people spend a greater proportion of their incomes on health-care costs than the "typical" family represented in the CPI market basket. Since health-care costs have been rising faster than the CPI, increases in social security payments linked to the CPI do not keep up with increases in health-care costs.

IV. In or Out of the Labor Force?

_____	Mr. Dimmen is not in the U.S. labor force since he is not a U.S. resident.
_____	Mr. Wolcutt is not looking for work and therefore would not be considered part of the labor force.
__X__	Mr. Stephans was laid off and is waiting for a recall, so he is part of the labor force.
_____	Thomas Buttking is not looking for work and therefore would not be considered part of the labor force.
__X__	Joe Shocker will start a new job within 30 days, so he is part of the labor force.

V. Illustrating the Business Cycle

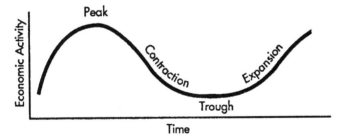

VI. Economic Reporting

1. A one-time increase in the index of leading indicators does not signal an expansion. Economists look for several consecutive months of a new direction in the leading indicators before forecasting a change in output. When these figures came out, most economists said the new numbers did not really suggest anything new.
2. New plant and equipment orders are a leading indicator. One would expect orders for new plants and equipment to increase when the economy enters an expansion. By themselves, the previous decline and subsequent flat performance suggest that the economy may be in a rut, but there is not enough evidence to tell.

3. Manufacturers' new orders are a leading indicator. By itself, a big increase might indicate that the economy is picking up, but several months of increase are needed to establish a pattern.
4. The GDP is the main measure of the economy's performance. The increase in the trade deficit indicates that net exports decreased. Since GDP = $C + I + G + X$, the GDP would be revised downward.

Chapter 9

MACROECONOMIC EQUILIBRIUM: AGGREGATE DEMAND AND SUPPLY

FUNDAMENTAL QUESTIONS

1. What factors affect aggregate demand?

   The nonprice determinants of aggregate demand are consumption, investment, government spending, and net exports. The downward slope of the aggregate demand curve is due to the wealth effect, the interest rate effect, and the international trade effect.

2. What causes the aggregate demand curve to shift?

   Anything that affects consumption, investment, government spending, or net exports will cause the aggregate demand curve to shift: changes in income, wealth, demographics, expectations, taxes, the interest rate, technology, the cost of capital goods, capacity utilization, foreign income and price levels, exchange rates, and government policies.

3. What factors affect aggregate supply?

   The **aggregate supply curve** shows the quantity of national output (or income) produced at different price levels. It has an upward slope because higher prices, *ceteris paribus,* mean higher profits, which induce producers to offer more output for sale.

4. Why does the short-run aggregate supply curve become steeper as real GDP increases?

   As the level of real GDP increases, more and more sectors of the economy approach capacity. In order to lure resources from other uses, firms must offer higher and higher resource payments. Prices must rise higher and higher to induce increases in output. Finally, no more output can be produced and existing output must be "rationed" to those who are willing to pay the highest prices.

5. Why is the long-run aggregate supply curve vertical?

   The **long-run aggregate supply curve** is vertical because in the long run there is no relationship between changes in the price level and changes in output. The economy has made all of its adjustments, and no further output can be produced with existing resources and technology. In particular, higher prices cannot induce more output.

6. What causes the aggregate supply curve to shift?

   The aggregate supply curve shifts if resource prices, technology, or expectations change.

7. What determines the equilibrium price level and real GDP?

   The equilibrium price level and real GDP are determined by the intersection of aggregate demand and aggregate supply.

Key Terms

demand-pull inflation
cost-push inflation
wealth effect
interest rate effect
international trade effect
aggregate demand curve
aggregate supply curve
long-run aggregate supply
curve (LRAS)

Quick-Check Quiz

Section 1: Aggregate Demand, Aggregate Supply, and Business Cycles

1. If aggregate demand increases,
   a. the equilibrium price and the level of real GDP will increase.
   b. the equilibrium price will increase, but the level of real GDP will decrease.
   c. the equilibrium price and the level of real GDP will decrease.
   d. the equilibrium price will decrease, but the level of real GDP will increase.
   e. unemployment will increase.

2. If aggregate supply increases,
   a. the equilibrium price and the level of real GDP will increase.
   b. the equilibrium price will increase, but the level of real GDP will decrease.
   c. the equilibrium price and the level of real GDP will decrease.
   d. the equilibrium price will decrease, but the level of real GDP will increase.
   e. demand-pull inflation will result.

3. Demand-pull inflation results from
   a. an increase in aggregate demand.
   b. a decrease in aggregate demand.
   c. an increase in aggregate supply.
   d. a decrease in aggregate supply.
   e. the price level rising because of higher production costs.

4. Cost-push inflation results from
   a. an increase in aggregate demand.
   b. a decrease in aggregate demand.
   c. an increase in aggregate supply.
   d. a decrease in aggregate supply.
   e. the price level rising because of increasing demand for output.

Section 2: Factors That Influence Aggregate Demand

1. Which of the following does *not* affect consumption?
   a. income
   b. wealth
   c. expectations
   d. the cost of capital goods
   e. taxation

2. Which of the following is *not* a determinant of investment?
   a. the interest rate
   b. technology
   c. disposable income
   d. the cost of capital goods
   e. capacity utilization

3. Which of the following will increase investment?
   a. an increase in the rate of capacity utilization
   b. an increase in interest rates
   c. an increase in disposable income
   d. an increase in the cost of capital goods
   e. a decrease in expected profits

4. Which of the following will *not* decrease investment?
   a. an increase in the cost of capital goods
   b. an improvement in technology
   c. an increase in interest rates
   d. unfavorable changes in tax policy
   e. rumors that the government will nationalize firms

5. Which of the following will increase consumption?
   a. a decrease in disposable income
   b. an increase in wealth
   c. gloomy expectations about the economy
   d. a decrease in population
   e. an increase in expected profits

6. Which of the following does the text cite as a determinant of government spending?
   a. population
   b. disposable income
   c. interest rates
   d. taxes
   e. The text does not cite any of these as determinants of government policy; it assumes that government authorities set government spending at whatever level they choose.

7. Which of the following is *not* a determinant of exports?
   a. foreign income
   b. domestic disposable income
   c. tastes
   d. government trade restrictions
   e. exchange rates

8. Which of the following will *not* cause an increase in exports?
   a. an increase in foreign incomes
   b. domestic currency depreciation
   c. a favorable change in tastes
   d. domestic currency appreciation
   e. a lowering of trade restrictions

9. Which of the following does *not* affect aggregate demand?
   a. consumption
   b. costs of production
   c. investment
   d. government spending
   e. net exports

Section 3: The Aggregate Demand Curve

1. Which of the following will increase aggregate demand?
   a. a decrease in wealth
   b. an increase in interest rates
   c. a decrease in foreign incomes
   d. appreciation of the domestic currency
   e. an increase in foreign price levels

2. Which of the following will *not* decrease aggregate demand?
   a. expectations that the economy is heading toward a recession
   b. depreciation of the domestic currency
   c. a fall in foreign incomes
   d. an increase in the cost of capital goods
   e. excess capacity in manufacturing

3. Which of the following will increase aggregate demand?
   a. an increase in taxes
   b. an increase in the proportion of middle-age households
   c. an increase in government spending
   d. a decrease in taxes
   e. items c and d above

4. Which of the following is a reason for the aggregate demand curve to slope downward?
   a. the substitution effect
   b. the income effect
   c. the interest rate effect
   d. the expectations effect
   e. the foreign price level effect

5. When prices increase, people and businesses need _____ money. They _____ bonds, causing interest rates to _____ and aggregate expenditures to _____ .
   a. more; buy; fall; rise
   b. more; sell; fall; rise
   c. more; buy; rise; fall
   d. more; sell; rise; fall
   e. less; buy; fall; rise

6. When the price level falls, domestic goods become _____ for foreigners. Net exports _____ , and aggregate expenditures _____ . This is called the _____ effect.
   a. cheaper; rise; rise; international trade
   b. cheaper; fall; fall; international trade
   c. cheaper; rise; fall; international trade
   d. more expensive; fall; fall; international trade
   e. cheaper; rise; rise; wealth

7. Which of the following does *not* cause aggregate demand to have a negative slope?
   a. wealth effect
   b. substitution effect
   c. income and substitution effects
   d. international trade effect
   e. interest rate effect

8. When the price level falls, the value of household and business assets _____ . Households and firms spend _____ , and aggregate expenditures _____ . This is called the _____ effect.
   a. increases; more; rise; income
   b. increases; more; rise; wealth
   c. decreases; less; fall; income
   d. decreases; less; fall; wealth
   e. decreases; more; rise; wealth

9. Which of the following do *not* cause aggregate demand to shift?
   a. changes in expectations
   b. changes in the price level
   c. changes in foreign incomes
   d. changes in foreign prices
   e. changes in government policy

Section 4: Aggregate Supply

1. The aggregate supply curve illustrates a _____ relationship between the quantity of national output and different price levels. This relationship is explained by the effect of _____ .
   a. negative; changing prices on profits
   b. positive; changing prices on profits
   c. negative; relative price changes
   d. positive; negative price changes
   e. positive; changes in interest rates

2. Which of the following will cause aggregate supply to shift?
   a. changes in the domestic price level
   b. changes in real GDP
   c. changes in foreign incomes
   d. changes in resource prices
   e. changes in national output

3. If a change in technology reduces costs, we move from _____ to _____ on the graph below.

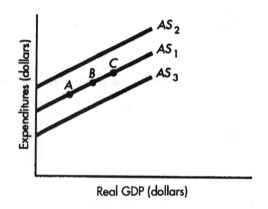

   a. point A; point B
   b. point B; point C
   c. point A; point C
   d. AS_1; AS_2
   e. AS_1; AS_3

4. The long-run aggregate supply curve is
   a. upward-sloping because of the effect of higher prices on profits.
   b. horizontal, reflecting excess capacity in all parts of the economy.
   c. upward-sloping, reflecting excess capacity in some parts of the economy.
   d. horizontal because there is no relationship between the price level and national income in the long run.
   e. vertical because there is no relationship between the price level and national income in the long run.

5. Which of the following statements is false?
   a. The long-run aggregate supply curve can shift to the right if new technologies are developed.
   b. The long-run aggregate supply curve can shift to the left if the quality of the factors of production decreases.
   c. The long-run aggregate supply curve is fixed at potential output and cannot shift.
   d. An increase in long-run aggregate supply will decrease the equilibrium price level.
   e. A decrease in long-run aggregate supply will decrease the equilibrium level of real GDP.

6. The slope of the aggregate supply curve is explained by
   a. relative price changes.
   b. the effect of changing prices on profits.
   c. the wealth effect.
   d. the interest rate effect.
   e. the international trade effect.

7. Which of the following will increase aggregate supply?
   a. an increase in resource prices
   b. a change in technology which increases productivity
   c. an increase in the price level
   d. a decrease in the price level
   e. anticipated higher prices

8. Which of the following will decrease aggregate supply?
   a. a decrease in foreign price levels
   b. new government regulations which require an expensive new technology to reduce pollutants
   c. appreciation of the domestic currency
   d. an increase in government spending
   e. a decrease in foreign incomes

Section 5: Aggregate Demand and Supply Equilibrium

1. A temporary increase in the equilibrium price level and the equilibrium level of income can result from
   a. an increase in aggregate demand.
   b. a decrease in aggregate demand.
   c. an increase in aggregate supply.
   d. a decrease in aggregate supply.
   e. a change in the price of resources.

2. A permanent decrease in inflation coupled with an increase in the equilibrium level of income can only result from
   a. an increase in aggregate demand.
   b. a decrease in aggregate demand.
   c. an increase in aggregate supply.
   d. a decrease in aggregate supply.
   e. a decrease in government spending.

3. Which of the following statements is true?
   a. In the long run, the short-run aggregate demand curve shifts so that changes in aggregate supply determine the price level, not the equilibrium level of income.
   b. In the long run, the short-run aggregate demand curve shifts so that changes in aggregate supply determine the equilibrium level of income, not the price level.
   c. In the long run, the equilibrium level of output never changes.
   d. In the long run, there is a positive relationship between the level of prices and the level of output.
   e. In the long run, the short-run aggregate supply curve shifts so that changes in aggregate demand determine the price level, not the equilibrium level of income.

Practice Questions and Problems

Section 1: Aggregate Demand, Aggregate Supply, and Business Cycles

1. _____ represents the total spending in the economy at alternative price levels.
2. _____ represents the total output of the economy at alternative price levels.
3. _____ inflation is inflation caused by increasing demand for output.
4. If aggregate demand falls, the equilibrium level of income _____ .
5. A(n) _____ in aggregate supply leads to an increase in the equilibrium level of national income.
6. An increase in the price level caused by increased costs of production is called _____ inflation.
7. The slope of the aggregate demand curve is _____ .
8. The slope of the aggregate supply curve is _____ (in the short run).

Section 2: Factors That Influence Aggregate Demand

1. If wealth decreases, consumption _____ .
2. _____ is spending by households.
3. If households expect an economic expansion, _____ increases.
4. If demographics change so that a greater percentage of the population consists of older households, consumption _____ .
5. As foreign income rises, net exports _____ .
6. If a new trade agreement with Japan succeeds in opening Japanese markets to U.S. goods, net exports will _____ .
7. _____ (Price effects, Nonprice effects) are reflected in movements along the aggregate demand curve; _____ (price effects, nonprice effects) are shifts in aggregate demand.

8. _____ equal exports minus imports.
9. When consumers expect future income to increase, consumption _____ (increases, decreases, does not change).
10. *Ceteris paribus,* economists expect consumption to _____ (rise, fall, not change) as the population increases.
11. As taxation increases, consumption _____ (rises, falls, does not change).
12. _____ is business spending on capital goods and inventories.
13. As household wealth increases, consumption _____ (increases, decreases).
14. List the five determinants of consumption.

_____
_____
_____
_____
_____

15. As the interest rate falls, the rate of return from an investment _____ (rises, falls).
16. As the cost of capital goods rises, the amount of investment _____ (rises, falls).
17. When capacity utilization is high, investment tends to _____ (rise, fall).
18. List the four determinants of investment.

_____
_____
_____
_____

19. When the domestic currency depreciates, imports _____ (rise, fall).
20. The higher the domestic income, the _____ (higher, lower) the net exports.
21. List the four determinants of net exports.

_____
_____
_____
_____

22. When domestic income increases, imports _____ (increase, decrease).

Section 3: The Aggregate Demand Curve

1. As the level of prices increases, the purchasing power of money _____ (increases, decreases) and the real value of assets _____ (increases, decreases). The _____ effect, or real-balance effect, predicts that the real value of aggregate expenditures will then _____ (rise, fall).

2. When prices increase, people _____ (buy, sell) bonds to get money. Bond prices _____ (increase, decrease), and interest rates _____ (rise, fall). The _____ effect suggests that aggregate expenditures will then _____ (rise, fall).

3. If domestic prices rise while foreign prices and foreign exchange rates remain constant, domestic goods will become _____ (less expensive, more expensive) for foreigners. Net exports will _____ (rise, fall), causing aggregate expenditures to _____ (rise, fall).

4. When the price level falls, aggregate expenditures _____ (rise, fall).

5. The _____ shows how the equilibrium level of expenditures changes as the price level changes.

6. If foreign prices fall, foreign goods become _____ (less expensive, more expensive), which causes _____ (a movement along the aggregate demand curve, a shift to the left of the aggregate demand curve).

7. A fall in the domestic price level causes _____ (a movement along the aggregate demand curve, a shift in aggregate demand to the left).

8. List the three types of price-level effects on total spending.
   _____
   _____
   _____

9. Positive expectations about the economy increase _____ and _____, which in turn _____ (increases, decreases) aggregate demand.

10. Higher foreign incomes cause _____ to rise, causing _____ (a movement along the aggregate demand curve, a shift in aggregate demand to the right).

Section 4: Aggregate Supply

1. The _____ shows the quantity of national output (or income) produced at different price levels.

2. The slope of the short-run aggregate supply curve is _____ because of the effect of changing prices on _____.

3. If the prices of output increase while all other prices remain unchanged, business profits will _____ (increase, decrease) and producers will produce _____ (more, less) output.
4. The _____ is the period of time when costs are variable.
5. The _____ is the period of time when all production costs remain constant.
6. List the three nonprice determinants of short-run aggregate supply.

_____

_____

_____

7. When the prices of resources fall, the short-run aggregate supply curve shifts to the _____ (right, left).
8. The _____ of the short-run aggregate supply curve reflects the fact that some sectors of the economy are approaching capacity.
9. Where the capacity output is reached, the short-run aggregate supply curve is a _____ line.
10. The _____ curve is a vertical line at the potential level of national income.
11. Draw a short-run aggregate supply curve on the graph below. Label your axes.

Section 5: Aggregate Demand and Supply Equilibrium

1. The equilibrium level of income is at the point where _____ equals _____ .
2. The short-run equilibrium level of income on the graph below is _____ .

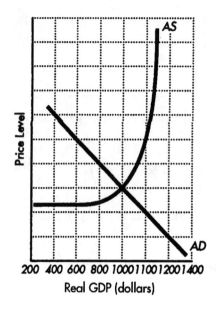

3. In the long run, there _____ (is, is not) a relationship between the level of prices and the level of output.
4. In the short run, changes in aggregate demand determine the level of prices and income. In the long run, changes in aggregate demand determine only the _____ .

Thinking About and Applying Macroeconomic Equilibrium: Aggregate Demand and Supply

I. Aggregate Demand and Its Determinants

Now that you have finished this chapter, you should be able to predict the effect on aggregate demand when one of its determinants changes. In the exercise below, decide which of the spending components each event affects, whether it increased or decreased the component, and whether it increased or decreased aggregate demand. Remember the determinants of each component of aggregate demand:

Consumption: income, wealth, expectations, demographics, taxes
Investment: interest rate, cost of capital goods, technology, capacity utilization
Government spending: set by government authorities
Net exports: foreign and domestic income, foreign and domestic prices, exchange rates, government policy

Events
1. Interest rates increase.
2. The dollar depreciates against foreign currencies.
3. The government increases its spending.
4. Foreign incomes rise.
5. The population increases more quickly.
6. Factories note a decline in the rate of capacity utilization.
7. The government imposes a nationwide sales tax on retail goods and services.
8. The cost of capital goods decreases.

	Component	Effect on Component	Effect on Aggregate Demand
1.	Investment	Decrease	Decrease
2.			
3.			
4.			
5.			
6.			
7.			
8.			

II. Aggregate Demand and Supply Equilibrium

Assume that the following are short-run situations.

1. On the graph below, show how an increase in aggregate demand could produce a higher output with no change in prices.

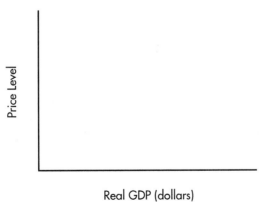

2. On the graph below, show a decrease in aggregate demand that produces a lower price level and lower real GDP.

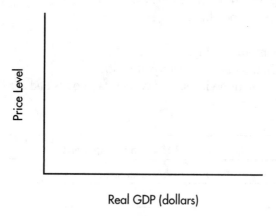

3. On the graph below, show how an increase in aggregate demand could result in higher prices at the same level of real GDP.

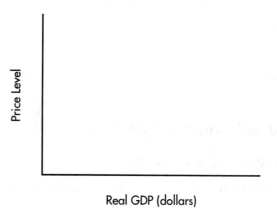

III. A Long-Run Analysis of the Effects of a Slump in Productivity

Many people have been concerned about the slower growth of productivity in recent years. Suppose that the growth of productivity in the United States not only slows, but actually decreases. This could result from declines in basic skills that some educators believe are surfacing in the nation's high schools. What will happen to the equilibrium price level and real GDP in the long run? Use the graph on the next page to analyze this problem. Be sure to label your axes.

IV. Sorting Out the Determinants of Aggregate Demand and Aggregate Supply

Place each of the items under the proper category. Some items can be placed in more than one category.

Wealth effect
Resource prices
Income
Taxes
Interest rates
International trade effect
Changes in technology

Wealth
Expectations
Interest rate effect
Price level
Demographics
Cost of capital goods
Capacity utilization

Domestic income
Foreign income
Domestic prices
Foreign prices
Exchange rate
Government policies
Government spending

Shifts Aggregate Demand	Shifts Aggregate Supply
_____ _____	_____ _____
_____ _____	_____
_____ _____	
_____ _____	
_____ _____	
_____ _____	
_____ _____	
_____	
Movement Along AD	**Movement Along AS**
_____ _____	_____
_____ _____	

Chapter 9   Homework Problems

Name _____

1. List the three effects that cause the aggregate demand curve to slope downward.

2. List the four components (the nonprice determinants) that make up aggregate demand.

3. List the three nonprice determinants of the short-run aggregate supply curve.

4. Sketch the short-run aggregate supply curve and explain why it has three regions (horizontal, rising, vertical).

5. a. The economy is currently in the equilibrium position shown on the graph below. For each event listed, predict the effect (increase, decrease, or remain the same) on the price level and real GDP.

   i. Government spending increases:

   price level _____   real GDP _____

   ii. Taxes increase:

   price level _____   real GDP _____

   iii. The interest rate decreases:

   price level _____   real GDP _____

   iv. Net exports decrease:

   price level _____   real GDP _____

b. Now suppose the economy is currently in the equilibrium position shown on the graph below. For each event listed, predict the effect (increase, decrease, or remain the same) on the price level and real GDP.

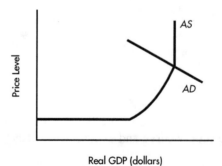

   i. Government spending increases:

   price level _____   real GDP _____

   ii. Taxes increase:

   price level _____   real GDP _____

   iii. The interest rate decreases:

   price level _____   real GDP _____

   iv. Net exports decrease:

   price level _____   real GDP _____

If your instructor assigns these problems, write your answers above, then tear out this page and hand it in.

Answers

Quick-Check Quiz

Section 1: Aggregate Demand, Aggregate Supply, and Business Cycles

1. a; 2. d; 3. a; 4. d
If you missed any of these questions, you should go back and review Section 1 of Chapter 9.

Section 2: Factors That Influence Aggregate Demand

1. d; 2. c; 3. a; 4. b; 5. b; 6. e; 7. b; 8. d; 9. b
If you missed any of these questions, you should go back and review Section 2 of Chapter 9.

Section 3: The Aggregate Demand Curve

1. e; 2. b; 3. e; 4. c; 5. d; 6. a; 7. c; 8. b; 9. b
If you missed any of these questions, you should go back and review Section 3 of Chapter 9.

Section 4: Aggregate Supply

1. b; 2. d; 3. e; 4. e; 5. c; 6. b; 7. b; 8. b
If you missed any of these questions, you should go back and review Section 4 of Chapter 9.

Section 5: Aggregate Demand and Supply Equilibrium

1. a; 2. c; 3. e
If you missed any of these questions, you should go back and review Section 5 of Chapter 9.

Practice Questions and Problems

Section 1: Aggregate Demand, Aggregate Supply, and Business Cycles

1. Aggregate demand
2. Aggregate supply
3. Demand-pull
4. falls
5. increase
6. cost-push
7. negative (downward-sloping)
8. positive (upward-sloping)

Section 2: Factors That Influence Aggregate Demand

1. decreases
2. Consumption
3. consumption
4. increases
5. increase
6. increase

7. Price effects; nonprice effects
8. Net exports
9. increases
10. rise
11. falls
12. Investment
13. increases
14. income
    wealth
    expectations
    demographics
    taxes
15. rises
16. falls
17. rise
18. interest rate
    technology
    cost of capital goods
    capacity utilization
19. fall
20. lower
21. foreign and domestic income
    foreign and domestic prices
    exchange rates
    government policy
22. increase

Section 3: The Aggregate Demand Curve

1. decreases; decreases; wealth; fall
2. sell; decrease; rise; interest rate; fall
3. more expensive; fall; fall
4. rise
5. aggregate demand curve
6. less expensive; a shift to the left of the aggregate demand curve
7. a movement along the aggregate demand curve
8. wealth effect
   interest rate effect
   international trade effect
9. consumption; investment; increases
10. exports; a shift in aggregate demand to the right

Section 4: Aggregate Supply

1. aggregate supply curve
2. positive, expected profits
3. increase; more
4. long run
5. short run

6. resource prices
   technology
   expectations
7. right
8. upward slope
9. vertical
10. long-run aggregate supply
11.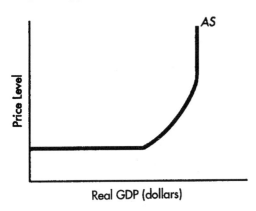

Section 5: Aggregate Demand and Supply Equilibrium

1. aggregate demand; aggregate supply
2. 1,000
3. is not
4. level of prices

Thinking About and Applying Macroeconomic Equilibrium: Aggregate Demand and Supply

I. Aggregate Demand and Its Determinants

	Component	Effect on Component	Effect on Aggregate Demand
1.	Investment	Decrease	Decrease
2.	Net exports	Increase	Increase
3.	Government spending	Increase	Increase
4.	Net exports	Increase	Increase
5.	Consumption	Increase	Increase
6.	Investment	Decrease	Decrease
7.	Consumption	Decrease	Decrease
8.	Investment	Increase	Increase

II. Aggregate Demand and Supply Equilibrium

1. You need to draw your aggregate demand curves so that the shifts are confined to the horizontal region of the short-run aggregate supply curve.

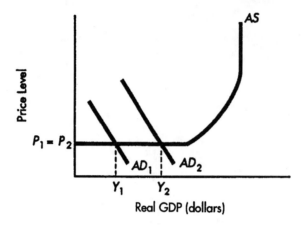

2. You need to draw your aggregate demand curves so that the shifts are confined to the upward-sloping region of the short-run aggregate supply curve.

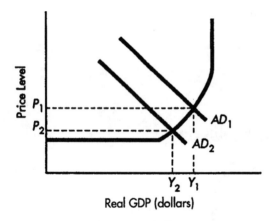

3. You need to draw your aggregate demand curves so that the shifts are confined to the vertical region of the short-run aggregate supply curve.

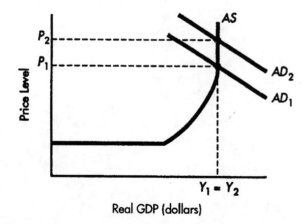

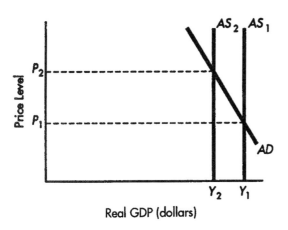

III. A Long-Run Analysis of the Effects of a Slump in Productivity

A decrease in productivity causes the long-run aggregate supply curve to shift to the left. If aggregate demand does not change, equilibrium real GDP will be lower and the price level will be higher—a very sorry prospect indeed.

IV. Sorting Out the Determinants of Aggregate Demand and Aggregate Supply

Shifts in Aggregate Demand		Shifts in Aggregate Supply	
Income	Domestic income	Resource prices	Expectations
Taxes	Foreign income	Changes in technology	
Interest rates	Domestic prices		
Wealth	Foreign prices		
Expectations	Exchange rate		
Demographics	Government policies		
Cost of capital goods	Government spending		
Capacity utilization			
Movement Along AD		**Movement Along AS**	
Wealth effect	Interest rate effect	Price level	
International trade effect	Price level		

Chapter 10

AGGREGATE EXPENDITURES

FUNDAMENTAL QUESTIONS

1. How are consumption and saving related?

   Households do three things with their income: spend it, save it, and pay taxes on it. Since households have no choice about paying taxes, economists usually look at after-tax, or disposable, income. **Consumption** and **saving** are the two components of disposable income. So if we know that disposable income is $1,000 and saving is $200, then we know that consumption must be $800.

   It is possible to spend more than your disposable income by borrowing or using past saving. If disposable income is again $1,000 and consumption is $1,100, than saving is –$100: you borrowed $100 or used $100 of past saving. Negative saving is called **dissaving.**

   Because consumption and saving together equal disposable income, any change (Δ) in disposable income equals the change in consumption plus the change in saving:

   $$\Delta C + \Delta S = \Delta Yd$$

   If we divide both sides by the change in disposable income, we have

   $$\Delta C/\Delta Yd + \Delta S/\Delta Yd = \Delta Yd/\Delta Yd$$

   or

   $$MPC + MPS = 1$$

   The change in consumption divided by the change in disposable income is called the **marginal propensity to consume (MPC).** It tells us how much consumption changes when income changes. If the MPC is .80, when disposable income changes by $100, consumption changes by $80. Likewise, the change in saving divided by the change in disposable income is called the **marginal propensity to save (MPS).** It tells us how much saving changes when income changes. If the MPS is .20, when disposable income changes by $100, saving changes by $20. Since the only things households can do with disposable income is save it and spend it, MPC + MPS = 1.

   There is another relationship between consumption and saving. Start with

   $$C + S = Yd$$

and divide both sides by disposable income:

$$C/Yd + S/Yd = Yd/Yd \quad \text{or} \quad APC + APS = 1$$

Consumption divided by disposable income is the **average propensity to consume (APC)**. It tells us the proportion of disposable income that is consumed. Likewise, saving divided by disposable income is the **average propensity to save (APS)** and tells us the proportion of income saved. Since disposable income can only be spent or saved, the two proportions must equal 1.

2. What are the determinants of consumption?

   The determinants of consumption are disposable income, **wealth,** expectations, demographics, and taxation. Consumption is a positive function of income, wealth, positive expectations about the economy, and population. If any of these determinants increase, consumption increases. Consumption is negatively related to negative expectations about the economy and taxes. If either of these factors increases, consumption decreases.

3. What are the determinants of investment?

   The determinants of investment are the interest rate, profit expectations, technological change, the cost of capital goods, and the rate at which capacity is utilized. Investment is a positive function of expected profit, technological change that reduces costs, and the rate at which capacity is utilized. If any of these factors increase, investment will increase. Investment is a negative function of interest rates and the cost of capital goods. If either of these determinants increases, investment will decrease. Because these determinants of investment are so variable over the business cycle, investment is the most volatile component of aggregate spending.

4. What are the determinants of government spending?

   Government spending is assumed to be autonomous of income. The government authorities set government spending according to political and other considerations at whatever level they choose.

5. What are the determinants of net exports?

   Net exports are exports minus imports. The determinants of net exports are foreign and domestic income, tastes, trade restrictions, and exchange rates. Net exports are a positive function of *foreign* income, tastes that favor exports, favorable changes in government restrictions on trade, and depreciation of the domestic currency. Net exports are negatively related to *domestic* income, tastes that favor imports, unfavorable changes in government restrictions on trade, and appreciation of the domestic currency.

6. What is the aggregate expenditures function?

   The aggregate expenditures function is the sum of the spending components in the economy: consumption plus investment plus government spending plus net exports.

$$AE = C + I + G + X$$

The aggregate expenditures function has a flatter (smaller) slope than $C + I + G$ because the net exports function has a negative slope.

Key Terms

consumption function
saving function
dissaving
autonomous consumption
marginal propensity to consume (MPC)
marginal propensity to save (MPS)
average propensity to consume (APC)
average propensity to save (APS)
wealth
marginal propensity to import (MPI)

Quick-Check Quiz

Section 1: Consumption and Saving

1. Consumption accounts for _____ percent of total expenditures in the U.S. economy.
    a. 20
    b. 15
    c. 68
    d. −1
    e. 35

2. Which of the following is a stock concept?
    a. GDP
    b. savings
    c. consumption
    d. investment
    e. net exports

3. Autonomous consumption
    a. depends on income.
    b. varies with the nonincome determinants of consumption.
    c. equals disposable income minus saving.
    d. occurs at the level of income at which all disposable income is being spent.
    e. occurs when consumption exceeds disposable income.

4. Which of the following is the equation for the marginal propensity to consume?
    a. change in consumption/change in income
    b. consumption/income
    c. change in consumption/change in disposable income
    d. consumption/disposable income
    e. 1 + MPS

5. Which of the following is the equation for the average propensity to save?
    a. change in saving/change in income
    b. saving/income
    c. change in saving/change in disposable income
    d. saving/disposable income
    e. 1 − MPC

Use the table below to answer questions 6 through 11.

Disposable Income	Consumption
$ 0	$1,000
2,000	2,700
4,000	4,400
6,000	6,100
8,000	7,800
10,000	9,500

6. Dissaving occurs at levels of income below
   a. $10,000.
   b. $8,000.
   c. $6,000.
   d. $4,000.
   e. $2,000.

7. Autonomous consumption is
   a. $1,000.
   b. $2,700.
   c. $4,400.
   d. $6,100.
   e. $7,800.

8. When disposable income is $6,000, saving is
   a. $–100.
   b. $100.
   c. $200.
   d. $500.
   e. $1,000.

9. The MPC is
   a. 1.35.
   b. 1.10.
   c. .975.
   d. .95.
   e. .85.

10. The MPS is
    a. .35.
    b. .15.
    c. .105.
    d. .05.
    e. .025.

11. If disposable income is $10,000, the APC is
    a. 1.11.
    b. 1.35.
    c. .975.
    d. .95.
    e. .85.

12. Which of the following will *not* increase consumption?
    a. Consumers expect the economy to pull out of the recession in the near future, as evidenced by the Consumer Confidence Index.
    b. An increase in property values increases household wealth.
    c. Medical advances allow many elderly people to live who otherwise would have died.
    d. Congress enacts a deficit reduction bill which increases taxes.
    e. A "baby boomlet" occurs when the original baby boomers grow up and have children.

13. The higher the MPC,
    a. the greater the MPS.
    b. the greater the fraction of any additional disposable income consumers will save.
    c. the greater the slope of the savings function.
    d. the flatter the slope of the consumption function.
    e. the greater the fraction of any additional disposable income consumers will spend.

14. Which of the following does *not* shift the consumption function?
    a. increases in wealth
    b. optimistic expectations about the economy
    c. an increase in disposable income
    d. an increase in taxes
    e. an increase in population

Section 2: Investment

1. Which of the following does *not* affect the equilibrium level of aggregate expenditures?
    a. business spending on capital goods
    b. planned inventory
    c. unplanned inventory
    d. capital purchases
    e. All of the above affect the equilibrium level of aggregate expenditures.

2. A firm must borrow $1,000 to buy a bottling machine and must pay 10 percent interest on the funds. The firm expects the machine to yield $1,188 in output. The rate of return on the investment is
    a. 1.188.
    b. 1.08.
    c. 1.088.
    d. .08.
    e. .088.

3. Which of the following will *not* increase investment?
   a. lower interest rates
   b. lower costs for capital goods
   c. expectations of a recession
   d. reinstatement of investment tax credits
   e. government subsidies to key industries

4. Which of the following will increase investment?
   a. expectations that the government will nationalize selected firms
   b. higher interest rates due to the Fed's fight against inflation
   c. repeal of investment tax credits
   d. decreases in capacity utilization
   e. invention of a powerful new computer chip

5. Which of the following is *not* a volatile component of investment?
   a. interest rates
   b. expectations
   c. technological change
   d. rate of capacity utilization
   e. All of the above are volatile components of investment spending.

Section 3: Government Spending

1. Government spending on goods and services is the _____ component of aggregate expenditures in the United States.
   a. largest
   b. second largest
   c. third largest
   d. fourth largest
   e. smallest

2. Government spending on goods and services
   a. is positively related to domestic income.
   b. is positively related to interest rates.
   c. is negatively related to disposable income.
   d. is negatively related to interest rates.
   e. is assumed to be autonomous of disposable income.

3. When plotted against disposable income, the government expenditures function has a(n) _____ slope.
   a. positive
   b. negative
   c. zero
   d. increasing
   e. decreasing

Section 4: Net Exports

1. Which of the following is false?
   a. Net exports cannot be negative.
   b. Net exports decline as domestic income increases.
   c. The net exports function has a negative slope.
   d. The net export function shifts with changes in foreign income.
   e. Imports are a positive function of domestic income.

2. Which of the following will *not* cause an increase in exports?
   a. an increase in foreign incomes
   b. domestic currency depreciation
   c. a favorable change in tastes
   d. domestic currency appreciation
   e. a lowering of trade restrictions

3. Which of the following is the equation for the marginal propensity to import?
   a. change in imports/change in income
   b. imports/income
   c. change in imports/change in disposable income
   d. imports/disposable income
   e. 1 – MPS

4. Which of the following will *not* shift the net exports function?
   a. changes in foreign income
   b. changes in tastes
   c. changes in domestic disposable income
   d. changes in exchange rates
   e. changes in government trade restrictions

Section 5: The Aggregate Expenditures Function

1. Which of the following is *not* a component of aggregate expenditures?
   a. consumption
   b. saving
   c. investment
   d. government spending
   e. net exports

2. Which of these functions is *not* drawn parallel to the others?
   a. C
   b. $C + I$
   c. $C + I + G$
   d. $C + I + G + X$
   e. All of the above are parallel lines.

3. Net exports
   a. are autonomous of disposable income.
   b. increase aggregate expenditures at relatively low levels of income.
   c. increase aggregate expenditures at relatively high levels of income.
   d. increase with disposable income.
   e. have the same slope as consumption.

Practice Questions and Problems

Section 1: Consumption and Saving

1. _____ equals consumption plus saving.
2. _____ is "not consuming" and is defined over a unit of time. _____ are an amount accumulated at a particular point in time.
3. GDP, consumption, saving, investment, government spending, and net exports are all _____ (stock, flow) concepts.
4. The primary determinant of consumption over any given period of time is _____ .
5. The _____ is the relationship between disposable income and consumption.
6. The _____ is the relationship between disposable income and saving.
7. _____ occurs when a households spends more than it earns in income, either by borrowing or by using savings.
8. Consumption and saving are _____ (positive, negative) functions of disposable income.
9. The level of consumption that does not depend on income is called _____ .
10. The relationship between change in consumption and change in disposable income is the _____ .
11. The _____ is equal to the change in saving divided by the change in disposable income.
12. MPC + MPS = _____ .
13. The MPC is the _____ of the consumption function.
14. The steeper the consumption function, the _____ the MPC.
15. The slope of the saving function is the _____ .
16. The _____ the saving function, the larger the MPS.
17. The _____ equals consumption divided by disposable income.
18. The APS equals _____ divided by _____ .
19. APC + APS = _____ .
20. The APS _____ (rises, falls) as disposable income rises.

21. Fill in the table below and answer the following questions.

Disposable Income	Consumption	Saving	APC	APS
$ 0	$1,000	$_____	_____	_____
1,000	1,800	_____	_____	_____
2,000	2,600	_____	_____	_____
3,000	3,400	_____	_____	_____
4,000	4,200	_____	_____	_____
5,000	5,000	_____	_____	_____
6,000	5,800	_____	_____	_____
7,000	6,600	_____	_____	_____
8,000	7,400	_____	_____	_____
9,000	8,200	_____	_____	_____
10,000	9,000	_____	_____	_____

a. What is the MPC? _____ the MPS? _____

b. Plot the consumption function on the graph below. Show on the graph the level of saving when disposable income is $9,000.

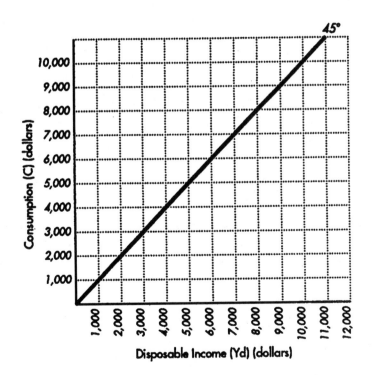

c. Plot the saving function on the graph below.

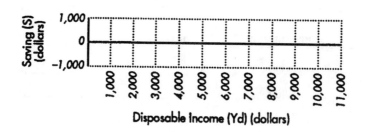

22. Use the graph below to answer the following questions.

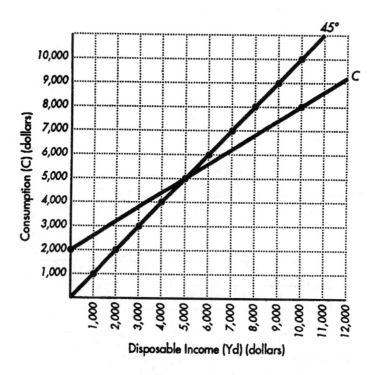

a. What is autonomous consumption? _____
b. What is the MPC? _____
c. What is savings when disposable income equals $10,000? _____

23. Disposable income is _____ income.

24. _____ is the value of all the assets owned by a household.

25. As household wealth increases, consumption _____ (increases, decreases) at every level of income.

26. The _____ is a measure of consumer opinion regarding the outlook for the economy.

27. When consumers expect future income to increase, autonomous consumption _____ (increases, decreases, does not change).

28. *Ceteris paribus,* economists expect consumption to _____ (rise, fall, not change) as the population increases.
29. Young households have _____ (larger, smaller, the same) MPCs than/as older households.
30. As taxation increases, autonomous consumption _____ (rises, falls, does not change).
31. List the five determinants of consumption.

    _____
    _____
    _____
    _____
    _____

32. Changes in the nonincome determinants of consumption affect the _____ (slope, intercept) of the consumption function.

Section 2: Investment

1. _____ is business spending on capital goods and inventories and is the most variable component of total spending.
2. The text assumes that investment is _____ of current income.
3. _____ investment combines with consumer, government, and foreign-sector spending to determine national income.
4. The higher the interest rate, the _____ (higher, lower) the rate of investment.
5. _____ is the profit from an investment divided by its cost.
6. As the interest rate falls, the rate of return from an investment _____ (rises, falls).
7. As the cost of capital goods rises, the amount of investment _____ (rises, falls).
8. When capacity utilization is high, investment tends to _____ (rise, fall).
9. List the five determinants of investment.

    _____
    _____
    _____
    _____
    _____

Section 3: Government Spending

1. Government spending on goods and services is the _____ largest component of aggregate expenditures in the United States.

2. The text assumes that government spending, like investment, is _____ of disposable income.

Section 4: Net Exports

1. _____ equal exports minus imports.
2. When net exports are positive, there is a _____ (deficit, surplus) on the merchandise and services accounts.
3. The text assumes that exports are _____ of current domestic income.
4. List the factors that affect exports.

   _____
   _____
   _____
   _____

5. When the domestic currency appreciates, exports _____ (rise, fall).
6. The greater domestic incomes, the _____ domestic imports.
7. The _____ equals the change in imports divided by the change in disposable income.
8. When the domestic currency depreciates, imports _____ (rise, fall).
9. The higher the domestic income, the _____ (higher, lower) net exports.
10. List the four determinants of net exports.

    _____
    _____
    _____
    _____

Section 5: The Aggregate Expenditures Function

1. _____ equals $C + I + G + X$.
2. Net exports _____ (increase, decrease) aggregate expenditures at relatively low levels of domestic income and _____ (increase, decrease) aggregate expenditures at relatively high levels of domestic income.
3. The aggregate expenditures function has a _____ (larger, smaller) slope than the consumption function.
4. The components of aggregate expenditures that are *not* autonomous are _____ and _____ .

5. Complete the table below and answer the following questions.

Y	C	I	G	X	AE
$1,000	$1,000	$30	$70	$ 100	$_____
2,000	1,900	30	70	0	_____
3,000	2,800	30	70	−100	_____
4,000	3,700	30	70	−200	_____
5,000	4,600	30	70	−300	_____
6,000	5,500	30	70	−400	_____

a. What is the MPC? _____
b. What is the MPS? _____
c. What is the MPI? _____

Thinking About and Applying Aggregate Expenditures

I. Sorting Out the Determinants of Aggregate Expenditures

Put the determinants of aggregate expenditures in their proper places in the table. Some determinants may be used in more than one place.

Trade restrictions
Technological change
Tastes
Disposable income
Foreign income

Expectations
Profit expectations
Capacity utilization
Wealth
Interest rate

Exchange rates
Domestic income
Demographics
Cost of capital goods
Taxation

Consumption	Investment	Government Spending	Net Exports

II. Aggregate Expenditures and Its Determinants

Now that you have finished this chapter, you should be able to predict the effect on aggregate expenditures when one of its determinants changes. In the exercise below, decide which of the spending components each event affects, whether it increased or decreased the component, and whether it increased or decreased aggregate expenditures. Remember the determinants of each component of expenditures:

Consumption: disposable income, wealth, expectations, demographics, taxation
Investment: interest rate, profit expectations, technological change, cost of capital goods, capacity utilization
Government spending: set by government authorities
Net exports: foreign and domestic income, tastes, trade restrictions, exchange rates

Events

1. Companies in Russia are hesitant to "put money in the ground and produce" because they "are put off by ever-changing tax laws, undependable partners, and political turmoil."

2. "Midsize firms plan to . . . spend more on capital equipment this year. . . ."

3. "There is considerable concern that the pileup of debt may act as a serious drag on the business expansion. . . . But . . . another consideration . . . is the level of savings. It is woefully low for what is presumed to be the early stages of a long expansion. . . . The U.S. rate is far below comparable rates prevailing in other major nations. . . . Consumers presumably will be reluctant to let their savings shrink very much more. . . ."

4. President Clinton's proposed $38 billion in new personal income taxes and $10 billion of additional corporate taxes is enacted.

5. President Clinton's $16 billion-plus increase in government spending bill is enacted.

6. "Industry operated at 79.9% of capacity last month, up from 79.7% in January."

	Component	Effect on Component	Effect on Aggregate Expenditures
1.	Investment	Decrease	Decrease
2.			
3.			
4.			
5.			
6.			

III. Determinants of Saving

The determinants of saving are the same as the determinants of consumption, since saving is "not consuming." There are reasons why Americans don't save. Translate the wording into the determinants of consumption (wealth, expectations, demographics, taxation). Here are some examples for you to try:

1. Members of Congress passed a proposal to allow families to put money into a savings plan tax free. _____

2. Tax laws generally benefit borrowing more than saving. _____

3. The spread of pension plans, social security benefits, and other items has reduced the need felt by many Americans to save. _____

4. Edward Yardeni says that the aging population will cause an increase in saving. _____

Chapter 10   Homework Problems

Name _____

1. State the five determinants of consumption.

2. State the five determinants of investment.

3. State the four determinants of net exports.

4. What determines government spending?

5. One of the purposes of economics is to help people analyze events in the real world and predict the effects of those events. Listed below are four brief quotations from the *Wall Street Journal* stories about economic events in the 1990s. Use your knowledge about the determinants of aggregate expenditures to predict which component of aggregate expenditures would be affected by each event listed, whether that component would be increased or decreased by the event, and whether the event would increase or decrease aggregate expenditures.

   a. "Foreigners, who poured billions of dollars into U.S. factories, real estate, and companies [in the 1980s], began pulling out some of that money...."

   b. "Interest rates shot up following the jobs report...."

   c. "The U.S. trade deficit deteriorated to $10.21 billion in March, the widest gap in nearly four years...."

   d. "Consumer confidence plunged to its lowest level since [late 1992]...."

   e. "Businesses stockpiled significantly more goods during the first quarter than originally thought, leading the Commerce Department to boost its estimate of the economy's growth rate...."

   f. "The Commerce Department also said that the rise in personal consumption in the first quarter was stronger than previously thought—6.1%...."

If your instructor assigns these problems, write your answers above, then tear out this page and hand it in.

Answers

Quick-Check Quiz

Section 1: Consumption and Saving

1. c; 2. b; 3. b; 4. c; 5. d; 6. b; 7. a; 8. a; 9. e; 10. b; 11. d; 12. d; 13. e; 14. c (An increase in disposable income would be reflected in a movement along the consumption function, not a shift in the curve.)

If you missed any of these questions, you should go back and review Section 1 of Chapter 10.

Section 2: Investment

1. c; 2. d (Rate of return = profit/cost. The cost is $1,000 + $100 in interest, so the rate of return is $88/$1,100 = .08); 3. c; 4. e; 5. e

If you missed any of these questions, you should go back and review Section 2 of Chapter 10.

Section 3: Government Spending

1. b; 2. e; 3. c

If you missed any of these questions, you should go back and review Section 3 of Chapter 10.

Section 4: Net Exports

1. a; 2. d; 3. c; 4. c (A change in domestic disposable income would be represented by a movement along the curve, not a shift in the curve.)

If you missed any of these questions, you should go back and review Section 4 of Chapter 10.

Section 5: The Aggregate Expenditures Function

1. b; 2. d; 3. b

If you missed any of these questions, you should go back and review Section 5 of Chapter 10.

Practice Questions and Problems

Section 1: Consumption and Saving

1. Disposable income
2. Saving; Savings
3. flow
4. disposable income
5. consumption function
6. saving function
7. Dissaving
8. positive
9. autonomous consumption
10. marginal propensity to consume (MPC)
11. marginal propensity to save (MPS)
12. 1
13. slope
14. larger

15. marginal propensity to save (MPS)
16. steeper
17. average propensity to consume (APC)
18. saving; disposable income
19. 1
20. rises
21. Note: The APC + APS will not always equal 1 due to rounding.

Disposable Income	Consumption	Saving	APC	APS
$ 0	$1,000	$–1,000	—	—
1,000	1,800	–800	1.8	–.8
2,000	2,600	–600	1.3	–.3
3,000	3,400	–400	1.13	–.13
4,000	4,200	–200	1.05	–.05
5,000	5,000	0	1.00	0
6,000	5,800	200	.97	.03
7,000	6,600	400	.94	.06
8,000	7,400	600	.93	.07
9,000	8,200	800	.91	.09
10,000	9,000	1,000	.90	.10

a. MPC = change in consumption/change in disposable income
       = $800/$1,000 = .8
   MPS = change in saving/change in disposable income
       = $200/$1,000 = .2 (or MPS = 1 – MPC = 1 – .8 = .2)
b.

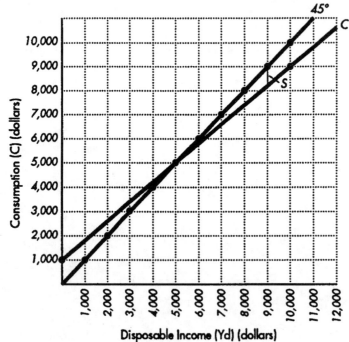

c.

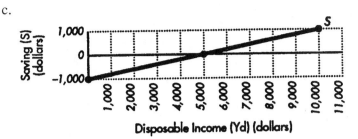

22. a. $2,000
    b. 3/5, or .6
    c. $2,000
23. after-tax
24. Wealth
25. increases
26. Consumer Confidence Index
27. increases
28. rise
29. larger
30. falls
31. disposable income
    wealth
    expectations
    demographics
    taxation
32. intercept

Section 2: Investment

1. Investment
2. autonomous (independent)
3. Planned
4. lower
5. Rate of return
6. rises
7. falls
8. rise
9. the interest rate
   profit expectations
   technological change
   the cost of capital goods
   the rate of capacity utilization

Section 3: Government Spending

1. second
2. autonomous (independent)

Section 4: Net Exports

1. Net exports
2. surplus
3. autonomous (independent)
4. foreign incomes
   tastes
   government trade restrictions
   exchange rates
5. fall
6. greater
7. marginal propensity to import (MPI)
8. fall
9. lower
10. foreign and domestic income
    tastes
    government trade restrictions
    exchange rates

Section 5: The Aggregate Expenditures Function

1. Aggregate expenditures (AE)
2. increase; decrease
3. smaller
4. consumption; net exports
5.

Y	C	I	G	X	AE
$1,000	$1,000	$30	$70	$ 100	$1,200
2,000	1,900	30	70	0	2,000
3,000	2,800	30	70	–100	2,800
4,000	3,700	30	70	–200	3,600
5,000	4,600	30	70	–300	4,400
6,000	5,500	30	70	–400	5,200

    a. MPC = change in consumption/change in disposable income
        = $900/$1,000 = .9
    b. MPS = 1 – MPC = 1 – .9 = .1
    c. MPI = change in imports/change in disposable income
        = $100/$1,000 = –.1

Thinking About and Applying Aggregate Expenditures

I. Sorting Out the Determinants of Aggregate Expenditures

Consumption	Investment	Government Spending	Net Exports
Tastes	Technological change		Tastes
Disposable income	Expectations		Trade restrictions
Expectations	Profit expectations		Foreign income
Wealth	Capacity utilization		Exchange rates
Demographics	Interest rate		Domestic income
Taxation	Cost of capital goods		

II. Aggregate Expenditures and Its Determinants

	Component	Effect on Component	Effect on Aggregate Expenditures
1.	Investment	Decrease	Decrease
2.	Investment	Increase	Increase
3.	Consumption	Decrease	Decrease

(The thought is that consumers will choose to distribute more of their incomes to savings, and therefore spend less at every level of income and save more out of additional income.)

	Component	Effect on Component	Effect on Aggregate Expenditures
4.	Consumption and investment	Decrease	Decrease
5.	Government spending	Increase	Increase
6.	Investment	Increase	Increase

III. Determinants of Saving

1. taxation
2. taxation
3. expectations about future incomes
4. demographics

Appendix to Chapter 10

AN ALGEBRAIC MODEL OF AGGREGATE EXPENDITURES

Summary

Each of the components of aggregate expenditures can be represented by an equation:

$$\text{Consumption: } C = C^a + c\, Y_d$$

where C^a is autonomous consumption and c is the MPC.

$$\text{Net exports: } EX^a - (IM^a + im\, Y_d)$$

where EX^a is autonomous exports, IM^a is autonomous imports, and im is the MPI.

Since investment and government spending are autonomous of income, they are represented by constants: I^a and G^a.

Ignore taxes so that $Y_d = Y$. Since $AE = C + I + G + X$, then

$$AE = (C^a + c\, Y) + I^a + G^a + (EX^a - IM^a - im\, Y)$$

Gathering like terms, we have

$$AE = C^a + I^a + G^a + EX^a - IM^a + (c - im)\, Y$$

Practice Questions and Problems

1. Consider the consumption function $C = \$45 + .8Y_d$. Autonomous consumption is _____ and the MPC is _____ .
   a. $45; .8
   b. $30; .9
   c. $.8; 45
   d. $45, .2
   e. None of the above are correct.

2. Consider the consumption function $C = \$500 + .75Y_d$. If disposable income equals $24,000, consumption equals _____ and saving equals _____.
   a. $18,000; $500
   b. $18,000; $6,000
   c. $18,500; $6,000
   d. $18,500; $5,500
   e. $31,333; $7,333

3. Consider the net exports function $\$15 - .15Y_d$. What is the marginal propensity to import?
   a. 15
   b. −15
   c. .15
   d. −.15
   e. 0

4. Consider the following:

   $C = \$50 + .90Y$
   $I = \$40$
   $G = \$60$
   $X = \$50 - .10Y$

   Construct the equation for aggregate expenditures.

   _____
   _____
   _____
   _____

   Plot the consumption and aggregate expenditures functions on the graph below. Note that the slope of aggregate expenditures is flatter than the slope of the consumption function.

   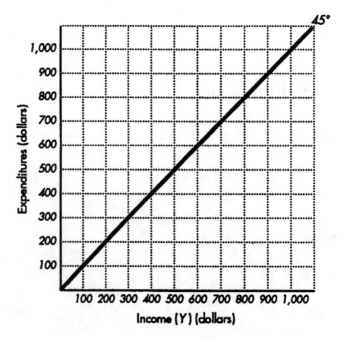

5. Consider the following equations:

   $C = \$2{,}000 + .65Y$
   $I^a = \$3{,}500$
   $G^a = \$7{,}000$
   $EX^a = \$750$
   $IM = \$250 + .12Y$

   a. What is the MPC? _____
   b. What is autonomous consumption? _____
   c. What is the MPI? _____
   d. If the level of income is $20,000, what is consumption?

   e. If the level of income is $20,000, what is savings?

   f. If the level of income is $20,000, what is net exports?

   g. Sum the functions to find the equation for aggregate expenditures.

Answers

1. a
2. d
3. c
4. $AE = C + I + G + X$
   $= (\$50 + .90Y) + \$40 + \$60 + (\$50 - .10Y)$
   $= \$200 + .80Y$

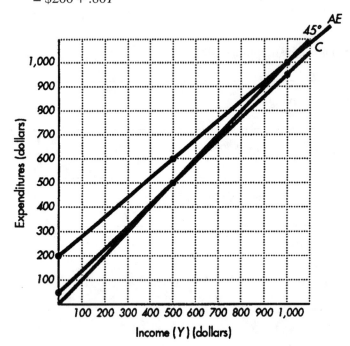

5. a. .65
   b. $2,000
   c. .12
   d. $C = \$2,000 + .65Y = \$2,000 + .65(\$20,000) = \$15,000$
   e. $S = Y - C = \$20,000 - \$15,000 = \$5,000$
   f. Net exports = exports − imports = $\$750 - (\$250 + .12Y)$
      $= \$500 - .12Y = \$500 - .12(\$20,000) = -\$1,900$
      (Imports are greater than exports.)
   g. $Y = C + I + G + X$
      $= \$2,000 + .65Y + \$3,500 + \$7,000 + \$750 - (\$250 + .12Y)$
      $= \$13,000 + .53Y$

Chapter 11

INCOME AND EXPENDITURES EQUILIBRIUM

FUNDAMENTAL QUESTIONS

1. What does equilibrium mean in macroeconomics?

   Equilibrium means that plans and reality coincide, and therefore people have no need to change their behavior. When aggregate expenditures are equal to income, people are planning to buy all that is currently being produced. Inventories stay at the level at which producers like to see them, so there is no need to increase or decrease production. Equilibrium is reached.

2. How do aggregate expenditures affect income or real GDP?

   Saying that aggregate expenditures exceed real GDP is the same as saying that planned expenditures exceed current output. If people are planning to buy more output than is currently being produced, the goods must come from somewhere. Producers replace their stock from inventories, and inventories fall. Since producers like to see a certain level of inventory, when inventories fall, producers increase production, increasing real GDP.

   If aggregate expenditures are less than real GDP, it means that people are planning to buy fewer goods and services than are currently being produced. Since not all goods and services will be sold, inventories will pile up. When producers see inventories building up, they decrease production, and real GDP falls.

3. What are the leakages from and injections to spending?

   Another way to determine macroeconomic equilibrium is to find where *leakages* from spending equal *injections* into spending. If injections are greater than leakages, aggregate expenditures are greater than real GDP. Inventories will fall, production will increase, and the increase in production leads to higher real GDP. If leakages are greater than injections, people are not planning to buy all the output that is produced. Inventories build up, production decreases, and real GDP falls.

   Leakages reduce autonomous expenditures. *Saving* is a leakage from spending. The more households save, the less they spend. Less household spending means less consumption, and consumption is one of the components of aggregate demand. *Taxes* transfer income away from households, forcing them to consume less, and are another leakage from spending. *Imports* reduce spending on domestic goods and services, and constitute the third leakage from spending.

   Injections into spending parallel the leakages. The saving of households is used by businesses for *investment,* which increases aggregate expenditures. The taxes collected by the government finance *government spending,* another component of aggregate expenditures. Besides U.S. spending on foreign goods, there is also foreign spending on U.S. goods. *Exports* also increase aggregate expenditures.

4. Why does equilibrium real GDP change by a multiple of a change in autonomous expenditures?

   The basic reason is that the change in expenditures becomes income for someone, who spends part of it and saves part of it. The part that the person spends becomes income to someone else, who saves part and spends part, and so on. To see how this works, let's assume that businesses decide to increase investment by $50 this year. Assume that the MPC is .75 and that this is a closed economy: exports and imports are both equal to zero. During the first round, the increase in investment is income to someone, so income increases by $50. The initial increase in income of $50 induces an increase in consumption of $37.50 (.75 × $50) and an increase in saving of $12.50 (.25 × $50). The $37.50 spent on domestic goods and services becomes income to someone else, who spends $28.13 (.75 × $37.50) and saves $9.38 (.25 × $37.50). The spiral continues, and the increases to income get smaller and smaller. In this example, all the increases in income sum to $200: four times the original increase in autonomous spending.

Round	Increase in Real GDP	Increase in Consumption	Increase in Saving
1—Increase in *I* of $50	$ 50	$ 37.5 = .75($50)	$12.5
2	$ 37.5	$ 28.125 = .75($37.5)	$ 9.375
3	$ 28.125	$ 21.09375	$ 7.03125
4	$ 21.09375	$ 15.820312	$ 5.273438
.	.	.	.
.	.	.	.
.	.	.	.
Total	$200	$150	$50

5. What is the spending multiplier?

   The **spending multiplier** measures the change in real GDP produced by a change in autonomous expenditures, and is equal to 1/(MPS + MPI).

6. What is the relationship between the GDP gap and the recessionary gap?

   The GDP gap is the difference between equilibrium GDP and potential GDP. It tells us the change in real GDP needed to get to potential GDP. The **recessionary gap** tells us the change in autonomous expenditures that is necessary to close the GDP gap.

7. How does international trade affect the size of the multiplier?

   The simple multiplier understates the true multiplier because it does not take into account the foreign repercussions of domestic spending. If Americans spend money on foreign goods, foreign incomes increase. The increase in foreign incomes increases U.S. exports, but the change in exports is not picked up by the simple multiplier.

8. Why does the aggregate expenditures curve shift with changes in the price level?

   The aggregate expenditures curve shifts with changes in the price level because of the wealth effect, interest rate effect, and international trade effect. When prices rise, purchasing power falls.

Since wealth is a determinant of consumption, consumption falls. Likewise, an increase in prices tends to increase interest rates, and this increase lowers investment spending. Finally, an increase in domestic prices makes domestic goods expensive for foreigners and thus decreases exports. Since consumption, investment, and net exports are all components of aggregate expenditures, aggregate expenditures fall.

Key Terms

spending multiplier   recessionary gap

Quick-Check Quiz

Section 1: Equilibrium Income and Expenditures

1. Actual expenditures always equal
    a. planned income.
    b. planned output.
    c. consumption.
    d. income and output.
    e. planned expenditures.

2. When aggregate expenditures exceed real GDP, inventories (rise, fall), production (increases, decreases), and national income (increases, decreases).
    a. rise; increases; increases
    b. rise; increases; decreases
    c. rise; decreases; increases
    d. fall; increases; increases
    e. fall; increases; decreases

3. The equilibrium level of real GDP is that point at which
    a. aggregate expenditures equal real GDP.
    b. real GDP equals output.
    c. unplanned spending equals aggregate expenditures.
    d. the aggregate expenditures curve lies above the 45-degree line.
    e. the aggregate expenditures curve lies below the 45-degree line.

4. Which of the following are *not* leakages from spending?
    a. saving
    b. investment
    c. taxes
    d. imports
    e. saving and taxes

5. For equilibrium to occur,
   a. investment must equal saving.
   b. government spending must equal taxes.
   c. exports must equal imports.
   d. leakages must equal injections.
   e. all of the above must occur.

6. When leakages exceed injections, planned spending is (less than, greater than) current real GDP, so production and real GDP (rise, fall).
   a. less than; rise
   b. less than; fall
   c. greater than; rise
   d. greater than; fall
   e. There is no relationship between planned spending and the equality of leakages and injections.

Section 2: Changes in Equilibrium Income and Expenditures

1. Assume that the MPC is .85 and the MPI is .10. What is the multiplier?
   a. 1.1764705
   b. 10
   c. 1.0526315
   d. 1.3333333
   e. 4.0

2. Suppose the MPC = .9 and the MPI = .15. If government spending decreased by $25, real GDP would _____ by _____ .
   a. increase; $100
   b. decrease; $100
   c. increase; $25
   d. decrease; $25
   e. decrease; $23.81

3. The equation for the recessionary gap is
   a. potential GDP + real GDP.
   b. real GDP – actual GDP.
   c. GDP gap/spending multiplier.
   d. spending multiplier/GDP gap.
   e. potential GDP/spending multiplier.

4. Suppose the potential GDP is $400 and the economy is at equilibrium at $350. The MPC = .8 and the MPI = .05. The GDP gap is $ _____ , the spending multiplier is _____ , and the recessionary gap is $ _____ .
   a. 50; 4; 12.50
   b. 12.50; 4; 50
   c. 50; 1.18; 42.50
   d. 42.58; 1.18; 50
   e. 50; .7692307; 65

5. Which of the following statements is true?
   a. The simple multiplier understates the actual multiplier in a closed economy.
   b. The simple multiplier overstates the actual multiplier in a closed economy.
   c. The simple multiplier understates the true multiplier because it does not take into account the foreign repercussions of domestic spending.
   d. The simple multiplier overstates the true multiplier because it does not take into account the foreign repercussions of domestic spending.
   e. The multiplier effect is lower with foreign repercussions than without.

6. The U.S. spending multiplier for Germany is .2. If U.S. investment decreases by $40, German equivalent real GDP will _____ by _____ .
   a. increase; $40
   b. decrease; $40
   c. increase; $8
   d. decrease; $8
   e. decrease; $200

Section 3: Aggregate Expenditures and Aggregate Demand

1. A drawback of the Keynesian model is that it
   a. assumes that shortages of goods and services will be met by rising prices.
   b. assumes that surpluses of goods and services will be met by rising prices.
   c. assumes that shortages of goods and services will be met by rising prices and increased production.
   d. assumes that shortages of goods and services will be met by rising prices and decreased production.
   e. is a fixed-price model.

2. Which of the following is a reason for the aggregate expenditures curve to shift with changes in the level of prices?
   a. the substitution effect
   b. the income effect
   c. the interest rate effect
   d. the expectations effect
   e. the foreign price level effect

3. When prices increase, people and businesses need _____ money. They _____ bonds, causing interest rates to _____ and aggregate expenditures to _____ .
   a. more; buy; fall; rise
   b. more; sell; fall; rise
   c. more; buy; rise; fall
   d. more; sell; rise; fall
   e. less; buy; fall; rise

4. When the price level falls, domestic goods become _____ for foreigners. Net exports _____, and aggregate expenditures _____. This is called the _____ effect.
   a. cheaper; rise; rise; international trade
   b. cheaper; fall; fall; international trade
   c. cheaper; rise; fall; international trade
   d. more expensive; fall; fall; international trade
   e. cheaper; rise; rise; wealth

5. When the price level falls, the value of household and business assets _____. Households and firms spend _____, and aggregate expenditures _____. This is called the _____ effect.
   a. increases; more; rise; income
   b. increases; more; rise; wealth
   c. decreases; less; fall; income
   d. decreases; less; fall; wealth
   e. decreases; more; rise; wealth

6. A higher price level _____ autonomous consumption, autonomous investment, and net exports, causing aggregate expenditures to _____. The aggregate expenditures curve would shift from AE_1 to _____ on the graph below.

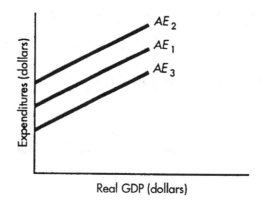

   a. increases; rise; AE_2
   b. increases; rise; AE_3
   c. increases; fall; AE_3
   d. decreases; fall; AE_2
   e. decreases; fall; AE_3

7. The Keynesian fixed-price model
   a. is represented by a vertical aggregate supply curve.
   b. describes an economy with substantial unemployment and excess capacity.
   c. is a comprehensive model used extensively by modern economists.
   d. assumes that increases in aggregate demand will be met by both increased output and higher prices.
   e. assumes that increases in aggregate demand will be met by increased output and lower prices.

Practice Questions and Problems

Section 1: Equilibrium Income and Expenditures

1. In macroeconomics, _____ is the level of income and expenditures that the economy tends to move toward and remain at until autonomous spending changes.
2. The aggregate expenditures function represents _____ expenditures at different levels of real GDP.
3. _____ expenditures always equal income and output because they reflect changes in inventories.
4. When planned spending on goods and services _____ the current value of output, the production of goods and services and real GDP increase.
5. When aggregate expenditures are less than real GDP, inventories _____ (become depleted, accumulate), production _____ (increases, decreases), and real GDP _____ (rises, falls).
6. The equilibrium level of real GDP is at the point where _____ equal _____ .
7. Leakages _____ autonomous aggregate expenditures.
8. The three types of leakages from spending are _____ , _____ , and _____ .
9. The three types of injections of spending into the income stream are _____ , _____ , and _____ .
10. For equilibrium to occur, total leakages must equal total _____ .
11. When leakages exceed injections, real GDP _____ (rises, falls).

Section 2: Changes in Equilibrium Income and Expenditures

1. Consumption changes by the _____ multiplied by the change in real GDP.
2. Imports change by the marginal propensity to import multiplied by the _____ .
3. The percentage of a change in income that is spent domestically is equal to _____ (use abbreviations).
4. The multiplier is equal to _____ (use abbreviations).
5. The greater the leakages, the _____ (greater, smaller) the multiplier.
6. An economy that does not trade with the rest of the world is called a(n) _____ economy.
7. According to the Keynesian view, equilibrium _____ (does, does not) necessarily occur at potential GDP.

8. The _____ is how much real GDP needs to change to yield equilibrium at potential real GDP. It is the _____ (horizontal, vertical) distance between equilibrium real GDP and potential real GDP.

9. The _____ is the change in spending necessary for equilibrium real GDP to rise to potential real GDP. It is the _____ (horizontal, vertical) distance between the aggregate expenditures curve and the 45-degree line at the potential real GDP level.

10. The simple multiplier [1/(MPS + MPI)] _____ (overstates, understates) the true multiplier effects of increases in autonomous spending because of the foreign repercussions of domestic spending.

11. U.S. spending increases have a _____ (larger, smaller) effect on foreign real GDP than foreign spending increases have on U.S. real GDP.

12. The _____ measures the change in real GDP produced by a change in autonomous spending.

Section 3: Aggregate Expenditures and Aggregate Demand

1. A drawback of the Keynesian model is that it assumes that the supply of goods and services in the economy always adjusts to aggregate expenditures. It is a _____ model.

2. Shortages of goods and services may be met by increased production or by _____ .

3. List the three reasons why the aggregate expenditures curve shifts with changes in the price level.
   _____
   _____
   _____

4. As the level of prices increases, the purchasing power of money _____ (increases, decreases) and the real value of assets _____ (increases, decreases). The _____ effect, or real-balance effect, predicts that the real value of aggregate expenditures will _____ (rise, fall).

5. When prices increase, people _____ (buy, sell) bonds to get money. Bond prices _____ (increase, decrease), and interest rates _____ (rise, fall). The _____ effect suggests that aggregate expenditures will _____ (rise, fall).

6. If domestic prices rise while foreign prices and foreign exchange rates remain constant, domestic goods will become _____ (less expensive, more expensive) for foreigners. Net exports will _____ (rise, fall), causing aggregate expenditures to _____ (rise, fall).

7. When the price level falls, aggregate expenditures _____ (rise, fall).

8. The _____ shows how the equilibrium level of expenditures changes as the price level changes.

9. Use the aggregate expenditures curves below to derive and plot the aggregate demand curve. Be sure to label your axes.

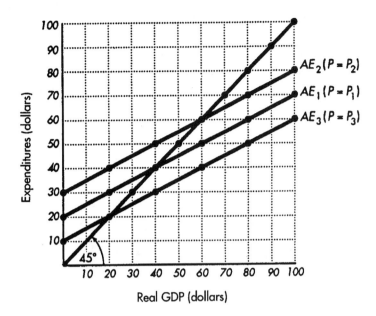

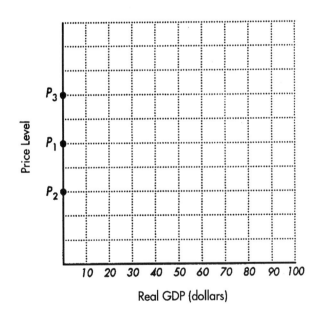

Thinking About and Applying Income and Expenditures Equilibrium

I. Aggregate Expenditures = Real GDP Approach

1. Complete the table below and answer the following questions.

Y	C	I	G	X	AE	Unplanned Change in Inventories	Change in Real GDP
$ 0	$ 40	$20	$30	$30	$ 120	$ −120	Increase
160	136	20	30	14	200	−40	Increase
180	148	20	30	12	210	−30	Increase
200	160	20	30	10	220	−20	Increase
220	172	20	30	8	230	−10	Increase
240	184	20	30	6	240	0	No change
260	196	20	30	4	250	+10	Decrease
280	208	20	30	2	260	+20	Decrease
300	220	20	30	0	270	+30	Decrease
320	232	20	30	−2	280	+40	Decrease

a. The equilibrium level of real GDP is __240__.

b. The MPC is __0.6__, and the MPS is __0.4__.

c. The MPI is __0.1__.

d. The spending multiplier is __2__.

e. If the potential GDP is $300, the GDP gap is __$60__ and the recessionary gap is __$30__.

f. Plot aggregate expenditures on the graph below. Show the GDP gap and the recessionary gap.

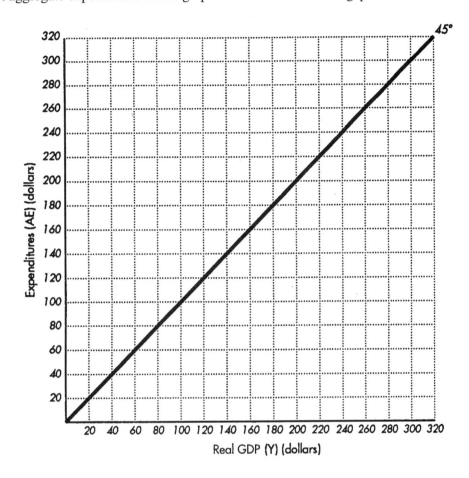

2. Use the graph below to answer the following questions. Assume that this is a closed economy and that government spending is $15 and investment is $5. Plot aggregate expenditures.

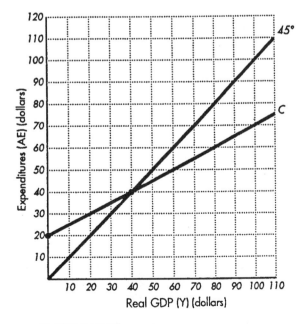

a. The equilibrium level of real GDP is _____.
b. The MPC is _____, and the MPS is _____.
c. The spending multiplier is _____.
d. If the potential GDP is $100, the GDP gap is _____ and the recessionary gap is _____.

II. Leakages = Injections Approach

1. Complete the table below and answer the following questions. Assume that investment equals $10, government spending is $20, and exports are $20.

Y	S	T	IM	Leakages	Injections	Change in Real GDP
$ 0	$-20	$0	$15	$ -5	$ 50	Increase
100	-5	0	25			
120	-2	0	27			
140	1	0	29			
160	4	0	31			
180	7	0	33			
200	10	0	35			
220	13	0	37			
240	16	0	39			
260	19	0	41			

a. The equilibrium level of real GDP is _____.
b. The MPS is _____, and the MPC is _____.
c. The MPI is _____.
d. The spending multiplier is _____.
e. If the potential GDP is $300, the GDP gap is _____ and the recessionary gap is _____.

2. Use the graph below to answer the following questions. Assume a closed economy with investment = $10, government spending = $20, and taxes = 0. Plot leakages and injections.

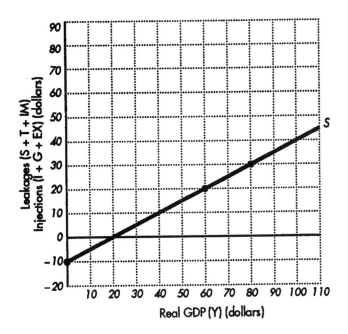

a. What is the MPS? _____ the MPC? _____
b. What is the spending multiplier? _____
c. What is the equilibrium level of real GDP? _____

Chapter 11   Homework Problems

Name _____

1. In the Keynesian model, what does aggregate expenditures have to equal for the economy to be in equilibrium?

2. List the leakages from spending in the Keynesian model.

3. List the injections into spending in the Keynesian model.

4. Suppose the economy is currently in equilibrium. Businesses decide they want to increase investment spending by $50 billion per year. Briefly explain why this $50 billion increase in spending will increase equilibrium real GDP by more than $50 billion.

5. In the United States, the president frequently gets the blame or the credit when the economy changes, although he has relatively little control over the economy. A growing economy is good for a president's chances of reelection, while an economy in recession makes winning reelection harder.

   The Federal Reserve System, an independent part of government that you'll learn more about in later chapters, has some control over interest rates through its control over monetary policy.

   Suppose that the Federal Reserve is thinking about raising interest rates in the near future. Use your knowledge of aggregate expenditures, and the diagram below, to determine the effect of an increase in interest rates on real GDP and figure out why a president would want to convince the Federal Reserve not to raise interest rates.

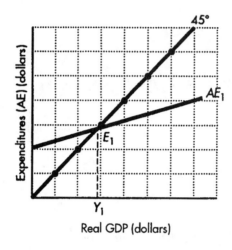

If your instructor assigns these problems, write your answers above, then tear out this page and hand it in.

Answers

Quick-Check Quiz

Section 1: Equilibrium Income and Expenditures

1. d; 2. d; 3. a; 4. b; 5. d; 6. b
If you missed any of these questions, you should go back and review Section 1 of Chapter 11.

Section 2: Changes in Equilibrium Income and Expenditures

1. e; 2. b; 3. c; 4. a; 5. c; 6. d
If you missed any of these questions, you should go back and review Section 2 of Chapter 11.

Section 3: Aggregate Expenditures and Aggregate Demand

1. e; 2. c; 3. d; 4. a; 5. b; 6. e; 7. b
If you missed any of these questions, you should go back and review Section 3 of Chapter 11.

Practice Questions and Problems

Section 1: Equilibrium Income and Expenditures

1. equilibrium
2. planned
3. Actual
4. exceeds
5. accumulate; decreases; falls
6. aggregate expenditures; real GDP (or output)
7. reduce
8. saving; taxes; imports
9. investment; government spending; exports
10. injections
11. falls

Section 2: Changes in Equilibrium Income and Expenditures

1. marginal propensity to consume (MPC)
2. change in real GDP
3. MPC − MPI
4. 1/(MPS + MPI)
5. smaller
6. closed
7. does not
8. GDP gap; horizontal
9. recessionary gap; vertical
10. understates
11. larger
12. spending multiplier

Section 3: Aggregate Expenditures and Aggregate Demand

1. fixed-price
2. rising prices
3. wealth effect
   interest rate effect
   international trade effect
4. decreases; decreases; wealth; fall
5. sell; decrease; rise; interest rate; fall
6. more expensive; fall; fall
7. rise
8. aggregate demand curve
9.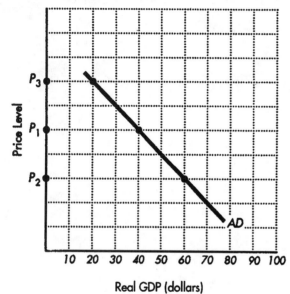

Thinking About and Applying Income and Expenditures Equilibrium

I. Aggregate Expenditures = Real GDP Approach

1.

Y	C	I	G	X	AE	Unplanned Change in Inventories	Change in Real GDP
$ 0	$ 40	$20	$30	$30	$120	$–120	Increase
160	136	20	30	14	200	–40	Increase
180	148	20	30	12	210	–30	Increase
200	160	20	30	10	220	–20	Increase
220	172	20	30	8	230	–10	Increase
240	184	20	30	6	240	0	No change
260	196	20	30	4	250	10	Decrease
280	208	20	30	2	260	20	Decrease
300	220	20	30	0	270	30	Decrease
320	232	20	30	–2	280	40	Decrease

a. $240
b. MPC = change in consumption/change in real GDP
   = $12/$20 = .6
   MPS = 1 – MPC = 1 – .6 = .4
c. MPI = change in imports/change in real GDP = 2/20 = .1
   (Since exports are autonomous, the change in net exports equals the change in imports.)
d. Spending multiplier = 1/(MPS + MPI) = 1/(.4 + .1) = 1/.5 = 2
e. GDP gap = potential GDP – real GDP
          = $300 – $240 = $60
   Recessionary gap = GDP gap/spending multiplier = $60/2 = $30

f.

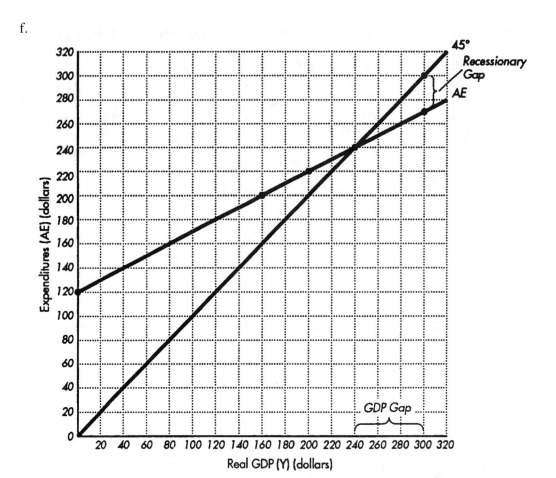

2.

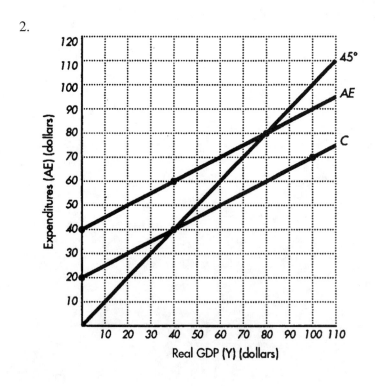

a. $80
b. .5; .5
c. 2
d. $20; $10

II. Leakages = Injections Approach

1.

Y	S	T	IM	Leakages	Injections	Change in Real GDP
$ 0	$-20	$0	$15	$-5	$50	Increase
100	-5	0	25	20	50	Increase
120	-2	0	27	25	50	Increase
140	1	0	29	30	50	Increase
160	4	0	31	35	50	Increase
180	7	0	33	40	50	Increase
200	10	0	35	45	50	Increase
220	13	0	37	50	50	No change
240	16	0	39	55	50	Decrease
260	19	0	41	60	50	Decrease

a. $220
b. MPS = change in saving/change in real GDP
   = $15/$100 = .15
   MPC = 1 − MPS = 1 − .15 = .85
c. MPI = change in imports/change in real GDP = $10/$100 = .1
d. Spending multiplier = 1/(MPS + MPI) = 1/(.15 + .1) = 1/.25 = 4
e. GDP gap = potential GDP − real GDP
          = $300 − $220 = $80
   Recessionary gap = GDP gap/spending multiplier = $80/4 = $20

2.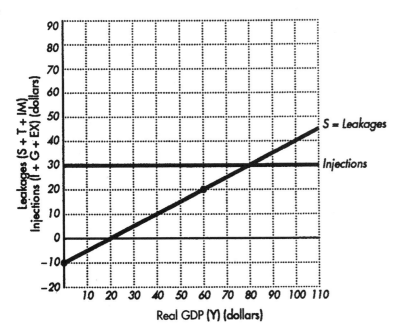

a. ½; ½
b. 2
c. $80

Appendix to Chapter 11

AN ALGEBRAIC MODEL OF INCOME AND EXPENDITURES EQUILIBRIUM

Summary

In Chapter 10, we learned that each of the components of aggregate expenditures can be represented by an equation. In that chapter we combined the equations to get an equation for aggregate expenditures:

$$AE = C^a + cY + I^a + G^a + EX^a - IM^a - im\, Y$$

Collecting like terms, we have

$$AE = C^a + I^a + G^a + EX^a - IM^a + (c - im)Yd$$

Since we know that aggregate expenditures must be equal to real GDP at macroeconomic equilibrium, we find equilibrium by setting

$$Y = AE$$
$$Y = C^a + I^a + G^a + EX^a - IM^a + (c - im)Yd$$
$$Y = [1/(1 - [c - im])] \times (C^a + I^a + G^a + EX^a - IM^a)$$

The first term on the right-hand side is the multiplier; the second term is autonomous expenditures.

Practice Questions and Problems

1. Given:

$$C = \$50 + .90Y$$
$$I = \$40$$
$$G = \$60$$
$$X = \$50 - .10Y$$

　　a. The equilibrium level of real GDP is _____ .

b. The spending multiplier is _____ .

c. If potential GDP is $1,250, the GDP gap is _____ and the recessionary gap is _____ .

2. Given:

$$C = \$100 + .8Y$$
$$I = \$50$$
$$G = \$60$$
$$X = \$70 - .15Y$$

a. The equilibrium level of real GDP is _____ .

b. The spending multiplier is _____ .

c. If potential GDP is $1,000, the GDP gap is _____ and the recessionary gap is _____ .

3. Use the information below to answer the following questions.

Autonomous consumption is $15,000.
The marginal propensity to consume is .85.
Gross investment is $3,750.
Government spending is $5,625.
Exports are $5,000.
Autonomous imports are $1,250.
The marginal propensity to import is .05.

a. The equilibrium level of real GDP is _____ .

b. The spending multiplier is _____ .

c. If potential GDP is $150,000, the GDP gap is _____ and the recessionary gap is _____ .

4. Use the information below to answer the following questions.

Autonomous consumption is $250.
The marginal propensity to consume is .95.
Gross investment is $65.
Government spending is $80.
Exports are $200.
Autonomous imports are $50.
The marginal propensity to import is .20.

a. The equilibrium level of real GDP is _____ .

b. The spending multiplier is _____ .

c. If potential GDP is $3,000, the GDP gap is _____ and the recessionary gap is _____ .

Answers

1. a. $Y = C + I + G + X$
        $Y = (\$50 + .90Y) + \$40 + \$60 + (\$50 - .10Y)$
        $Y = \$200 + .80Y$
        $.20Y = \$200$
        $Y = \$1,000$
    b. Spending multiplier = $1/(MPS + MPI) = 1/(.1 + .1) = 1/.2 = 5$
    c. GDP gap = potential GDP – actual GDP = $\$1,250 - \$1,000 = \$250$
        Recessionary gap = GDP gap/spending multiplier = $\$250/5 = \$50$
2. a. $Y = C + I + G + X$
        $Y = (\$100 + .8Y) + \$50 + \$60 + (\$70 - .15Y)$
        $Y = \$280 + .65Y$
        $.35Y = \$280$
        $Y = \$800$
    b. Spending multiplier = $1/(MPS + MPI)$
        $= 1/(.2 + .15) = 1/.35 = 2.8571428$
    c. GDP gap = potential GDP – actual GDP
        $= \$1,000 - \$800 = \$200$
        Recessionary gap = GDP gap/spending multiplier
        $= \$200/2.8571428$
        $= \$70$
3. a. $C = \$15,000 + .85Y$
        $I^a = \$3,750$
        $G^a = \$5,625$
        $X = E^a - I^a - imY = \$5,000 - \$1,250 - .05Y = \$3,750 - .05Y$
        $Y = C + I + G + X = \$15,000 + .85Y + \$3,750 + \$5,625 + \$3,750 - .05Y$
        $Y = \$28,125 + .8Y$
        $.2Y = \$28,125$
        $Y = \$140,625$
    b. Spending multiplier = $1/(MPS + MPI) = 1/(.15 + .05) = 1/.2 = 5$
    c. GDP gap = potential GDP – actual GDP
        $= \$150,000 - \$140,625$
        $= \$9,375$
        Recessionary gap = GDP gap/spending multiplier = $\$9,375/5$
        $= \$1,875$
4. a. $C = \$250 + .95Y$
        $I^a = \$65$
        $G^a = \$80$
        $X = E^a - I^a - imY = \$200 - \$50 - .20Y = \$150 - .20Y$
        $Y = C + I + G + X = \$250 + .95Y + \$65 + \$80 + \$150 - .20Y$
        $Y = \$545 + .75Y$
        $.25Y = \$545$
        $Y = \$2,180$
    b. Spending multiplier = $1/(MPS + MPI) = 1/(.05 + .20) = 1/.25 = 4$

c. GDP gap = potential GDP − actual GDP
   = $3,000 − $2,180
   = $820
   Recessionary gap = GDP gap/spending multiplier = $820/4
   = $205

Sample Test I
Chapters 6–11
(*Economics* Chapters 6–11)

1. The value of intermediate goods and services is not counted in GDP
   a. because this would lead to an understatement of the true value of GDP.
   b. because only the value of raw materials is included in the computations of GDP.
   c. because it is difficult to keep track of the precise values of intermediate goods and services in an economy.
   d. because the value of the final good already incorporates the value added of the intermediate goods and services used in production.
   e. because intermediate goods and services are sold only in the underground economy.

2. A motorcycle built in 1999 and sold in 2000
   a. is not counted as part of 1999 inventory.
   b. must be subtracted from the calculations of 2000 GDP.
   c. increases the value of national output for 1999.
   d. is ignored in all GDP measurements to avoid double-counting.
   e. is added to 2000 GDP and excluded from 1999 output computations.

Consider the following table for questions 3 and 4:

GDP Data	
Wages	$1,500,000
Net exports	400,000
Interest income	300,000
Corporate profits	500,000
Capital consumption allowance	50,000
Rental income	550,000
Net factor income from abroad	150,000
Indirect business taxes	200,000
Personal income taxes	350,000
Gross domestic investment	650,000

3. What is GDP?
   a. $2,650,000
   b. $2,800,000
   c. $3,100,000
   d. $3,250,000
   e. $3,450,000

4. What is net national product?
   a. $2,600,000
   b. $2,750,000
   c. $2,850,000
   d. $3,050,000
   e. $3,200,000

Consider the following table for questions 5 through 7:

Year	Nominal GDP	Price Data Price Index
1996	$1,300	90
1997	1,500	100
1998	1,650	110
1999	1,900	125
2000	2,100	140

5. What is the base year?
   a. 1996
   b. 1997
   c. 1998
   d. 1999
   e. 2000

6. What is real GDP for 1999?
   a. $1,250
   b. $1,520
   c. $1,775
   d. $1,900
   e. $2,020

7. Between 1999 and 2000,
   a. real output and prices have fallen.
   b. real output has grown and prices have remained constant.
   c. real output has fallen and prices have risen.
   d. real output and prices have risen.
   e. real output has grown and prices have fallen.

8. Other things being equal, the U.S. current account deficit will fall when
   a. Germany imports wine from France.
   b. Great Britain exports beer to the United States.
   c. the United States provides humanitarian aid to Somalia.
   d. Japan buys soft-drink products from the United States.
   e. French investors sell U.S. government bonds.

9. If the exchange rate moves from FF5.5 = $1 to FF6.0 = $1, then
   a. U.S. imports of French products are likely to increase.
   b. French imports of U.S. products are likely to increase.
   c. the French franc has appreciated in value against the U.S. dollar.
   d. fewer French francs are needed to purchase one U.S. dollar.
   e. U.S. residents are likely to lower their demand for French currency.

10. The expansionary phase of a business cycle tends to be associated with
    a. declining price levels.
    b. lower real output.
    c. an economic trough.
    d. a higher number of discouraged workers.
    e. lower cyclical unemployment.

11. Who is most likely to be a winner during inflationary periods?
    a. a white-collar worker earning a fixed income
    b. commercial banks
    c. a retired person who lives on a fixed social security payment
    d. a married couple that owes $100,000 on a mortgage
    e. an investor in U.S. Treasury bills

12. Potential real GDP is equal to
    a. the reciprocal of the price level.
    b. the level of output that would be produced at zero unemployment.
    c. actual real GDP if the economy operates at the natural rate of unemployment.
    d. real output at zero percent inflation.
    e. the GDP gap minus actual real GDP.

13. If the rate of inflation exceeds increases in nominal income, then
    a. the purchasing power of a dollar has declined.
    b. the standard of living has risen.
    c. the nominal interest rate is negative.
    d. the real value of money has risen.
    e. the economy is at a peak.

14. Other things being equal, a decline in the domestic price level will result in
    a. a rightward shift of the aggregate demand curve.
    b. a reduction in aggregate expenditures.
    c. a movement down the aggregate demand curve.
    d. a leftward shift of the aggregate demand curve.
    e. a decline in the slope of the aggregate demand curve.

15. If personal income taxes are expected to fall, then, other things being equal,
    a. consumption expenditures will fall and real GDP will decline.
    b. consumption expenditures will rise and real output will increase for any given price level.
    c. consumption expenditures will rise and the price level will decline.
    d. consumption expenditures will remain unchanged, but the aggregate quantity of goods and services supplied will rise.
    e. consumption expenditures will fall and the aggregate quantity of goods and services demanded will rise.

Refer to the following figure for questions 16 and 17.

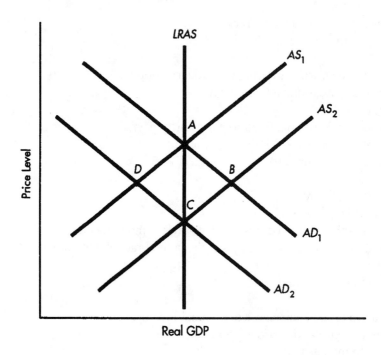

16. The short-run effects of a decrease in government spending are best described by a movement from
    a. A to D.
    b. C to B.
    c. A to B.
    d. A to C.
    e. C to A.

17. The long-run effects of a decrease in government spending are best described by a movement from
    a. C to D to A.
    b. C to B.
    c. D to A to B.
    d. C to B to A.
    e. A to D to C.

18. When the aggregate supply curve is vertical,
    a. the economy has zero unemployment.
    b. an increase in aggregate demand will lead to an increase in the price level but no change in potential real GDP.
    c. there is a large amount of cyclical unemployment.
    d. a decrease in aggregate demand will lead to a decrease in potential real GDP and a decrease in inflation.
    e. the equilibrium level of real GDP is solely determined by the position of the aggregate demand curve.

19. In the Keynesian model of macroeconomics, an increase in disposable income is associated with
    a. an increase in consumption and a decrease in saving.
    b. a decrease in both consumption and saving.
    c. an increase in both consumption and saving.
    d. a decrease in consumption and an increase in saving.
    e. an increase in consumption and no change in saving.

20. The slope of the saving function
    a. measures the fraction of disposable income that is saved.
    b. equals 1 + APS.
    c. measures the amount of saving that does not depend on disposable income.
    d. equals 1 − MPC.
    e. is the inverse of the marginal propensity to consume.

21. Other things being equal, an increase in investment spending in the Keynesian framework results in all of the following *except*
    a. a higher intercept of the $C + I + G + X$ function.
    b. a higher equilibrium level of real GDP.
    c. a rise in aggregate demand.
    d. a steeper slope of the aggregate expenditures function.
    e. an upward shift of the $C + I + G + X$ function.

22. In the Keynesian model, the equilibrium level of real GDP occurs at the point where
    a. $S + T + IM < G + I + EX$.
    b. planned aggregate expenditures exceed actual aggregate expenditures.
    c. MPS + MPI = 1.
    d. autonomous aggregate expenditures are zero.
    e. $AE = C + I + G + X$.

23. Suppose the MPS equals 0.5 and the MPI equals 0.3. Then a $400 increase in government spending will
    a. raise the equilibrium level of real GDP by $500.
    b. lower the equilibrium level of real GDP by $400.
    c. raise the equilibrium level of real GDP by $320.
    d. lower the equilibrium level of real GDP by $500.
    e. lower the equilibrium level of real GDP by $320.

Refer to the following figure for questions 24 and 25.

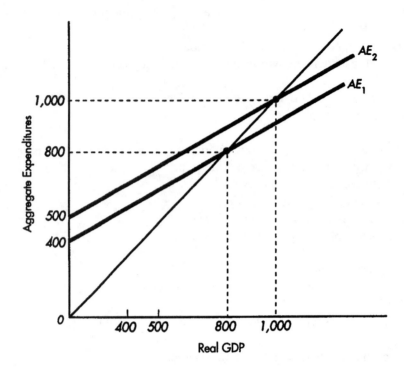

24. If aggregate expenditures are equal to AE_1 and potential real GDP is at $1,000,
    a. the GDP gap is zero.
    b. actual real GDP exceeds potential real GDP by $200.
    c. the economy operates at the natural rate of unemployment.
    d. there exists a recessionary gap equal to $100.
    e. aggregate expenditures must be increased by $200 to bring the economy to the point of full employment of resources.

25. Suppose that we allow for a changing price level as spending increases. Then to close the GDP gap, aggregate expenditures would have to
    a. increase by exactly $100.
    b. increase by more than $100.
    c. increase by less than $100.
    d. increase by exactly $200.
    e. remain unchanged at AE_1.

Answers to Sample Test

1. d (Chapter 6, Section 1.a; *Economics* Chapter 6)
2. c (Chapter 6, Section 1.a; *Economics* Chapter 6)
3. c (Chapter 6, Section 1.a; *Economics* Chapter 6)
4. d (Chapter 6, Section 1.a; *Economics* Chapter 6)
5. b (Chapter 6, Section 2.b; *Economics* Chapter 6)
6. b (Chapter 6, Section 2.b; *Economics* Chapter 6)
7. d (Chapter 6, Section 2.b; *Economics* Chapter 6)
8. d (Chapter 7, Section 2.b; *Economics* Chapter 7)
9. a (Chapter 7, Section 1.b; *Economics* Chapter 7)
10. e (Chapter 8, Section 2.c; *Economics* Chapter 8)
11. d (Chapter 8, Section 3.b; *Economics* Chapter 8)
12. c (Chapter 8, Section 2.d; *Economics* Chapter 8)
13. a (Chapter 8, Section 3.b; *Economics* Chapter 8)
14. c (Chapter 9, Section 2.e; *Economics* Chapter 9)
15. b (Chapter 9, Section 3.b; *Economics* Chapter 9)
16. a (Chapter 9, Section 5.a; *Economics* Chapter 9)
17. e (Chapter 9, Section 5.b; *Economics* Chapter 9)
18. b (Chapter 9, Section 5.b; *Economics* Chapter 9)
19. c (Chapter 10, Section 1.b; *Economics* Chapter 10)
20. d (Chapter 10, Section 1.c; *Economics* Chapter 10)
21. d (Chapter 10, Section 5.a; *Economics* Chapter 10)
22. e (Chapter 10, Section 5; *Economics* Chapter 10)
23. a (Chapter 11, Section 2.a; *Economics* Chapter 11)
24. d (Chapter 11, Section 2.b; *Economics* Chapter 11)
25. b (Chapter 11, Section 2.c; *Economics* Chapter 11)

Sample Test II
Chapters 6–11
(*Economics* Chapters 6–11)

1. Since barter transactions are excluded from GDP measures,
   a. GDP is not a very useful measure of a nation's output.
   b. double-counting in calculating GDP is avoided.
   c. the economy's total production tends to be overestimated.
   d. the value-added method is preferred over the expenditures approach in determining a nation's productive activity.
   e. GDP tends to underestimate national output.

2. Suppose a data processing consultant buys a computer for $2,000 to write a new accounting program. The finished program then is sold to a software firm for $9,500. The software firm, in turn, earns total revenues of $25,000 from retail sales of the accounting program. What is the total value added associated with the accounting program?
   a. $9,500
   b. $11,500
   c. $25,000
   d. $34,500
   e. $36,500

3. If $C = \$3,500$, $I = \$900$, $G = \$700$, $X = \$200$, and net factor income from abroad = $100, then GDP is
   a. $3,500.
   b. $5,100.
   c. $5,200.
   d. $5,300.
   e. $5,400.

4. If real GDP is $5,000 and the GDP price index for the same year equals 125, we can conclude that
   a. the price level has not changed relative to the base year.
   b. nominal GDP equals $4,000.
   c. the price level has fallen relative to the base year.
   d. nominal GDP equals $3,000.
   e. nominal GDP equals $6,250.

5. Suppose that Ms. Weber in Berlin, Germany, receives a $300 check from an uncle in Chicago for her eighteenth birthday. In the U.S. balance of payments, this transaction would be classified as
   a. a $300 credit to the merchandise account.
   b. a $300 debit to the services account.
   c. a $300 debit to the merchandise account.
   d. a $300 debit to the unilateral transfers account.
   e. a $300 credit to the investment income account.

6. When a nation is a net creditor to the rest of the world,
   a. it runs a surplus in its current account.
   b. it consumes more than it produces.
   c. it runs a surplus in its capital account.
   d. it borrows more funds from foreigners than it is owed.
   e. it runs a government budget surplus.

7. An increase in the French franc price of the U.S. dollar implies that
   a. the dollar has depreciated against the franc.
   b. the franc value in terms of the dollar has risen.
   c. the franc has appreciated against the dollar.
   d. the dollar value in terms of the franc has fallen.
   e. the franc has depreciated against the dollar.

8. The recessionary phase of a business cycle is always followed immediately by
   a. a peak.
   b. an expansion.
   c. a trough.
   d. a contraction.
   e. a boom period.

9. Suppose that there are 250 million U.S. residents. Of those, 150 million are in the labor force, 10 million are discouraged workers, 5 million are underemployed, and 15 million are officially unemployed. Then the unemployment rate equals
   a. 6 percent.
   b. 9 percent.
   c. 10 percent.
   d. 12 percent.
   e. 20 percent.

10. Suppose that you expect an inflation rate of 4 percent next year. Mike asks to borrow $1,000 from you for one year, and you charge him an interest rate of 8 percent to cover your costs. However, the inflation rate next year turns out to be 5 percent. This implies that
    a. you will earn a lower real return than expected.
    b. you will earn a higher real return than expected.
    c. Mike will lose purchasing power.
    d. you will earn the same return on the loan as initially expected.
    e. real income will be redistributed from Mike to you.

11. Which type of unemployment is assumed to be zero in measuring the "natural rate of unemployment"?
    a. seasonal unemployment
    b. frictional unemployment
    c. structural unemployment
    d. cyclical unemployment
    e. potential unemployment

12. Which of the following results in a movement along the aggregate demand curve?
    a. an increase in government spending
    b. an increase in foreign income
    c. pessimistic consumer expectations
    d. a decline in investment spending
    e. a decline in the domestic price level

13. Other things being equal, demand-pull inflation
    a. is the result of a leftward shift of the aggregate demand curve.
    b. is associated with an economic expansion.
    c. has the same macroeconomic effects as cost-push inflation.
    d. is the result of a leftward shift of the aggregate supply curve.
    e. brings about higher unemployment.

14. When aggregate demand decreases and the aggregate supply curve is upward-sloping and unchanged, this implies that
    a. the equilibrium price level falls and the equilibrium level of real GDP rises.
    b. the equilibrium price level rises and the equilibrium level of real GDP remains unchanged.
    c. both the equilibrium price level and the equilibrium level of real GDP fall.
    d. both the equilibrium price level and the equilibrium level of real GDP rise.
    e. the equilibrium price level rises and the equilibrium level of real GDP falls.

Use the following figures to answer questions 15 and 16.

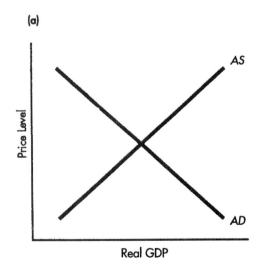
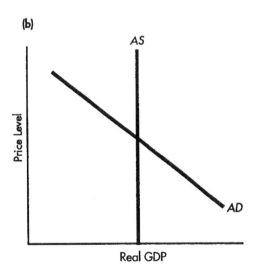

15. Evaluate which statement with respect to the figure is *not* correct.
    a. The graph shows a short-run macroeconomic equilibrium.
    b. The shape of the aggregate supply curve implies fixed production costs.
    c. Increases in the equilibrium price level would raise profits for producers.
    d. Other things being equal, an upward shift of the aggregate demand curve would result in increased real GDP and a higher price level.
    e. Over time, as production costs adjust, the upward-sloping aggregate supply curve will turn into a vertical line.

16. The macroeconomic equilibrium illustrated in the figure implies that
    a. aggregate demand is the sole determinant of equilibrium real GDP.
    b. there are unemployed resources in the economy.
    c. AS is a short-run aggregate supply curve.
    d. input costs adjust instantaneously to changes in the price level.
    e. the economy operates at a level of zero unemployment.

17. The aggregate demand curve
    a. is characterized by a positive slope.
    b. relates aggregate expenditures to changes in aggregate supply.
    c. shifts down when consumer income declines.
    d. is identical to the demand curve for a single good.
    e. is downward-sloping because of a domestic substitution effect.

18. Other things being equal, it is generally assumed that an increase in domestic real GDP causes
    a. a rise in domestic net exports.
    b. a rise in domestic imports.
    c. a decline in the domestic price level.
    d. a rise in domestic exports.
    e. a rise in the domestic spending multiplier.

19. Suppose that disposable income increases from $500 to $1,000 while saving increases from $20 to $100. Then the MPC must be equal to
    a. 0.16.
    b. 0.20.
    c. 0.50.
    d. 0.84.
    e. 1.00.

20. A decline in expected future income will act to decrease
    a. the slope of the consumption function.
    b. the slope of the aggregate expenditures function.
    c. autonomous consumption.
    d. aggregate supply.
    e. the APC.

21. Which of the following is *not* a determinant of investment spending?
    a. capacity utilization
    b. household wealth
    c. the cost of capital
    d. interest rates
    e. technological changes

22. If the marginal propensity to consume is 0.6 and the marginal propensity to import equals 0.1, then the spending multiplier equals
    a. 0.7.
    b. 1.0.
    c. 1.43.
    d. 1.67.
    e. 2.0.

Use the following figure to answer question 23.

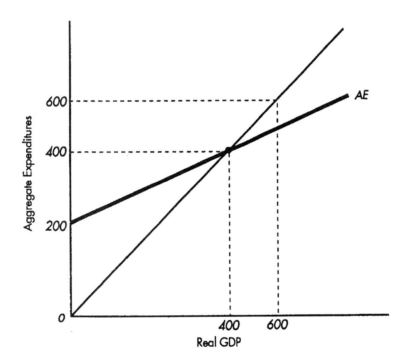

23. If aggregate expenditures are equal to $400,
    a. business inventories will decrease.
    b. the economy has reached the equilibrium level of real GDP.
    c. businesses will decrease output.
    d. planned expenditures are less than the actual real GDP level.
    e. leakages exceed injections.

24. When foreign repercussions of domestic imports are insignificant, we can conclude that
    a. the domestic economy is relatively open to trade.
    b. the real-world spending multiplier is closely approximated by the reciprocal of MPS + MPI.
    c. the real-world multiplier is smaller than the reciprocal of MPS + MPI.
    d. the multiplier effect of autonomous expenditures tends toward zero.
    e. the domestic economy is strongly affected by business cycle fluctuations in other countries.

25. A major criticism of the Keynesian model is the assumption of
    a. a vertical aggregate supply curve.
    b. a downward-sloping aggregate demand curve.
    c. fixed input costs.
    d. a horizontal aggregate supply curve.
    e. a zero unemployment rate.

Answers to Sample Test

1. e (Chapter 6, Section 1.a; *Economics* Chapter 6)
2. c (Chapter 6, Section 1.a; *Economics* Chapter 6)
3. d (Chapter 6, Section 1.a; *Economics* Chapter 6)
4. e (Chapter 6, Section 2.b; *Economics* Chapter 6)
5. d (Chapter 7, Section 2.b; *Economics* Chapter 7)
6. a (Chapter 7, Section 2.c; *Economics* Chapter 7)
7. e (Chapter 7, Section 1.b; *Economics* Chapter 7)
8. c (Chapter 8, Section 1.a; *Economics* Chapter 8)
9. c (Chapter 8, Section 2.a; *Economics* Chapter 8)
10. a (Chapter 8, Section 3.b; *Economics* Chapter 8)
11. d (Chapter 8, Section 2.d; *Economics* Chapter 8)
12. e (Chapter 9, Section 3.a; *Economics* Chapter 9)
13. b (Chapter 9, Section 1.a; *Economics* Chapter 9)
14. c (Chapter 9, Section 5.a; *Economics* Chapter 9)
15. e (Chapter 9, Section 5.a; *Economics* Chapter 9)
16. d (Chapter 9, Section 5.b; *Economics* Chapter 9)
17. c (Chapter 9, Section 3.b; *Economics* Chapter 9)
18. b (Chapter 10, Section 4.c; *Economics* Chapter 10)
19. d (Chapter 10, Section 1.c; *Economics* Chapter 10)
20. c (Chapter 10, Section 1.e; *Economics* Chapter 10)
21. b (Chapter 10, Section 1.e; *Economics* Chapter 10)
22. e (Chapter 11, Section 2.a; *Economics* Chapter 11)
23. b (Chapter 11, Section 1.a; *Economics* Chapter 11)
24. b (Chapter 11, Section 2.c; *Economics* Chapter 11)
25. d (Chapter 11, Section 3.c; *Economics* Chapter 11)

Chapter 12

FISCAL POLICY

FUNDAMENTAL QUESTIONS

1. How can fiscal policy eliminate a GDP gap?

   Fiscal policy can eliminate a GDP gap by increasing government spending (which directly increases aggregate demand) or by decreasing taxes (which increases consumption). The changes in government spending and taxes have a multiplier effect on income.

2. How has U.S. fiscal policy changed over time?

   Government spending has increased from 3 percent of the GDP before the Great Depression to approximately 19 percent of the GDP.

3. What are the effects of budget deficits?

   Budget deficits can be harmful to the economy. If the deficit is financed by borrowing, interest rates may be driven up and private domestic investment may be crowded out. Higher interest rates make U.S. financial instruments attractive to foreigners, and the resulting increase in the demand for dollars may cause the dollar to appreciate. The appreciation of the dollar decreases net exports. Greater interest costs as a result of the deficit may decrease national wealth if the debt is held by foreign residents and the debt did not increase investment and productive capacity in the United States.

4. How does fiscal policy differ across countries?

   Industrial countries spend more of their budgets on social programs than do developing countries, and they depend more on direct taxes and less on indirect taxes as sources of revenue.

Key Terms

crowding out
discretionary fiscal policy

automatic stabilizer
progressive tax

transfer payment
value-added tax (VAT)

Quick-Check Quiz

Section 1: Fiscal Policy and Aggregate Demand

1. Which of the following affects aggregate demand only *indirectly*?
   a. consumption
   b. investment
   c. taxes
   d. government spending
   e. net exports

2. Taxes affect the level of aggregate demand primarily through changing the level of _____ , which alters _____ .
   a. disposable income; consumption
   b. disposable income; investment
   c. disposable income; government spending
   d. government spending; consumption
   e. government spending; investment

3. A(n) _____ in government spending or a(n) _____ in taxes lowers the level of expenditures at every price and shifts the aggregate demand curve to the _____ .
   a. decrease; increase; right
   b. decrease; increase; left
   c. increase; decrease; right
   d. increase; decrease; left
   e. decrease; decrease; left

4. Assuming no effects on aggregate supply, if the government decreases government spending and increases taxes in an attempt to reduce the federal government budget deficit, aggregate demand will shift to the _____ , the price level will either remain constant or _____ , and the level of national income will _____ .
   a. left; increase; increase
   b. left; increase; decrease
   c. left; decrease; increase
   d. left; decrease; decrease
   e. right; decrease; decrease

5. A decrease in taxes may cause aggregate supply to shift to the _____ , causing the level of prices to _____ and the level of national income to _____ .
   a. right; fall; rise
   b. right; fall; fall
   c. right; rise; rise
   d. left; fall; rise
   e. left; rise; fall

6. Government spending financed by _____ will have a greater expansionary effect than government spending financed by _____ if the public _____ base current spending on future tax liabilities.
   a. taxes; issuing money; does
   b. taxes; borrowing; does not
   c. taxes; borrowing; does
   d. borrowing; taxes; does
   e. borrowing; taxes; does not

7. Increases in government spending financed by _____ may drive _____ interest rates and decrease _____ .
   a. taxes; up; consumption
   b. taxes; down; consumption
   c. borrowing; down; investment
   d. borrowing; up; investment
   e. borrowing; down; net exports

8. Expansionary fiscal policy refers to
   a. decreasing government spending and decreasing taxes.
   b. decreasing government spending and increasing taxes.
   c. increasing government spending and increasing taxes.
   d. increasing government spending and decreasing taxes.
   e. increasing government spending and increasing the money supply.

9. An increase in government spending
   a. has the same effect on aggregate demand as an increase in taxes.
   b. will result in a lower level of prices if the aggregate supply curve is horizontal.
   c. shifts aggregate demand to the right.
   d. decreases aggregate expenditures.
   e. is not likely to result in higher prices or a higher level of real GDP.

10. If the aggregate supply curve slopes up before reaching potential real GDP,
    a. the effect of government spending on real GDP is enhanced.
    b. the government must increase its spending by more than the recessionary gap to reach potential real GDP.
    c. the government must increase its spending by the amount of the recessionary gap to reach real GDP.
    d. prices will remain constant as government spending increases.
    e. prices will decrease as government spending increases.

11. Which of the following statements is true?
    a. If the price level rises as real GDP rises, the multiplier effects of any given change in aggregate expenditures are larger than they would be if the price level remained constant.
    b. Spending and tax multipliers overestimate the change in expenditures needed to close a recessionary gap.
    c. If aggregate supply shifts in response to an increase in government spending financed by an increase in taxes, the effects of government spending may be enhanced.
    d. David Ricardo stated that the effects of a deficit financed by an increase in taxes are different from the effects of a deficit financed by borrowing.
    e. The spending multiplier overestimates the expansionary effect of an increase in government spending unless the economy is in the Keynesian region of short-run aggregate supply.

Section 2: Fiscal Policy in the United States

1. Discretionary fiscal policy refers to
    a. government spending at the discretion of the president.
    b. government spending at the discretion of the Congress.
    c. elements of fiscal policy that automatically change in value as national income changes.
    d. government spending at the discretion of the president and the Congress.
    e. changes in government spending and taxation aimed at achieving an economic policy goal.

2. Which of the following is *not* a harmful effect of government deficits?
    a. lower private investment as a result of crowding out
    b. lower net exports as a result of the appreciation of the dollar
    c. increased investment caused by foreign savings placed in U.S. bonds
    d. an increase in saving caused by anticipated future increases in taxes
    e. an increase in imports

3. Which of the following is *not* an example of an automatic stabilizer?
    a. unemployment insurance
    b. lump-sum taxes
    c. progressive taxes
    d. food stamps
    e. welfare benefits

4. The following tax table represents a _____ tax schedule.

Income	Tax Payment
$100	$ 45
200	80
300	105
400	120

    a. regressive
    b. progressive
    c. proportional
    d. lump-sum
    e. constant rate

5. Which of the following is *not* an expected result of government budget deficits?
   a. increases in saving
   b. increases in imports
   c. decreases in investment
   d. increases in consumption
   e. decreases in exports

Section 3: Fiscal Policy in Different Countries

1. Which of the following statements is false?
   a. Historically, government spending has played an increasingly larger role over time in industrial countries.
   b. Government plays a larger role in investment spending in developing countries.
   c. Developed countries rely more on their governments to provide the infrastructure of the economy than do developing countries.
   d. State-owned enterprises account for a larger percentage of economic activity in developing countries than in developed countries.
   e. Industrial nations spend a larger percentage of their budgets on social programs than do developing countries.

2. Which of the following statements is true?
   a. Developing countries rely more heavily on direct taxes than do developed countries.
   b. Developing countries rely more heavily on indirect taxes than do developed countries.
   c. Developing countries rely more heavily on personal income taxes than do developed countries.
   d. Developing countries rely more heavily on social security taxes than do developed countries.
   e. Developed countries rely more heavily on import and export taxes than do developing countries.

Practice Questions and Problems

Section 1: Fiscal Policy and Aggregate Demand

1. Fiscal policy is changing _____ and _____ .
2. The _____ gave the federal government the responsibility for creating and maintaining low inflation and unemployment.

3. Assume the economy is in equilibrium at Y_e. In an attempt to reduce the federal government budget deficit, the government reduces government spending and increases taxes. Further assume that changes in fiscal policy *will* affect aggregate supply and that the change in aggregate demand will be greater than the change in aggregate supply. Show the effects of deficit reduction on the graph below.

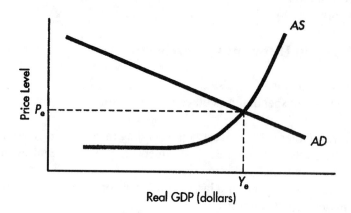

   a. Aggregate demand will shift to the _____ (right, left), and aggregate supply will shift to the _____ (right, left).

   b. The equilibrium level of national income will _____ (rise, fall), and the equilibrium price level will _____ (rise, fall).

4. Taxes affect aggregate expenditures indirectly by changing _____ ; this change alters _____ .

5. Increases in government spending may drive interest rates _____ , thereby _____ investment.

6. If government spending increases by the same amount as taxes, the effect is _____ (expansionary, contractionary).

7. An increase in government spending or a decrease in taxes causes the aggregate demand curve to shift to the _____ .

8. When prices go up, the multiplier effect of an increase in spending is _____ (enhanced, reduced). The spending and tax multipliers _____ (understate, overstate) the effect of a change in aggregate expenditures.

9. List the three ways government spending may be financed.
   _____
   _____
   _____

10. An increase in taxes may shift aggregate supply to the _____ .

11. The graph below shows equilibrium at Y_1 and P_1. Show the effect of government spending financed by taxes if the aggregate supply curve *is* affected by the change in taxes.

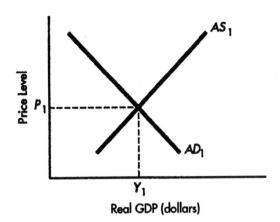

12. A government borrows funds by _____ (buying bonds from, selling bonds to) the public.

13. _____ refers to the notion that the effects on the economy are the same whether the government finances its spending through tax increases or through borrowing.

14. Ricardian equivalence assumes that aggregate demand will decrease as a result of government spending financed by borrowing because people will increase _____ to pay for future taxes.

15. An increase in government spending that reduces private spending is called _____ .

16. Crowding out may occur if government borrowing drives up _____ .

Section 2: Fiscal Policy in the United States

1. Fiscal policy in the United States is a product of the budget process, which involves the _____ and _____ branches of government.

2. As part of the budget process, federal agencies submit their budgets to the _____ (OMB), which reviews and modifies each agency's requests and consolidates all of the proposals into a single budget.

3. The _____ (CBO) reports to Congress on the validity of the economic assumptions made in the president's budget.

4. The federal budget is determined as much by _____ as by economics.

5. List the two kinds of fiscal policy.

   _____
   _____

6. _____ refers to changes in government spending and taxation aimed at achieving a policy goal.

7. _____ are elements of fiscal policy that automatically change in value as national income changes.

8. Historically, except in times of war, the federal government deficit increased the most during _____.

9. Government deficits can harm the economy by dampening _____ and _____.

10. As income falls, automatic stabilizers _____ spending.

11. _____ are taxes that are a flat dollar amount regardless of income.

12. With _____ taxes, as income rises, so does the rate of taxation.

13. With _____ taxes, the tax rate falls as income rises.

14. With _____ taxes, the tax rate is constant as income rises.

15. Look at the tax payment schedules below. Which is progressive? _____ Regressive? _____ Proportional? _____

Income	A Tax Payment	B Tax Payment	C Tax Payment
$100	$10	$ 50	$ 10
200	20	80	30
300	30	90	60
400	40	100	100

16. _____ taxes are an example of an automatic stabilizer.

17. A _____ is a payment to one person that is funded by taxing others.

18. In the first half of the 1990s, federal spending has been about _____ percent of the GDP.

Section 3: Fiscal Policy in Different Countries

1. Government plays a bigger role in investment spending in the _____ (developing, industrial) countries. Give two reasons why this should be so.
   _____
   _____

2. Low-income countries _____ (do, do not) spend a greater percentage of their budgets on social programs as compared with industrialized countries.

3. The relative cost of an education is _____ (higher, lower) in developing countries than it is in industrial countries.

4. _____ taxes are taxes on individuals and firms.

5. _____ taxes are taxes on goods and services.
6. _____ taxes are hard to collect in developing countries because so much of household production is for personal consumption.
7. In general, developing countries rely more heavily on _____ (direct, indirect) taxes than do developed countries.
8. VAT stands for _____, an indirect tax imposed on each sale at each stage of production.

Thinking About and Applying Fiscal Policy

I. Reducing the Deficit

Your text discusses the possible harmful effects of budget deficits. Since a budget deficit results from government spending that is greater than tax revenues, reducing the deficit implies reducing government spending, increasing taxes, or both. But, to quote Publius Syrus, "There are some remedies worse than the disease" (Maxim 301). Since reducing government spending and increasing taxes reduces aggregate demand, the economy might be thrown into a recession if spending cuts and tax increases are adopted.

1. Consider the graph below, where the economy is at equilibrium at P_1 and Y_1. Show what will happen if spending cuts and tax increases are implemented.

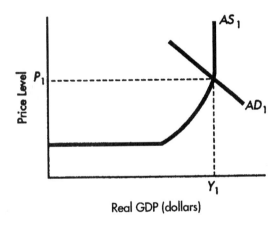

What will happen to equilibrium real GDP and price level?

_____
_____
_____
_____

2. Now consider an economy operating in the vertical region of the aggregate supply curve. Can you draw a curve that illustrates tax increases and spending cuts but does *not* throw the economy into a recession?

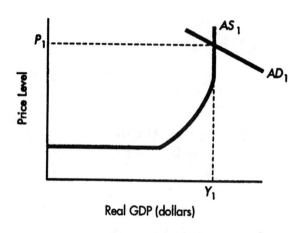

II. Clinton's Economic Stimulus Package

a. Former President Clinton's initial 1993 budget was referred to as an "economic stimulus package." From what you know about fiscal policy, if the president's goal was economic stimulus, you would expect this package to consist of increases in _____ and decreases in _____ .

b. The plan was also referred to as a "deficit reduction plan." Why might the president want to reduce the deficit?

c. If the goal is to reduce the deficit, _____ would be increased and _____ would be decreased.

d. Does it seem possible to reduce the deficit while stimulating the economy at the same time?

e. The president proposed halving capital-gains taxes for investors in some small businesses, and would have expanded the bill's proposed write-off for small businesses' equipment purchases. These tax breaks are intended to _____ (increase, decrease) which component of aggregate expenditures? What effect would that change have on real GDP?

___

___

___

III. Using Fiscal Policy to *Stabilize* the Economy

Assume you are a member of Congress. You receive the following data on the economy:

	Year-Ago Quarter	Last Quarter	Estimate for Quarter Now Ending
Real GDP (in billions of 1987 dollars)	3,906	4,148	4,279
Consumer price index	217	222	228
Unemployment rate	6.7%	5.6%	4.9%

You also know that the index of leading economic indicators is rising.

a. On the basis of these statistics, this economy is at which stage of the business cycle: trough, expansion, peak, or contraction? Briefly defend your answer.

b. Fiscal policy should be used to (increase/decrease) aggregate demand. *Circle one.*

c. What fiscal policy would you recommend? Be specific!

Chapter 12 Homework Problems

Name _____

1. What is fiscal policy, and what parts of the government determine what fiscal policy will be?

2. What are the three ways the government can finance a budget deficit?

3. If the government wants to stimulate the economy (increase equilibrium real GDP), how should it change government spending and taxes?

4. Use the aggregate demand–aggregate supply model to describe why the fiscal policy you recommended above will increase equilibrium GDP.

5. In 1965, the U.S. government began spending more money on both the "War on Poverty" and the war in Vietnam, without a corresponding increases in taxes. Suppose that in 1965 the U.S. economy was in the position shown on the diagram below.

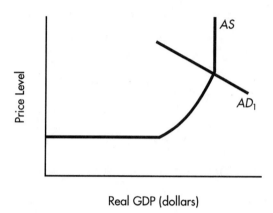

a. Sketch in the expected effect of the 1965 increase in government spending. What will happen to the price level and real GDP?

b. If the deficit were financed by borrowing within the United States, what would be the effect on investment?

If your instructor assigns these problems, write your answers above, then tear out this page and hand it in.

Answers

Quick-Check Quiz

Section 1: Fiscal Policy and Aggregate Demand

1. c; 2. a; 3. b; 4. d; 5. a; 6. e; 7. d; 8. d; 9. c; 10. b; 11. e
If you missed any of these questions, you should go back and review Section 1 of Chapter 12.

Section 2: Fiscal Policy in the United States

1. e; 2. c; 3. b; 4. a; 5. d
If you missed any of these questions, you should go back and review Section 2 of Chapter 12.

Section 3: Fiscal Policy in Different Countries

1. c; 2. b
If you missed either of these questions, you should go back and review Section 3 of Chapter 12.

Practice Questions and Problems

Section 1: Fiscal Policy and Aggregate Demand

1. taxation; government spending
2. Employment Act of 1946
3.

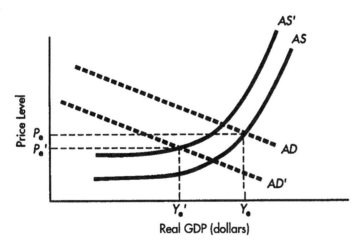

   a. left; left
   b. fall; fall
4. disposable income; consumption
5. up; decreasing
6. expansionary
7. right
8. reduced; overstate

9. taxes
   change in government debt (borrowing)
   change in the stock of government-issued money
10. left
11.

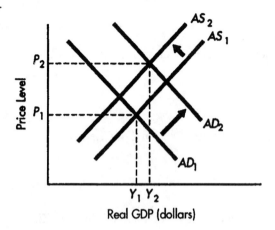

12. selling bonds to
13. Ricardian equivalence
14. saving
15. crowding out
16. interest rates

Section 2: Fiscal Policy in the United States

1. legislative; executive
2. Office of Management and Budget
3. Congressional Budget Office
4. politics
5. discretionary fiscal policy
   automatic stabilizers
6. Discretionary fiscal policy
7. Automatic stabilizers
8. recessions
9. investment; net exports
10. increase
11. Lump-sum taxes
12. progressive
13. regressive
14. proportional

; B; A

To determine what kind of tax it is, we must first calculate the tax *rate* at each level of income.

	A		B		C	
Income	Tax Payment	Tax Rate	Tax Payment	Tax Rate	Tax Payment	Tax Rate
$100	$10	.10	$ 50	.50	$ 10	.10
200	20	.10	80	.40	30	.15
300	30	.10	90	.30	60	.20
400	40	.10	100	.25	100	.25

Since A's tax *rate* is constant at .10, A is a proportional tax schedule. B's tax *rate* decreases with income, so B is a regressive tax. C's tax *rate* increases with income, so C is a progressive tax schedule.

Note: If you look at just the *dollar* amount of taxes paid, all three schedules look "progressive" because the dollar amount of tax payments increases as income increases. But we classify these taxes according to how the tax *rate* changes as income increases.

Progressive

transfer payment

4

on 3: Fiscal Policy in Different Countries

developing. State-owned enterprises account for a larger percentage of economic activity in developing countries as compared with industrial countries. Also, developing countries rely on their governments, as opposed to private investment, to build their infrastructure.

do not

higher

Direct

Indirect

Personal income

indirect

value-added tax

Thinking About and Applying Fiscal Policy

I. Reducing the Deficit

1.

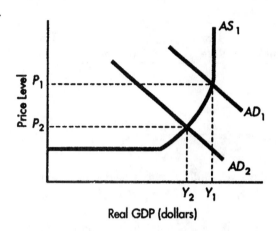

   Government spending cuts and tax increases both decrease aggregate demand. If the economy is operating in the Keynesian or intermediate regions, decreasing aggregate demand will decrease real GDP. If the economy is in the intermediate range, the price level will decline. If it is in the Keynesian region, there will be no change in the price level. These are the dire results that the economic analysts fear.

2.

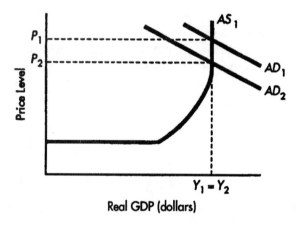

   If the economy is operating in the vertical region of short-run aggregate supply (above), a decrease in aggregate demand may bring only a decrease in the price level with no decrease in real GDP.

II. Clinton's Economic Stimulus Package

a. government spending; taxes
b. Many economists argue that deficits raise interest rates, which in turn can depress investments and net exports. Decreases in investment and net exports reduce aggregate demand, which conflicts with the president's goal of stimulating the economy.
c. taxes; government spending
d. Since economic stimulus calls for increasing government spending and decreasing taxes, and deficit reduction calls for decreasing government spending and increasing taxes, the two goals seem incompatible.
e. These tax breaks are intended to increase investment, thereby increasing aggregate demand and equilibrium real GDP.

III. Using Fiscal Policy to Stabilize the Economy

a. Expansion. Unemployment has been decreasing while inflation and real GDP have been increasing. Since the index of leading economic indicators is rising, the economy probably has not reached its peak.
b. Fiscal policy should be used to decrease aggregate demand. Remember that the goal is to smooth out the ups and downs of the business cycle.
c. To decrease aggregate demand, taxes must be cut and government spending must be increased.

Appendix to Chapter 12

AN ALGEBRAIC EXAMINATION OF THE BALANCED-BUDGET CHANGE IN FISCAL POLICY

Summary

The spending multiplier is $1/(MPS + MPI)$. The tax multiplier is $-(MPC - MPI) \times 1/(MPS + MPI)$. If we have equal changes in taxes and government spending, the multiplier equals the spending multiplier plus the taxation multiplier:

$$1/(MPS + MPI) + [-(MPC - MPI) \times 1/(MPS + MPI)]$$

or

$$[1 - (MPC - MPI)] \times 1/(MPS + MPI)$$

Simplifying, we have

$$(1 - MPC + MPI) \times 1/(MPS + MPI)$$

Since $MPS = 1 - MPC$, we can substitute

$$(MPS + MPI) \times 1/(MPS + MPI)$$

which equals 1.

Practice Questions and Problems

1. Given:

    $C = 50 + .90Y$
    $I = 40$
    $G = 60$
    $X = 50 - .10Y$

    Verify that the balanced budget multiplier equals 1.

2. a. In the late 1990s, the *Wall Street Journal* reported that the Democrats claimed a reduction of $516 billion for their deficit reduction package, split equally between spending cuts and tax increases. If the marginal propensity to consume is 90 percent and the marginal propensity to import is 10 percent, how much will equilibrium income decrease as a result of this deficit reduction package? Assume that the economy is in the horizontal segment of the aggregate supply curve and that the aggregate supply curve will not shift as a result of the package.

    b. Former President Clinton hopes that private investment will increase enough to offset the dampening effects of deficit reduction. How much would private investment have to increase to offset the effects of deficit reduction?

Answers

1. The MPC = .9, so the MPS = .1.
   The MPI = .1.
   The spending multiplier is
   1/(MPS + MPI) = 1/(.1 + .1) = 1/.2 = 5.
   The taxation multiplier is
   – (MPC – MPI) × 1/(MPS + MPI)
   = – (.9 – .1) × 1/(.1 + .1) = – .8/.2 = –4.
   Adding the two multipliers together, we get 5 + –4 = 1.

2. a. The $516 billion for deficit reduction is equally split between decreases in government spending and increases in taxes, so government spending decreases by $258 billion and taxes increase by $258 billion ($516 ÷ 2). The spending multiplier is 1/(MPS + MPI), so a decrease in government spending of $258 billion will lead to a decrease in equilibrium income of $1,290 billion (−258/.2). The tax multiplier is − (MPC − MPI)/(MPS + MPI), so a tax increase of $258 billion will lead to a decrease of $1,032 billion [258(−.8/.2)]. Taken together, the total decrease in equilibrium income will be $2,322 billion.
   b. To offset a decrease in equilibrium income of $2,322 billion, private investment would have to increase by $464.4 billion (2,322/5).

Chapter 13

MONEY AND BANKING

FUNDAMENTAL QUESTIONS

1. What is money?

   Money is anything that is generally acceptable to sellers in exchange for goods and services. Money serves as a medium of exchange, a unit of account, a store of value, and a standard of deferred payment.

2. How is the U.S. money supply defined?

   There are three definitions of the U.S. money supply. The narrowest definition, the **M1 money supply,** consists of currency, travelers' checks, demand deposits, and other checkable deposits. M2 adds savings deposits, small-denomination time deposits, and retail money market mutual fund balances. M3 equals M2 plus large time deposits, repurchase agreements, Eurodollar deposits, and institution-only money market mutual fund balances.

3. How do countries pay for international transactions?

   Countries use the foreign exchange market to convert national currencies to pay for trade. They also use **international reserve assets,** like gold, or **international reserve currencies,** like the dollar.

4. Why are banks considered intermediaries?

   Banks act as middlemen between savers and borrowers. They accept deposits from savers and use those deposits to make loans to borrowers.

5. How does international banking differ from domestic banking?

   Domestic banking is heavily regulated, whereas international banking is not. Because they are not restricted by regulations, international banks can usually offer depositors and borrowers better terms than can domestic banks.

6. How do banks create money?

   Banks create money by making loans up to the amount of their excess reserves. The banking system can increase the money supply by the **deposit expansion multiplier** times the **excess reserves** in the system.

Key Terms

money
liquid asset
currency substitution
credit
M1 money supply
transactions account
international reserve asset
international reserve currency
European currency unit (ECU)
composite currency
special drawing right (SDR)
Federal Deposit Insurance Corporation (FDIC)
Eurocurrency market (offshore banking)
international banking facility (IBF)
fractional reserve banking system
required reserves
excess reserves
deposit expansion multiplier

Quick-Check Quiz

Section 1: What Is Money?

1. Which of the following is *not* one of the functions of money?
    a. a medium of exchange
    b. a unit of account
    c. a resource for production
    d. a store of value
    e. a standard of deferred payment

2. A $34 price tag on a sweater is an example of money functioning as a
    a. medium of exchange.
    b. unit of account.
    c. resource for production.
    d. store of value.
    e. standard of deferred payment.

3. For money to function as a store of value, it is most important that it have which of the following properties?
    a. durability
    b. divisibility
    c. portability
    d. ability to be easily identified as genuine
    e. optimal scarcity

4. Which of the following is *not* a component of the M1 money supply?
    a. demand deposits
    b. other checkable deposits
    c. currency
    d. certificates of deposit
    e. travelers' checks

5. Which of the following is *not* a transactions account?
   a. negotiable order of withdrawal
   b. credit union share draft account
   c. savings account
   d. automated transfer system account
   e. demand deposit at a commercial bank

6. In 2000 currency represented _____ percent of the M1 money supply.
   a. 1
   b. 47
   c. 35
   d. 36
   e. 10

7. Which of the following accounts are offered by savings and loans?
   a. negotiable orders of withdrawal
   b. credit union share draft accounts
   c. money market deposit accounts
   d. automated transfer system accounts
   e. demand deposits at commercial banks

8. Demand deposits made up _____ percent of the M1 money supply in 2000.
   a. 1
   b. 28
   c. 35
   d. 71
   e. 30

9. Which of the following is *not* a component of the M2 money supply?
   a. retail money market mutual fund balances
   b. small-denomination time deposits
   c. checkable deposits
   d. savings deposits
   e. large time deposits

10. Which of the following is *not* a component of the M3 money supply?
    a. Eurodollar deposits
    b. value of stocks and bonds
    c. RPs
    d. institution-only money market mutual fund balances
    e. M2

11. The European currency unit is an average of the values of individual European currencies. Which of the following is *not* one of the currencies?
    a. the U.K. pound
    b. the Spanish peseta
    c. the Luxembourg franc
    d. the Danish krone
    e. the Greek drachma

Section 2: Banking

1. Which of the following statements is false?
   a. The 1980 Depository Institutions Deregulation and Monetary Control Act was intended to stimulate competition among financial intermediaries.
   b. The 1980 Depository Institutions Deregulation and Monetary Control Act narrowed the distinctions between commercial banks and thrifts.
   c. The 1980 Depository Institutions Deregulation and Monetary Control Act eliminated many of the differences between state banks and national banks.
   d. The 1980 Depository Institutions Deregulation and Monetary Control Act created the Federal Deposit Insurance Corporation.
   e. The 1980 Depository Institutions Deregulation and Monetary Control Act permitted thrift institutions to offer many of the same services as commercial banks.

2. Which of the following statements is true?
   a. The laws regulating international banks typically are very restrictive, whereas domestic banks go relatively unregulated.
   b. Offshore banking, called the Eurocurrency market, refers to international banking transactions among the seven Western European industrial powers.
   c. Offshore banks are typically able to offer a higher return on deposits and a lower rate on loans than domestic banks.
   d. International banking is dominated by the United States and the United Kingdom.
   e. U.S. banks that participate in international banking on U.S. soil are subject to the same regulations as domestic banks.

3. Which of the following statements is false?
   a. The FDIC does not permit banks to fail, for fear of causing a bank panic.
   b. Many states permit entry to banks located out of state.
   c. A Eurodollar is a dollar-denominated deposit outside the U.S. banking industry.
   d. International banking is riskier than domestic banking.
   e. International banking facilities are not physical entities.

Section 3: Banks and the Money Supply

1. Deposits at the Third National Bank are $200,000, and the reserve requirement is 10 percent. Cash reserves equal $50,000. Required reserves equal
   a. $40,000.
   b. $20,000.
   c. $50,000.
   d. $30,000.
   e. $10,000.

2. Deposits at the ABC Bank are $600,000, and the reserve requirement is 20 percent. Cash reserves equal $160,000. Excess reserves equal
   a. $120,000.
   b. $160,000.
   c. $32,000.
   d. $40,000.
   e. $128,000.

3. Deposits at the XYZ Bank are $400,000, and the reserve requirement is 20 percent. Cash reserves equal $6,000. The deposit expansion multiplier is
   a. .20.
   b. .80.
   c. 5.
   d. 1.25.
   e. 1.

4. The deposit expansion multiplier will be larger the
   a. smaller the reserve requirement.
   b. greater the currency drain.
   c. greater the percentage of excess reserves held by banks.
   d. larger the bank.
   e. greater the value of the assets held by the bank.

5. The Golden State Bank has cash reserves of $110,000, deposits of $200,000, and loans of $90,000. The reserve requirement is 5 percent. This bank can make additional loans up to the amount of
   a. $4,500.
   b. $10,000.
   c. $5,500.
   d. $100,000.
   e. $190,000.

6. Suppose that excess reserves in the Stranda National Bank are $15,000 and the reserve requirement is 4 percent. The maximum amount that the money supply can be increased is
   a. $60,000.
   b. $600.
   c. $375,000.
   d. $15,000.
   e. $72,000.

7. Banks increase the money supply by
   a. cashing checks.
   b. making loans.
   c. providing currency.
   d. printing money.
   e. printing money and coining currency.

8. A bank has $200,000 in deposits and $10,000 in cash. The reserve requirement is 4 percent. The bank's required reserves are _____, and its excess reserves are _____.
   a. $400; $199,600
   b. $199,600; $400
   c. $8,000; $192,000
   d. $2,000; $8,000
   e. $8,000; $2,000

Practice Questions and Problems

Section 1: What Is Money?

1. _____ is anything that is generally acceptable to sellers in exchange for goods and services.
2. A(n) _____ asset is an asset that can easily be exchanged for goods and services.
3. List the four functions of money.

   _____

   _____

   _____

   _____

4. _____ is the direct exchange of goods and services for other goods and services.
5. The use of money as a medium of exchange lowers _____ costs.
6. Money eliminates the need for a _____, which is necessary for barter to work.
7. For money to be an effective medium of exchange, it must be _____ and _____.
8. The use of money as a unit of account lowers _____ costs.
9. For money to be an effective store of value, it must be _____.
10. _____ is the use of foreign money as a substitute for domestic money when the domestic money has a high rate of inflation.
11. _____ is available savings that are lent to borrowers to spend.
12. List the four components of the M1 money supply.

    _____

    _____

    _____

    _____

13. A checking account at a bank or other financial institution that can be drawn on to make payments is called a _____ account.
14. Currency represented _____ percent of the M1 money supply in 2000.
15. The U.S dollar is backed by _____. This type of monetary system is called a _____ monetary system.
16. Money that has an intrinsic value is called _____ money.
17. _____ is the tendency to hoard currency as its commodity value increases.
18. Travelers' checks accounted for _____ percent of the M1 money supply in 2000.
19. _____ pay no interest and must be paid immediately on the demand of the depositor.

20. _____ are checking accounts at financial institutions that pay interest and give the depositor check-writing privileges.
21. _____ (NOW) accounts are interest-bearing checking accounts offered by savings and loan institutions.
22. _____ (ATS) accounts are accounts at commercial banks that combine an interest-bearing savings account with a non-interest-bearing checking account.
23. Credit unions offer their members interest-bearing checking accounts called _____ .
24. _____ are nonprofit savings and loan institutions.
25. Demand deposits made up _____ percent of the M1 money supply in 2000.
26. List the four components of the M2 money supply.

_____
_____
_____
_____

27. A _____ is an agreement between a bank and a customer under which the customer buys U.S. government securities from the bank and later sells them back to the bank.
28. Deposits denominated in dollars but held outside the U.S. domestic bank market are called _____ deposits.
29. _____ deposits are deposits at banks and at savings and loans that earn interest but offer no check-writing privileges.
30. Small-denomination time deposits are also called _____ .
31. _____ combine the deposits of many individuals and invest them in government Treasury bills and other short-term securities.
32. List the five components of the M3 money supply.

_____
_____
_____
_____
_____

33. Sales contracts between developed countries are usually invoiced in the national currency of the _____ , whereas sales between a developed and a developing country are usually invoiced in the currency of the _____ .
34. An asset used to settle debts between governments is called an _____ asset.
35. Currencies that are held to settle debts between governments are called _____ currencies.

36. The _____ is a unit of account used by the industrial nations of western Europe to settle debts between them.

37. A _____ currency is a unit of account whose value is an average of the values of certain national currencies.

38. The value of the _____ is an average of the values of the U.S. dollar, the French franc, the German mark, the Japanese yen, and the U.K. pound.

Section 2: Banking

1. Thrift institutions include _____, _____, and _____.
2. _____ banks are banks chartered by the federal government, whereas _____ banks are chartered under state law.
3. A bank is allowed to operate in only one location in a _____ banking state.
4. The _____ is a federal agency that insures deposits in commercial banks so that depositors do not lose their deposits when a bank fails.
5. The international deposit and loan market is often called the _____ or _____.
6. Typically, domestic banks are subject to _____ regulations, whereas offshore banks are subject to _____ regulation.
7. _____ (Domestic/Offshore) banks are usually able to offer better terms to their customers.
8. Eurodollar transactions are _____ (more risky/less risky) than domestic transactions in the United States because of the lack of regulation and deposit insurance.
9. A bank _____ occurs when depositors, fearing a bank's closing, rush to withdraw their funds.
10. _____ are permitted to take part in international banking activities on U.S. soil.
11. The _____ (1980) eliminated many of the differences between commercial banks and thrift institutions and between state banks and national banks.

Section 3: Banks and the Money Supply

1. In a _____ banking system, banks keep less than 100 percent of their deposits on reserve.
2. A financial statement that records a firm's assets and liabilities is called a _____.
3. _____ are what the firm owns, and _____ are what the firm owes.
4. In the United States, reserve requirements are set by the _____.
5. _____ reserves are the cash reserves a bank must keep on hand or on deposit with the Fed.
6. _____ reserves are total reserves minus required reserves.
7. A bank is _____ when it has zero excess reserves.
8. The deposit expansion multiplier equals _____ (formula).

9. The deposit expansion multiplier tells us the _____ (maximum, minimum) change in total deposits when a new deposit is made.

10. If people withdraw deposits from banks, _____ occurs and the deposit expansion multiplier will be less than the reciprocal of the reserve requirement.

11. Any single bank can lend only up to the amount of its _____ .

12. Banks increase the money supply by _____ .

13. McDougall Bank and Trust has vault cash in the amount of $300,000, loans of $900,000, and deposits of $1,200,000.

   a. Prepare a balance sheet for this bank.

   _____

   _____

   _____

   _____

   b. If the bank maintains a reserve requirement of 5 percent, what is the largest new loan it can make?

   _____

   c. What is the maximum amount the money supply can be increased by the banking system due to McDougall Bank and Trust's new loan? _____

14. The State Bank of Oswald has cash reserves of $5,000, loans of $495,000, and deposits of $500,000. The bank maintains a reserve requirement of 1 percent.

   a. Calculate this bank's excess reserves.

   _____

   b. The bank receives a new deposit of $100,000. What is the largest loan the bank can make?

   _____

   c. What is the maximum amount the money supply can be increased as a result of the State Bank of Oswald's new loan? _____

Thinking About and Applying Money and Banking

I. Sorting Out the Monetary Aggregates

Put *M3* next to items that are included *only* in M3, *M2* next to items included in M2 and M3, and *M1* next to items common to all three monetary aggregates.

_____ RPs

_____ Demand deposits

_____ Savings deposits

_____ Large time deposits

_____ Institution-only money market mutual funds

_____ Currency

_____ Eurodollars

_____ Small-denomination time deposits

_____ Demand deposits

_____ Retail money market mutual funds

_____ Other checkable deposits

_____ Travelers' checks

II. The Components of the Monetary Aggregates

The table below lists the components of the monetary aggregates in billions of dollars.

Large time deposits	356.7
Travelers' checks	8.1
Institution-only money market mutual funds	178.0
Savings deposits	1,135.0
Demand deposits	406.5
Other checkable deposits	420.0
Eurodollars	52.2
Currency	357.3
RPs	100.8
Retail money market mutual funds	372.1
Small-denomination time deposits	826.9

Calculate M1, M2, and M3.

M1 _____

M2 _____

M3 _____

Chapter 13   Homework Problems

Name _____

1. In terms of its function within an economy, what is money?

2. What are the four functions of money?

3. What are the four components of the M1 money supply?

4. How do banks create money?

5. a. The Bank of Dimmenland was fully loaned up until it received a new deposit of $10,000. Like all banks in this economy, the Bank of Dimmenland has its reserve ratio set by law at 5 percent. How much are the Bank of Dimmenland's excess reserves now, and how large a loan can it make?

b. The Bank of Dimmenland makes a loan of $9,500 to Randy Haydon, who pays $9,500 to Family Motors to buy a used BMW. Family Motors deposits the $9,500 in the Bank of Clarkville. How much excess reserves does the Bank of Clarkville gain from the deposit, and how large a loan can it make based on those excess reserves?

c. What is the deposit expansion multiplier for this economy, and by how much can the initial deposit of $10,000 expand the money supply in this economy?

If your instructor assigns these problems, write your answers above, then tear out this page and hand it in.

Answers

Quick-Check Quiz

Section 1: What Is Money?

1. c; 2. b; 3. a; 4. d; 5. c; 6. b; 7. a; 8. e; 9. e; 10. b; 11. a
If you missed any of these questions, you should go back and review Section 1 of Chapter 13.

Section 2: Banking

1. d; 2. c; 3. a
If you missed any of these questions, you should go back and review Section 2 of Chapter 13.

Section 3: Banks and the Money Supply

1. b; 2. d; 3. c; 4. a; 5. d; 6. c; 7. b; 8. e
If you missed any of these questions, you should go back and review Section 3 of Chapter 13.

Practice Questions and Problems

Section 1: What Is Money?

1. Money
2. liquid
3. medium of exchange
   unit of account
   store of value
   standard of deferred payment
4. Barter
5. transactions
6. double coincidence of wants
7. portable; divisible
8. information
9. durable
10. Currency substitution
11. Credit
12. currency
    traveler's checks
    demand deposits
    other checkable deposits (OCDs)
13. transactions
14. 47
15. the confidence of the public; fiduciary
16. commodity
17. Gresham's Law
18. less than 1
19. Demand deposits
20. Other checkable deposits (OCDs)
21. Negotiable order of withdrawal

22. Automated transfer system
23. share drafts
24. Mutual savings banks
25. 30
26. M1
    savings deposits
    small-denomination time deposits (certificates of deposit, or CDs)
    retail money market mutual fund balances
27. repurchase agreement
28. Eurodollar
29. Savings
30. certificates of deposit
31. Retail money market mutual fund balances
32. M2
    large time deposits
    RPs
    Eurodollar deposits
    institution-only money market mutual fund balances
33. exporter; developed country
34. international reserve
35. international reserve
36. European currency unit (ECU)
37. composite
38. special drawing right (SDR)

Section 2: Banking

1. savings and loans; mutual savings banks; credit unions
2. National; state
3. unit
4. Federal Deposit Insurance Corporation (FDIC)
5. Eurocurrency market; offshore banking
6. restrictive; little or no
7. Offshore
8. more risky
9. panic
10. International Banking Facilities (IBFs)
11. Depository Institutions Deregulation and Monetary Control Act

Section 3: Banks and the Money Supply

1. fractional reserve
2. balance sheet
3. Assets; liabilities
4. Federal Reserve Board

5. Required
6. Excess
7. loaned up
8. 1/reserve requirement
9. maximum
10. currency drain
11. excess reserves
12. making loans
13. a.

Assets		Liabilities	
Cash	$ 300,000	Deposits	$1,200,000
Loans	900,000		
Total	$1,200,000	Total	$1,200,000

    b. $240,000
       Required reserves = .05($1,200,000) = $60,000. Excess reserves = total reserves − required reserves = $300,000 − $60,000 = $240,000. Since a bank can make loans up to the amount of its excess reserves, this bank can loan out $240,000.
    c. $4,800,000
       The deposit expansion multiplier = 1/reserve requirement = 1/.05 = 20. Change in the money supply = deposit expansion multiplier x excess reserves = 20($240,000) = $4,800,000.

14. a. Required reserves = .01($500,000) = $5,000. Excess reserves = $5,000 − $5,000 = 0.
    b. Cash = $105,000. Deposits = $600,000. Required reserves = .01($600,000) = $6,000. Excess reserves = $105,000 − $6,000 = $99,000.
    c. Deposit expansion multiplier = 1/.01 = 100. Maximum amount of money that can be created = deposit expansion multiplier × excess reserves = 100($99,000) = $9,900,000.

Thinking About and Applying Money and Banking

I. Sorting Out the Monetary Aggregates

M3	RPs
M1	Demand deposits
M2	Savings deposits
M3	Large time deposits
M3	Institution-only money market mutual funds
M1	Currency
M3	Eurodollars
M2	Small-denomination time deposits
M1	Demand deposits
M2	Retail money market mutual funds
M1	Other checkable deposits
M1	Traveler's checks

II. The Components of the Monetary Aggregates

M1 = Currency + travelers' checks + demand deposits + other checkable deposits
  = 357.3 + 8.1 + 406.5 + 420.0 = 1,191.9

M2 = M1 + savings deposits + small-denomination time deposits + retail money market mutual funds
  = 1,191.9 + 1,135.0 + 826.9 + 372.1
  = 3,525.9

M3 = M2 + large time deposits + RPs + Eurodollars
   + institution-only money market mutual funds
  = 3,525.9 + 356.7 + 100.8 + 52.2 + 178.0
  = 4,163.6

Chapter 14

MONETARY POLICY

FUNDAMENTAL QUESTIONS

1. What does the Federal Reserve do?

    The Federal Reserve is the central bank of the United States. As such, the Fed accepts deposits from and makes loans to financial institutions, acts as a banker for the federal government, supervises the banking system, and controls the money supply.

    The **Federal Open Market Committee (FOMC)** is the policy-making body of the Federal Reserve. It consists of the seven-member Federal Reserve Board and five of the twelve Federal Reserve Bank presidents, who serve on a rotating basis. The FOMC issues directives to the Federal Reserve Bank of New York, which implements its directives.

2. How is monetary policy set?

    The Fed's ultimate policy objective is economic growth with stable prices, but it cannot control output or the price level directly. Instead, the Fed uses the money supply as an intermediate target. It controls the money supply, which in turn affects real GDP and the level of prices.

3. What are the tools of monetary policy?

    The tools of monetary policy are the reserve requirement, the **discount rate,** and **open market operations.** The reserve requirement is the percentage of deposits that financial institutions must keep on hand or at the Fed. The higher the reserve requirement, the smaller the amount of deposits banks can create and the smaller the money supply. The discount rate is the rate of interest the Fed charges banks. If the Fed wants to increase the money supply, it lowers the discount rate. Open market operations are the buying and selling of bonds to change the money supply. The Fed buys bonds if it wants to increase the money supply and sells bonds to decrease the money supply. Open market operations are the Fed's most important tool.

4. What role do central banks play in the foreign exchange market?

    Central banks may intervene in the foreign exchange market to stabilize or change exchange rates. For example, the Fed might buy francs to bolster the price of the franc if U.S. goods and services became too expensive for the French.

5. What are the determinants of the demand for money?

    There are three aspects to the demand for money. Consumers and firms demand money in order to conduct transactions (the **transactions demand for money**), to take care of emergencies (the **precautionary demand for money**), and to be able to take advantage of a fall in the price of an asset that they want (the **speculative demand for money**).

The amount of money held depends on the interest rate and nominal income. Increases in nominal income generate a greater volume of transactions, so more money is needed. The demand for money is therefore positively related to nominal income. The interest rate is the opportunity cost of holding money. A higher interest rate means that it costs more to hold money, so less money will be held. The demand for money is negatively related to the interest rate.

6. How does monetary policy affect the equilibrium level of real GDP?

   Monetary policy refers to controlling the money supply. An increase in the money supply decreases interest rates, which increases consumption and investment. The increases in consumption and investment increase aggregate demand, which increases the equilibrium level of real GDP. A decrease in the money supply increases interest rates, which decreases consumption and investment. The decreases in consumption and investment decrease aggregate demand, which decreases the equilibrium level of real GDP. So increases in the money supply are expansionary, whereas decreases in the money supply are contractionary.

Key Terms

Federal Open Market Committee (FOMC)
intermediate target
equation of exchange
velocity of money
quantity theory of money
FOMC directive

legal reserves
federal funds rate
discount rate
open market operations
foreign exchange market intervention
sterilization

transactions demand for money
precautionary demand for money
speculative demand for money

Quick-Check Quiz

Section 1: The Federal Reserve System

1. Which of the following is *not* a function of the Fed?
   a. accepting deposits from banks
   b. making loans to banks
   c. controlling taxes
   d. acting as a banker for the federal government
   e. controlling the money supply

2. The _____ is/are the policy-making entity of the Fed.
   a. Federal Reserve chairman
   b. Federal Reserve Board
   c. twelve Federal Reserve district banks
   d. twelve Federal Reserve Bank presidents
   e. FOMC

3. The Fed's most important function is
   a. providing services to the banking community.
   b. controlling the money supply.
   c. supervising the banking community.
   d. clearing checks.
   e. holding bank reserves.

Section 2: Implementing Monetary Policy

1. The ultimate goal of monetary policy is
   a. economic growth with stable prices.
   b. stable exchange rates.
   c. stable interest rates.
   d. a low federal funds rate.
   e. steady growth in bank reserves.

2. According to the equation of exchange,
   a. if the money supply increases and velocity is constant, real GDP must rise.
   b. if the money supply increases and velocity is constant, nominal GDP must rise.
   c. an increase in the money supply causes an increase in the price level.
   d. an increase in the money supply causes an increase in real GDP and higher prices.
   e. if the money supply increases, nominal GDP must rise.

3. To increase the money supply, the Fed would
   a. increase the reserve requirement and the discount rate, and sell bonds.
   b. increase the reserve requirement and the discount rate, and buy bonds.
   c. decrease the reserve requirement and the discount rate, and sell bonds.
   d. decrease the reserve requirement and the discount rate, and buy bonds.
   e. increase the reserve requirement, decrease the discount rate, and buy bonds.

4. Consider the First National Bank of Rozzelle. The bank has deposits of $600,000, loans of $500,000, vault cash of $30,000, and deposits at the Fed of $70,000. The reserve requirement is 4 percent. The bank's legal reserves are _____ , and excess reserves are _____ . The deposit expansion multiplier is _____ , and the banking system could create a maximum of _____ in new money.
   a. $30,000; $6,000; 25; $150,000
   b. $30,000; $26,000; 25; $650,000
   c. $100,000; $96,000; 25; $2,400,000
   d. $100,000; $76,000; 4; $304,000
   e. $100,000; $76,000; 25; $1,900,000

5. If the Fed wants to decrease the money supply, it can
   a. buy bonds.
   b. sell bonds.
   c. lower the reserve requirement.
   d. lower the federal funds rate.
   e. lower the discount rate.

6. Suppose that the U.K. pound is currently equivalent to $1.596 and that the Fed wants the dollar to depreciate versus the pound. The Fed will most likely
   a. buy dollars.
   b. buy pounds.
   c. sell dollars.
   d. sell pounds.
   e. ask the U.K. central bank to buy pounds.

7. If the Fed intervened in the foreign currency market to buy another currency, the domestic money supply would _____ and the Fed might _____ bonds to offset its foreign currency operations. This process is called _____ .
   a. decrease; buy; sterilization
   b. decrease; sell; sterilization
   c. increase; sell; sterilization
   d. increase; buy; sterilization
   e. increase; sell; depreciation

Section 3: Monetary Policy and Equilibrium Income

1. A student who cashes a check at the student union in order to go shopping is an example of the
   a. transactions demand for money.
   b. speculative demand for money.
   c. precautionary demand for money.
   d. income effect.
   e. substitution effect.

2. An increase in the interest rate will cause
   a. an increase in the demand for money.
   b. an increase in the quantity demanded of money.
   c. a decrease in the demand for money.
   d. a decrease in the quantity demanded of money.
   e. an increase in the supply of money.

3. A decrease in nominal income will cause
   a. an increase in the demand for money.
   b. an increase in the quantity demanded of money.
   c. a decrease in the demand for money.
   d. a decrease in the quantity demanded of money.
   e. a decrease in the supply of money.

4. The supply of money is
   a. a positive function of interest rates.
   b. a negative function of interest rates.
   c. a positive function of income.
   d. a negative function of income.
   e. independent of income and interest rates.

5. A bond selling for $998 pays $54.89 in interest annually. The current interest rate is
   a. .18.
   b. .055.
   c. .82.
   d. .945.
   e. .125.

6. If the interest rate is above the equilibrium rate, there is an excess _____ money. People will _____ bonds, and the interest rate will _____.
   a. demand for; sell; rise
   b. demand for; sell; drop
   c. demand for; buy; drop
   d. supply of; buy; drop
   e. supply of; sell; rise

7. If the Fed wants to increase equilibrium income, it should _____ the supply of money, which will _____ interest rates. The change in interest rates will _____ consumption and investment, causing aggregate demand to _____.
   a. decrease; increase; decrease; decrease
   b. decrease; decrease; increase; increase
   c. increase; decrease; increase; increase
   d. increase; increase; decrease; decrease
   e. increase; increase; increase; increase

8. Consider the graph below. The demand for money is Md_1, and the supply of money is Ms_1. The equilibrium interest rate is i_1, and the equilibrium quantity of money is M_1. If income decreases,

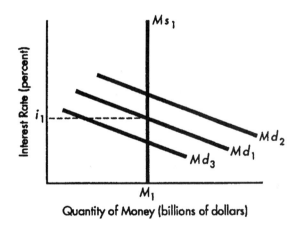

   a. the demand for money shifts to Md_2, and the interest rate and equilibrium quantity rise.
   b. the demand for money shifts to Md_2, and the interest rate rises.
   c. the demand for money shifts to Md_3, and the interest rate and equilibrium quantity fall.
   d. the demand for money shifts to Md_3, and the interest rate falls.
   e. the supply of money shifts to the left, the interest rate rises, and the equilibrium quantity of money falls.

9. A bond sells for $990 and has a yield of 8.5 percent. The bond must be paying _____ in interest annually.
   a. $84.15
   b. $8,415
   c. $8.415
   d. $116.47
   e. $1,164.71

Practice Questions and Problems

Section 1: The Federal Reserve System

1. The Federal Reserve System was intended to be a _____ (centralized, decentralized) system.
2. There are _____ Federal Reserve districts, each with its own Federal Reserve Bank.
3. Monetary policy is largely set by the _____ .
4. The chairman of the Federal Reserve Board of Governors is appointed by the _____ and serves a _____ -year term. Governors serve _____ -year terms.
5. Each of the Fed's twelve district banks has a _____ -member board of directors.
6. The _____ is the official policy-making body of the Federal Reserve System. It consists of the Board of Governors plus _____ of the Federal Reserve Bank presidents.
7. List the six main functions of the Fed.
   _____
   _____
   _____
   _____
   _____
   _____
8. The most important function of the Fed is _____ .
9. The Federal Reserve is the _____ bank of the United States.
10. The _____ has been called the second most powerful person in the United States.
11. The president of the _____ Federal Reserve Bank is always a member of the FOMC.

Section 2: Implementing Monetary Policy

1. The goal of monetary policy is _____ with _____ .
2. An _____ is an objective used to achieve some ultimate policy goal.
3. $MV = PQ$ is the _____ .

4. The _____ of money is the average number of times each dollar is spent on final goods and services in a year.

5. The _____ states that if the money supply increases and the velocity of money is constant, nominal GDP must rise.

6. In the late 1970s and early 1980s, the M1 velocity of money _____ (fluctuated erratically, remained relatively stable).

7. The Fed monitors _____ , _____ , and _____ and considers them in setting policy.

8. The Federal Reserve Bank of _____ implements monetary policy for the Fed.

9. A(n) _____ is instructions issued by the FOMC to the Federal Reserve Bank in New York to implement monetary policy.

10. List the three tools the Fed uses to change reserves.

_____

_____

_____

11. Large banks must hold a _____ (greater, smaller) percentage of deposits in reserve than do small banks.

12. _____ deposits are time deposits held by business firms.

13. Legal reserves consist of _____ and _____ .

14. The Fed can reduce the money-creating potential of the banking system by _____ (raising, lowering) the reserve requirement.

15. The _____ rate is the rate of interest the Fed charges banks. In other countries, this rate is called the _____ rate.

16. Banks borrow from other banks in the _____ market.

17. If the Fed wants to increase the money supply, it _____ (raises, lowers) the discount rate.

18. _____ are the buying and selling of government bonds by the Fed and are the Fed's major monetary policy tool.

19. To increase the money supply, the Fed _____ (buys, sells) bonds.

20. _____ indicate how the money supply should react to a change in the short-run target.

21. The Fed has been using _____ as its short-run operating target since the fall of 1979.

22. _____ is the buying and selling of foreign exchange by a central bank in order to move exchange rates up or down.

23. If the Fed wants the dollar to appreciate against the yen, it will buy _____ (dollars, yen).

24. _____ is the use of open market operations to offset the effects of a foreign exchange market intervention on the domestic money supply.

25. If the Fed wishes to support a foreign currency, it _____ (increases, decreases) the domestic money supply, unless offsetting operations are undertaken.

26. List the four other factors that the Fed considers in its FOMC directives.

    _____
    _____
    _____
    _____

27. The Bank of McDonald has the following balance sheet:

Assets		Liabilities	
Vault cash	$ 20,000	Deposits	$400,000
Deposits in the Fed	30,000		
Loans	350,000		

    If this bank's reserve requirement is 5 percent,

    a. legal reserves are _____.
    b. required reserves are _____.
    c. excess reserves are _____.
    d. the deposit expansion multiplier is _____.
    e. this bank can create _____ of additional deposits.
    f. the banking system could create a maximum of _____.

28. _____ are checking accounts and other deposits that can be used to pay third parties.

Section 3: Monetary Policy and Equilibrium Income

1. The _____ demand for money is a demand to hold money in order to spend it on goods and services.

2. The _____ demand for money is a demand to hold money to take care of emergencies.

3. The _____ demand for money is created by uncertainty about the value of other assets.

4. The demand for money depends on _____ and _____.

5. There is a(n) _____ relationship between the interest rate and the quantity of money demanded.

6. The greater the nominal income, the _____ (greater, smaller) the demand for money.

7. The _____ sets the money supply.

8. The supply of money _____ (does, does not) depend on interest rates and nominal income.

9. The formula for the current interest rate of a bond is _____ .
10. A bond pays $200 a year in interest and sells for $2,500. The current interest rate is _____ .
11. As bond prices increase, the current interest rate _____ .
12. A decrease in the money supply causes interest rates to _____ (rise, fall), which causes consumption and investment to _____ (rise, fall). The changes in consumption and investment cause aggregate demand to _____ (increase, decrease), which causes equilibrium income to _____ (rise, fall). Use the graphs below to illustrate the sequence of events following a decrease in the money supply.

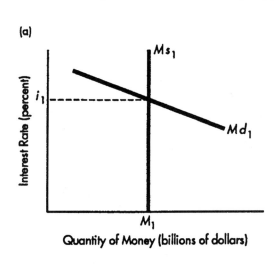

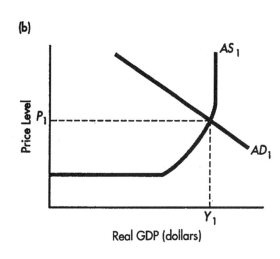

13. Norm and Debbie keep 1.5 months' income in a NOW account for emergencies. This is an example of the _____ demand for money.
14. A young couple cash in a bond to buy a crib and changing table to prepare for the birth of their first child. This is an example of the _____ demand for money.
15. If nominal income increases, the demand for money _____ (shifts to the left, does not change, shifts to the right).
16. You read in the *Wall Street Journal* that the bond markets rallied yesterday (bond prices increased). Interest rates must have _____ (increased, decreased).
17. A bond sells for $975 and pays $68.25 in interest annually. The current rate of interest is _____ . If the bond market plummets (demand falls), the price of this bond will _____ (rise, fall) and the interest rate will _____ (rise, fall).

Thinking About and Applying Monetary Policy

I. More on Foreign Exchange Market Intervention

If the Fed feels that the price of the dollar in terms of Japanese yen is unacceptably high, it may choose to intervene directly in the foreign exchange markets. To bolster the yen, the Fed will _____ (buy, sell) yen. In the process, the domestic money supply will _____ (increase, decrease).

In the absence of any sterilization actions by the Fed, domestic interest rates will _____ (increase, decrease) as a result of the change in the money supply. The change in domestic interest rates will _____ (increase, decrease) the demand for U.S. securities. The dollar will _____ (appreciate, depreciate) in value. The effect of the change in the money supply has _____ (reinforced, opposed) the Fed's actions in the foreign exchange market.

II. Bond Prices and Interest Rates

a. Fill in the gaps in this typical article from the *Wall Street Journal:*

"The benchmark 30-year Treasury bond rose more than ¼ point to 106, a gain of more than $2.50 for a bond with a $1,000 face amount. Its yield, which moves in the _____ (same, opposite) direction from the price, _____ (rose, fell) to 6.65%...."

b. "More investors and economists are beginning to believe that interest rates are headed higher, although many think long-term bond yields won't move as fast as short-term rates.... Mr. Olsen... believes there will be a significant sell-off in the bond market."

Why would higher interest rates precipitate a significant sell-off in the bond market?

_____

_____

Chapter 14   Homework Problems

Name _____

1. What is the central bank of the United States called, and what does it do?

2. What is the name of the policy-making body at the central bank, who are its members, and what is its ultimate policy objective?

3. What are the three tools of monetary policy? Which one is most important?

4. Each of the following is an example of one of the three reasons why people demand money. Write in the matching reason.
   a. Ashley is going to the grocery store to buy tonight's dinner.

   b. Shawn is saving money so he can buy a new refrigerator when they go on sale.

   c. Joel is putting 5 percent of his paycheck in the bank in case he loses his job.

5. Suppose you read the following headline in the newspaper:

   "Fed Worried about Inflation; Considering Raising Interest Rates"

   a. If the Fed wanted interest rates to rise, would it want to increase or decrease the money supply?

   b. Would the Fed change the money supply by buying or selling bonds? Why?

   c. If interest rates did go up, what would you expect to happen to each of the following, and why?
      i. The price of bonds

      ii. Aggregate demand

      iii. Real GDP

      iv. The price level

If your instructor assigns these problems, write your answers above, then tear out this page and hand it in.

Answers

Quick-Check Quiz

Section 1: The Federal Reserve System

1. c; 2. e; 3. b
If you missed any of these questions, you should go back and review Section 1 of Chapter 14.

Section 2: Implementing Monetary Policy

1. a; 2. b (Answer a is false, and the others are true only if certain assumptions are made. For c to be true, velocity must be constant and the economy must be at full employment, so that Q cannot rise. For d to be true, velocity must be constant and there must be some unemployment in the economy. Answer e may be true if velocity is constant.); 3. d; 4. e [LR = vault cash + deposits at the Fed = $30,000 + $70,000 = $100,000. $RR = rD = .04(\$600,000) = \$24,000$. $ER = LR - RR = \$100,000 - \$24,000 = \$76,000$. The deposit expansion multiplier = $1/r = 1/.04 = 25$. The change in the money supply = $1/r(ER) = 25(\$76,000) = \$1,900,000$.]; 5. b; 6. b (The Fed can keep this up indefinitely, since it can create dollars to buy pounds. It does not need the help of the U.K. central bank to depreciate the dollar.); 7. c
If you missed any of these questions, you should go back and review Section 2 of Chapter 14.

Section 3: Monetary Policy and Equilibrium Income

1. a; 2. d; 3. c; 4. e; 5. b; 6. d; 7. c; 8. d; 9. a
If you missed any of these questions, you should go back and review Section 3 of Chapter 14.

Practice Questions and Problems

Section 1: The Federal Reserve System

1. decentralized
2. twelve
3. Board of Governors
4. president; four; fourteen
5. nine
6. Federal Open Market Committee (FOMC); five
7. provides currency
   holds reserves
   clears checks
   supervises commercial banks
   acts as a banker for the federal government
   controls the money supply
8. controlling the money supply
9. central
10. Fed chairperson
11. New York

Section 2: Implementing Monetary Policy

1. economic growth; stable prices
2. intermediate target
3. equation of exchange
4. velocity
5. quantity theory of money
6. fluctuated erratically
7. commodity prices; interest rates; foreign exchange rates
8. New York
9. FOMC directive
10. reserve requirement
    discount rate
    open market operations
11. greater
12. Nonpersonal time
13. vault cash; deposits in the Fed
14. raising
15. discount; bank
16. federal funds
17. lowers
18. Open market operations
19. buys
20. Short-run operating targets
21. bank reserves
22. Foreign exchange market intervention
23. dollars
24. Sterilization
25. increases
26. federal funds rate
    growth of real GDP
    rate of inflation
    foreign exchange rate of the dollar
27. a. $50,000 ($LR$ = vault cash + deposits in the Fed = $20,000 + $30,000)
    b. $20,000 [$RR = rD = .05(\$400,000)$]
    c. $30,000 ($ER = LR - RR = \$50,000 - \$20,000$)
    d. 20 ($1/r = 1/.05$)
    e. $30,000 (the amount of ER)
    f. $600,000 [change in money supply = deposit expansion multiplier × excess reserves = 20($30,000)]
28. Transactions accounts

Section 3: Monetary Policy and Equilibrium Income

1. transactions
2. precautionary
3. speculative
4. nominal income; interest rates
5. inverse

6. greater
7. Federal Reserve
8. does not
9. annual interest payment/bond price
10. .08 (annual interest payment/bond price = $200/$2,500 = .08)
11. decreases
12. rise; fall; decrease; fall

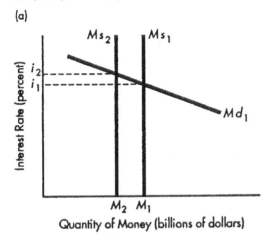
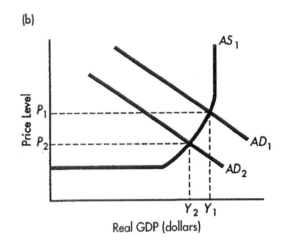

13. precautionary
14. transactions
15. shifts to the right
16. decreased
17. .07 (annual interest payment/bond price = $68.25/$975 = .07); fall; rise

Thinking About and Applying Monetary Policy

I. More on Foreign Exchange Market Intervention

buy; increase; decrease; decrease; depreciate; reinforced

II. Bond Prices and Interest Rates

a. opposite; fell
b. Bond prices drop as interest rates rise. If owners of bonds expect higher interest rates, they will want to sell their bonds before the prices of the bonds decrease.

Chapter 15

MACROECONOMIC POLICY: TRADEOFFS, EXPECTATIONS, CREDIBILITY, AND SOURCES OF BUSINESS CYCLES

FUNDAMENTAL QUESTIONS

1. Is there a tradeoff between inflation and the unemployment rate?

   The **Phillips curve** is a graph showing the relationship between the inflation rate and the rate of unemployment. In the short run, the Phillips curve has a downward slope, indicating a possible tradeoff between inflation and unemployment. In the long run, the Phillips curve is vertical, indicating that no such tradeoff is possible.

2. How does the tradeoff between inflation and the unemployment rate vary from the short to the long run?

   The short-run downward slope of the Phillips curve is caused by shifts in aggregate demand while aggregate supply stays constant. In the long run no tradeoffs are possible because adaptations are made and the aggregate supply curve shifts.

3. What is the relationship between unexpected inflation and the unemployment rate?

   Unexpected inflation can decrease unemployment in three ways. If workers have constant **reservation wages** and constant expectations about inflation, an unexpected increase in inflation raises nominal wages without raising real wages. Workers do not realize that inflation has increased, so they accept smaller real wages and unemployment decreases.

   When aggregate demand is greater than expected, inventories fall and prices on remaining goods in stock are higher. Businesses hire new workers to increase production to offset the falling inventories.

   If wage contracts exist, employers must adjust employment to changing conditions. If revenues fall, employers must reduce costs, either by lowering wages or by getting rid of workers. If a wage contract precludes lowering wages, a decrease in inflation will result in unemployment.

4. How are macroeconomic expectations formed?

   Adaptive expectations are expectations based on past experience. People expect things to be as they were before, and they take nothing else into account. **Rational expectations** are formed using all available information, including, but not limited to, past events.

5. What makes government policies credible?

   A government's policies are credible only if they are not **time inconsistent.** People will refuse to believe the announcements of a government that changes its policies when conditions change. The central bank of a country can achieve credibility by fixing the growth rate of the money supply by law or by creating incentives for policymakers to follow through on announced plans.

6. Are business cycles related to political elections?

   Some economists believe in the existence of a political business cycle, in which the incumbent administration stimulates the economy just before the election. After the election, unemployment and inflation rise. There is no conclusive evidence of political business cycles in the United States.

7. How do real shocks to the economy affect business cycles?

   The economy can expand or contract as a result of changes in real economic variables, such as the weather, technology, and so forth. These real shocks are to be distinguished from discretionary fiscal and monetary policies.

8. How is inflationary monetary policy related to government fiscal policy?

   The government must finance its spending through taxes, borrowing, or changes in the money supply. If the government cannot or will not borrow and deficits continue, monetary policy must be inflationary.

Key Terms

Phillips curve
reservation wage
adaptive expectation
rational expectation
time inconsistent
shock
monetary reform

Quick-Check Quiz

Section 1: The Phillips Curve

1. According to the short-run Phillips curve,
   a. inflation is inversely related to unemployment.
   b. inflation is positively related to unemployment.
   c. inflation is not related to unemployment.
   d. high inflation necessarily requires high unemployment.
   e. low inflation and low unemployment can occur at the same time.

2. The long-run Phillips curve
   a. is downward-sloping, illustrating the possibility of trading off higher inflation for lower unemployment.
   b. is upward-sloping, indicating that high unemployment is associated with rising prices.
   c. is horizontal, indicating that no tradeoff is possible between unemployment and inflation in the long run.
   d. is vertical, indicating no relationship between inflation and unemployment in the long run.
   e. is horizontal, indicating an infinite number of tradeoffs between inflation and unemployment.

3. Which of the following statements is false?
   a. In the long run, as the economy adjusts to an increase in aggregate demand, there is a period in which national income falls and the price level rises.
   b. The tradeoff between unemployment and inflation worsened from the 1960s through the 1970s.
   c. A decrease in aggregate supply is reflected in a movement along the Phillips curve.
   d. The long-run Phillips curve is a vertical line at the natural rate of unemployment.
   e. The tradeoff between unemployment and inflation disappears in the long run.

Section 2: The Role of Expectations

1. Unexpected inflation can affect the unemployment rate through
   a. the income effect.
   b. the substitution effect.
   c. the wealth effect.
   d. wage contracts.
   e. the interest rate effect.

2. Which of the following could *not* cause a movement along the Phillips curve?
   a. a change in inflation that is not expected by workers
   b. an unexpected increase in inflation that causes inventories to decline
   c. wage contracts that did not correctly anticipate the inflation rate
   d. an anticipated rise in nominal wages
   e. All of the above cause movements along the short-run Phillips curve.

3. Which of the following is an example of rational rather than adaptive expectations?
   a. The crowd expects a 95 percent free-throw shooter to sink the free throw to win the state basketball championship.
   b. A professor has been 10 minutes late to class three times in a row. Students come to the fourth class 10 minutes late.
   c. The fans of a pro football team that had four wins, ten losses, and one tie last year find another team to root for this year.
   d. Stockholders of a firm that had losses three years in a row sell off their stocks.
   e. A company with a poor earnings record over the past five years finds itself swamped by investors when word of its new superproduct leaks out.

4. Which of the following is false?
   a. The short-run effect of unexpected disinflation is rising unemployment.
   b. The short-run Phillips curve assumes a constant reservation wage and a constant expected rate of inflation.
   c. The tradeoff between inflation and unemployment comes from expected inflation.
   d. Inventory fluctuations may cause a movement along the Phillips curve.
   e. If wages were flexible, unexpected changes in aggregate demand might be reflected more in wage adjustments than in employment adjustments.

Section 3: Credibility and Time Inconsistency

1. The central bank announces a low-monetary-growth policy. If the goal of the central bank is to keep unemployment as low as possible, it will follow a
   a. low-money-growth policy if a low-wage contract is signed.
   b. high-money-growth policy if a low-wage contract is signed.
   c. low-money-growth policy if a high-wage contract is signed.
   d. high-money-growth policy if a high-wage contract is signed.
   e. high-money-growth policy no matter which labor contract is signed.

2. Which of the following statements is false?
   a. The Federal Reserve has a credibility problem because of time inconsistency.
   b. The Fed is required to follow the plans it announces to Congress in conformance with the Full Employment and Balanced Growth Act (1978).
   c. If the public does not believe the Fed, the Fed's policies may not have their intended effect.
   d. The Fed's policies could gain credibility if Congress were to pass a law requiring the Fed to increase the money supply at a fixed rate.
   e. If the Fed abandoned the goal of reducing unemployment below the natural rate, the problem of inflation would disappear.

Section 4: Sources of Business Cycles

1. Which of the following statements is true?
   a. Economists have clear evidence that political business cycles occur in the United States.
   b. The effort to exploit the short-run Phillips curve for political gain would shift the Phillips curve in a manner consistent with recent data.
   c. The end result of the political business cycle is that the economy returns to its original equilibrium price level and output after the election.
   d. Real business cycles are caused by discretionary monetary policy.
   e. Real business cycles are caused by discretionary fiscal policy.

2. Which of the following would *not* be a cause of a real business cycle?
   a. a decrease in government borrowing
   b. a drought in the Midwest
   c. oil prices skyrocketing as a result of an accident on the world's largest offshore oil rig
   d. a labor strike that cripples the steel industry
   e. an improvement in the technology for solar energy that yields a lightweight solar battery that can be used to power cars for long trips

3. The existence of a political business cycle implies that, prior to the election, the incumbent administration would
   a. increase aggregate demand by increasing government spending and the money supply.
   b. increase aggregate demand by increasing government spending and decreasing the money supply.
   c. increase aggregate demand by decreasing government spending and the money supply.
   d. decrease aggregate demand by increasing government spending and the money supply.
   e. decrease aggregate demand by increasing government spending and decreasing the money supply.

Section 5: The Link Between Monetary and Fiscal Policies

1. The government budget constraint
   a. always holds true.
   b. demonstrates that there is no link between fiscal and monetary policy.
   c. demonstrates that an expansionary fiscal policy implies a contractionary monetary policy.
   d. shows that the change in the money supply equals government spending minus borrowing.
   e. demonstrates that monetary reform will always halt inflation.

2. Which of the following is false?
   a. In most developed countries, monetary and fiscal policies are conducted by separate independent agencies.
   b. Fiscal policy can impose an inflationary burden on monetary policy.
   c. In typical developing countries, monetary and fiscal policies are controlled by the same central authority.
   d. Using money to finance deficits has produced severe deflation in many countries.
   e. Monetary control is not possible until fiscal policy is under control.

Practice Questions and Problems

Section 1: The Phillips Curve

1. The _____ illustrates the inverse relationship between inflation and the unemployment rate.

2. The Phillips curve tradeoff between inflation and unemployment _____ (does, does not) persist over the long run.

3. Over the long run, the Phillips curve is _____ .

4. Plot the following unemployment and inflation data on the graph below. Be sure to label your axes.

	Inflation Rate	Unemployment Rate
1974	14.6	5.6
1975	13.5	8.5
1976	9.3	7.7
1977	11	7.1
1978	13.9	6.1

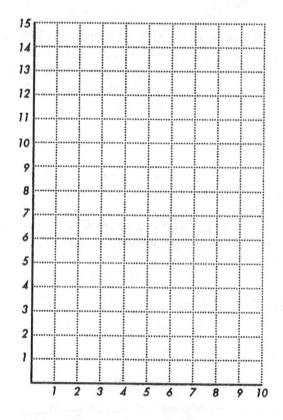

Does your graph imply the existence of a short-run Phillips curve during this period? _____

5. The downward slope of the short-run Phillips curve is caused by shifts in _____ , with _____ remaining constant.

Section 2: The Role of Expectations

1. A(n) _____ is the lowest wage that an unemployed worker is willing to accept.
2. List the two assumptions underlying the short-run Phillips curve.

_____

_____

3. The _____ wage is the number of dollars earned; the _____ wage is the purchasing power of those dollars.
4. If people's expectations about inflation do not change, the short-run effect of disinflation is rising _____ .
5. The short-run tradeoff between inflation and unemployment comes from _____ inflation.
6. Unexpected inflation can affect the employment rate in the following three ways:

_____

_____

_____

7. As economic conditions change, firms with expiring wage contracts can adjust _____ to those conditions; firms with existing contracts must adjust _____ to those conditions.
8. _____ expectations are expectations that are determined by what has happened in the recent past.
9. _____ expectations are based on all available relevant information.
10. Your economics professor bases her first exam solely on material from the textbook. Before the second exam, she announces that this exam will be based primarily on lecture material. If you only study the textbook, you are acting on the basis of _____ expectations.
11. When the inflation rate is unexpectedly high, unemployment _____ .
12. If wages were always flexible, unexpected changes in aggregate demand would be met by _____ adjustments rather than by _____ adjustments.

Section 3: Credibility and Time Inconsistency

1. _____ gives the Fed a credibility problem.
2. If the public does not believe the low-money-growth plans of the central bank, high-wage contracts will always be signed and the central bank will always have to follow a _____ -money-growth policy to maintain the natural rate of unemployment.
3. The central bank could eliminate the problem of _____ if it eliminated the goal of reducing unemployment below its natural rate.
4. List two ways to establish the credibility of the Fed.

_____

_____

5. A plan is _____ when it changes over time in response to changing conditions.

Section 4: Sources of Business Cycles

1. The _____ refers to macroeconomic policy used to promote the reelection of incumbent politicians.

2. The _____ refers to a business cycle that is not related to discretionary policy actions.

3. The political business cycle argument suggests that incumbent administrations follow _____ macroeconomic policies just before an election.

4. Economists _____ (do, do not) agree on whether a political business cycle exists in the United States.

5. A(n) _____ is an unexpected change in a variable.

6. A(n) _____ is an expansion and contraction of the economy caused by a change in the weather, technology, or other real factors.

7. List some examples of real shocks.
   _____

Section 5: The Link Between Monetary and Fiscal Policies

1. Write the equation for the government budget restraint.
   _____

2. A _____ is a new monetary policy that includes the introduction of a new monetary unit.

3. The only way to reduce the amount of money being created is to reduce the _____ minus _____.

4. The government can finance its spending by _____ , _____ , or _____ .

Thinking About and Applying Macroeconomic Policy: Tradeoffs, Expectations, Credibility, and Sources of Business Cycles

I. Expectations and Government Spending Cuts

In a *Wall Street Journal* editorial titled "Hurry Up and Wait," former president Ronald Reagan complained that the Clinton administration wanted to "hurry up" with tax increases, but that the deficit reduction through spending cuts wasn't scheduled to take place for four or five years. Mr. Reagan urged the budget makers to put spending cuts in the same year as tax increases, not at some point down the road. He implied that people should not believe in future spending cuts, because when he was president, Congress agreed to make such cuts but never did.

a. Mr. Reagan expected this Congress to renege on its promise to cut government spending down the road because Congress did not follow through with spending cuts promised in 1982. Expectations formed in this way are called _____ expectations.

b. At the time of the editorial's publication, the Clinton administration hoped to persuade the public to believe that the deficit would be reduced through cuts in government spending in the future. Mr. Clinton said he learns from mistakes. The Clinton administration hoped that the public would consider new information and have _____ expectations.

II. War on Inflation

The leader of a developing nation has declared war on inflation by issuing a series of belt-tightening measures. Capital gains taxes will be enforced, lending and deposit rates at banks will be raised, and government spending will be slashed.

Use the government's budget constraint to explain how these measures will affect inflation.

Chapter 15   Homework Problems

Name _____

1. What relationship does the Phillips curve show?

2. a. How does the Phillips curve relationship work in the short run?

   b. How does the Phillips curve relationship work in the long run?

3. Label the following events as fiscal policy (F), monetary policy (M), or real shocks (R).
   ___ a. The Fed raises the discount rate.
   ___ b. The price of oil falls 25% as a new oil field comes into production.
   ___ c. Expensive new pollution-control requirements are put into effect.
   ___ d. Taxes are reduced.
   ___ e. Government spending is cut to reduce the budget deficit.
   ___ f. The FOMC decides to buy more bonds.

4. a. For the last twenty-five years, U.S. politicians have been saying that they will reduce the federal budget deficit. Over that period, the deficit has not been reduced. As a result of this experience, some people conclude that the deficit will never go down. What type of expectations do these people demonstrate?

   b. In an election, control of the Congress and presidency pass to a different political party, which promises that "things will be different" now. Some people now conclude that the budget deficit will go down in the future. What type of expectations do these people demonstrate?

5. In the summers of 1993 and 1995, heavy rains and flooding significantly reduced agricultural production in the U.S. Midwest.

   Sketch a short-run aggregate demand–aggregate supply diagram, with the economy currently in the rising part of the aggregate supply curve. Be sure to label your axes.

   Next, sketch in the effect of the reduced agricultural production.

   Finally, use your diagram to predict the effect of the heavy rain and flooding on the equilibrium price level and real GDP.

If your instructor assigns these problems, write your answers above, then tear out this page and hand it in.

Answers

Quick-Check Quiz

Section 1: The Phillips Curve

1. a; 2. d; 3. c
If you missed any of these questions, you should go back and review Section 1 of Chapter 15.

Section 2: The Role of Expectations

1. d; 2. d (Only unanticipated inflation makes the inflation-unemployment tradeoff possible.); 3. e; 4. c
If you missed any of these questions, you should go back and review Section 2 of Chapter 15.

Section 3: Credibility and Time Inconsistency

1. e; 2. b
If you missed either of these questions, you should go back and review Section 3 of Chapter 15.

Section 4: Sources of Business Cycles

1. b; 2. a; 3. a
If you missed any of these questions, you should go back and review Section 4 of Chapter 15.

Section 5: The Link Between Monetary and Fiscal Policies

1. a; 2. d
If you missed either of these questions, you should go back and review Section 5 of Chapter 15.

Practice Questions and Problems

Section 1: The Phillips Curve

1. Phillips curve
2. does not
3. vertical

4.

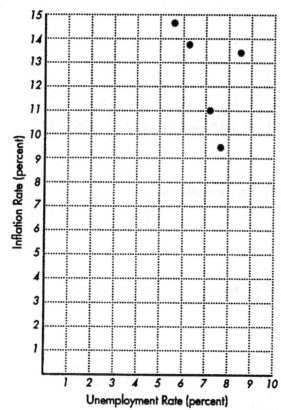

Since the curve does slope down, there is evidence of a short-run Phillips curve tradeoff between inflation and unemployment.
5. aggregate demand; aggregate supply (Note that aggregate supply does shift in the long run.)

Section 2: The Role of Expectations

1. reservation wage
2. constant expected rate of inflation
   constant reservation wage
3. nominal; real
4. unemployment
5. unexpected
6. wage expectations
   inventory fluctuations
   wage contracts
7. wages; employment
8. Adaptive
9. Rational
10. adaptive
11. decreases
12. wage; employment

Section 3: Credibility and Time Inconsistency

1. Time inconsistency
2. high
3. inflation
4. Pass a law requiring the Fed to maintain a certain growth rate in the money supply. Create incentives for Fed policymakers to follow through with low-money-growth plans, so that the Fed establishes a reputation for consistency.
5. time inconsistent

Section 4: Sources of Business Cycles

1. political business cycle
2. real business cycle
3. expansionary
4. do not
5. shock
6. real business cycle
7. technological change, changes in tastes, labor strikes, or weather

Section 5: The Link Between Monetary and Fiscal Policies

1. $G = T + B + \Delta M$
2. monetary reform
3. fiscal deficit; borrowing
4. taxing; borrowing; creating money

Thinking About and Applying Macroeconomic Policy: Tradeoffs, Expectations, Credibility, and Sources of Business Cycles

I. Expectations and Government Spending Cuts

a. adaptive
b. rational

II. War on Inflation

$$\Delta M = (G - T) - B$$

If G is decreased and T is increased, $(G - T)$ will be smaller. If there is no change in government borrowing, the change in the money supply will be negative and inflation will decrease.

Chapter 16

MACROECONOMIC VIEWPOINTS: NEW KEYNESIAN, MONETARIST, AND NEW CLASSICAL

FUNDAMENTAL QUESTIONS

1. What do Keynesian economists believe about macroeconomic policy?

   Keynesians believe the following:
   Wages and prices are not flexible in the short run.
   The economy is not always in equilibrium.
   The government must take an active role in the economy to stabilize aggregate demand.
   The private sector, especially investment, is an important source of shifts in aggregate demand.
   The aggregate supply curve is not horizontal, but slopes upward as real GDP approaches its potential level.

2. What role do monetarists believe the government should play in the economy?

   Monetarists believe that the economy is inherently stable and that government intervention in the economy makes business cycles worse. They therefore favor minimal government intervention in the economy.

3. What is new classical economics?

   New classical economists emphasize rational expectations and believe that the economy tends toward equilibrium. They also believe that fiscal and monetary policies can change the equilibrium level of real GDP only if the changes are unexpected. Any predictable policy simply affects prices. Government policy should therefore target a low, stable rate of inflation.

4. How do theories of economics change over time?

   Economic theories develop in response to new economic situations or perceived failings in old theories. Thus Keynesian theory evolved to explain the Great Depression, and monetarist and new classical economics evolved to explain the problem of simultaneous unemployment and inflation.

Key Terms

Keynesian economics
monetarist economics
classical economics
new classical economics

Quick-Check Quiz

Section 1: Keynesian Economics

1. Which of the following is *not* common to Keynesian and new Keynesian economists?
   a. the belief that wages and prices are not flexible in the short run
   b. the belief that the aggregate supply curve is a horizontal line
   c. the belief that monetary policy should be used to manage aggregate demand
   d. the belief that fiscal policy should be used to stabilize aggregate demand
   e. the belief that disequilibrium occurs in the labor market

2. Keynesians
   a. believe that the price system efficiently allocates resources.
   b. believe that monetary policy operates with long and variable lags.
   c. emphasize rational expectations.
   d. believe that the government needs to take an active role in managing aggregate demand.
   e. believe that only unexpected changes in the money supply affect real national income.

Section 2: Monetarist Economics

1. Monetarists believe that
   a. fiscal policy is an effective way to manage aggregate demand.
   b. the government should use only monetary policy to achieve its goals of low inflation and economic growth.
   c. government intervention should be kept to a minimum.
   d. the government should change monetary and fiscal policies to suit current conditions.
   e. government policies have an effect on real GDP only if the changes are unanticipated.

2. Monetarists
   a. have great faith that the market system allocates resources efficiently.
   b. believe that government intervention accentuates business cycles.
   c. believe that the government should follow a fixed rule for monetary growth.
   d. believe that government intervention in the economy is ineffective because of long and variable lags.
   e. All of these statements are true.

3. The effect lag
   a. is the time it takes for the effects of a policy to work their way through the economy once the policy is implemented.
   b. is the time it takes for policymakers to realize there is a problem.
   c. is the time it takes for policymakers to formulate a policy once they recognize there is a problem.
   d. is the time from when policymakers realize there is a problem until the effects of the policy work their way through the economy.
   e. is the time from when policymakers formulate a policy until the effects of the policy work their way through the economy.

Section 3: New Classical Economics

1. New classical economists agree with Keynesians that
   a. wages and prices are flexible.
   b. the aggregate supply curve is vertical.
   c. markets are always in equilibrium.
   d. any predictable macroeconomic policy has an effect only on prices.
   e. monetary and fiscal policies can achieve a low, stable rate of inflation.

2. New classical economics and classical economics both
   a. emphasize rational expectations.
   b. assume perfect information.
   c. assume a horizontal aggregate supply curve.
   d. believe that wages and prices are flexible.
   e. believe that formal rules should govern economic policymaking.

3. Monetarists and new classical economists agree that
   a. only unexpected changes in prices have effects on real GDP.
   b. wages and prices are not flexible in the short run.
   c. any predictable macroeconomic policy has an effect only on prices.
   d. attempts by the government to manage aggregate demand make business cycles worse.
   e. the government should not try to affect the equilibrium level of real output.

Section 4: Comparison and Influence

1. Which of the following favor an active role for government in promoting low inflation and economic growth?
   a. only Keynesians
   b. only monetarists
   c. only new classical economists
   d. monetarists and new classical economists
   e. monetarists and Keynesians

2. Which of the following believe that wages and prices are flexible in the short run?
   a. only Keynesians
   b. only monetarists
   c. only new classical economists
   d. monetarists and new classical economists
   e. monetarists and Keynesians

3. Which of the following emphasize rational expectations?
   a. only Keynesians
   b. only monetarists
   c. only new classical economists
   d. monetarists and new classical economists
   e. monetarists and Keynesians

4. Which theory(ies) developed as a response to the problem of unemployment and inflation at the same time?
   a. only Keynesians
   b. only monetarists
   c. only new classical economists
   d. monetarists and new classical economists
   e. monetarists and Keynesians

5. Which of the following believe that the economy tends toward equilibrium at potential real GDP?
   a. only Keynesians
   b. only monetarists
   c. only new classical economists
   d. monetarists and new classical economists
   e. monetarists and Keynesians

6. Which of the following favor fixed rules for money growth?
   a. only Keynesians
   b. only monetarists
   c. only new classical economists
   d. monetarists and new classical economists
   e. monetarists and Keynesians

7. Which of the following believe that monetary and fiscal policies are effective only if people cannot anticipate the changes?
   a. only Keynesians
   b. only monetarists
   c. only new classical economists
   d. monetarists and new classical economists
   e. monetarists and Keynesians

Practice Questions and Problems

Section 1: Keynesian Economics

1. _____ economics focuses on the role government plays in stabilizing the economy by managing aggregate demand.

2. New Keynesians _____ (do, do not) believe that wages and prices are flexible in the short run.

3. New Keynesians believe that the economy _____ (is, is not) always in equilibrium.
4. New Keynesian economists _____ (do, do not) believe that the government must play an active role in stabilizing the economy.

Section 2: Monetarist Economics

1. _____ is the leading monetarist economist.
2. Monetarists believe that changes in the money supply directly affect _____ and _____.
3. Monetarists believe that fiscal and monetary policies have only _____ effects on real GDP.
4. Monetarists believe that, in the long run, a change in the money supply will affect only the _____.
5. Monetarists believe that the economy _____ (does, does not) tend toward equilibrium at a level consistent with the natural rate of unemployment.
6. Monetarists _____ (do, do not) believe that the government needs to play an active role in stabilizing the economy.
7. In recent years, the inflation rate seemed to follow changes in the growth rate of the money supply with a lag of _____ or _____ years.
8. _____ lag is the time it takes policymakers to realize that a problem exists.
9. _____ lag is the time it takes policymakers to formulate an appropriate policy once they realize that a problem exists.
10. The _____ lag is the time it takes for the effects of the policy to work through the economy.
11. Monetarists believe that government attempts at achieving full employment and low inflation make the business cycle _____ .
12. Instead of discretionary fiscal and monetary policies, monetarists advocate fiscal and monetary _____ .
13. Monetarists emphasize the role of the _____ in determining equilibrium income and prices.
14. Monetarists believe that government intervention makes the economy worse because of the existence of long and variable _____ .

Section 3: New Classical Economics

1. Classical economists believed that the aggregate supply curve was _____ and that changes in aggregate demand affected only the _____ level, not the level of _____ .
2. Classical economists believed that prices and wages _____ (were, were not) perfectly flexible.

3. New classical economists believe that wages and prices _____ (are, are not) flexible.

4. New classical economists emphasize _____ expectations. Classical economists assumed _____ information.

5. It is much easier for policymakers to make unexpected changes in policy if expectations are formed _____ rather than _____ .

6. New classical economists believe that the economy _____ (does, does not) tend toward equilibrium at a level consistent with the natural rate of unemployment.

7. New classical economists believe that during recessions low real wages cause workers to substitute _____ activities for work.

8. New classical economists believe that changes in fiscal and monetary policy can affect the equilibrium level of real GDP only if those changes are _____ .

9. New classical economists believe that any predictable policy simply affects _____ .

10. New classical economists believe that the goal of monetary and fiscal policies should be a low, stable rate of _____ .

Section 4: Comparison and Influence

1. Macroeconomic theories develop in response to _____ in existing theories.

2. Only _____ economics supports an active role for government; the other two theories suggest that government should not intervene.

3. _____ and _____ economists believe that the economy tends toward equilibrium at the natural rate of unemployment.

Thinking About and Applying Macroeconomic Viewpoints: New Keynesian, Monetarist, and New Classical

I. The Roots of "Freshwater" Economists

"Freshwater" economists are named for the origins of this group at universities along the shores of the Great Lakes. Like other economic theories, the theory of this group incorporates parts of economic theories that came before it. For each tenet of "freshwater" economic thought, place a *K* if the tenet has Keynesian roots, an *M* if it has monetarist roots, and an *N* if it has new classical roots. A tenet may have more than one letter next to it.

1. The government should not tinker with (or fine-tune) the economy. _____

2. Consumers, workers, business executives, and investors anticipate changes in the economy faster than the government and can adjust to them better on their own. _____

3. People anticipate the effects of changes in government policy and sometimes blunt the government's objectives in devising ways to accommodate the changes. _____
4. Recessions are not a problem, and the government can't do anything about them anyway. _____
5. Tax cuts have no effect on consumption. _____
6. "Freshwater" economists are rational expectationalists. _____
7. There is a lag before Congress recognizes that there is a problem and acts, and another lag before the acts have effects. _____
8. Government intervention could accentuate the business cycle. _____
9. Free markets work. _____

II. Comparing and Contrasting New Keynesians, Monetarists, and New Classical Economists

Place a *K* next to statements associated with new Keynesians, an *M* next to statements associated with monetarists, and an *N* next to statements associated with new classical economists.

_____ Fiscal and monetary policies can change the equilibrium level of real GDP only if those changes are unexpected.

_____ Monetary and fiscal policies should be set according to formal rules.

_____ Wages and prices are inflexible.

_____ When real wages are lower, people voluntarily substitute nonlabor activities for employment.

_____ The private sector is an important source of shifts for aggregate demand.

_____ Money affects income and consumption directly.

_____ The economy tends toward equilibrium at the level of potential real GDP.

_____ Since economic policy acts with a long and variable lag, government should not attempt discretionary monetary and fiscal policies.

_____ The economy is subject to disequilibrium in labor and goods markets.

_____ Wages are flexible.

_____ Expectations are formed using all available information, not just past experience.

_____ Any predictable expansionary fiscal or monetary policy affects only prices.

_____ Fiscal and monetary policies should aim for a low, stable rate of inflation.

_____ In the long run, real GDP will be at a level consistent with the natural level of unemployment.

_____ Government intervention is necessary to achieve high employment and low, stable inflation.

Chapter 16   Homework Problems

Name _____

1. For each group of economists listed below, decide whether they would agree (A) or disagree (D) with the following statement:

    "The economy tends toward equilibrium without government interference."

    _____ new Keynesian economists

    _____ monetarist economists

    _____ new classical economists

2. For each group of economists listed below, decide whether they would agree (A) or disagree (D) with the following statement:

    "Wages and prices are not very flexible in the short run."

    _____ new Keynesian economists

    _____ monetarist economists

    _____ new classical economists

3. For each group of economists listed below, decide whether they would agree (A) or disagree (D) with the following statement:

    "Government policy can affect the price level."

    _____ new Keynesian economists

    _____ monetarist economists

    _____ new classical economists

4. For each group of economists listed below, decide whether they would agree (A) or disagree (D) with the following statement:

    "Government policy can effectively control real GDP by stabilizing aggregate demand."

    _____ new Keynesian economists

    _____ monetarist economists

    _____ new classical economists

5. John Maynard Keynes once wrote that "practical men . . . are the slaves of some defunct economist." Which group or groups of economists (defunct or not) discussed in Chapter 16 are each of the politicians below relying on for their comments?

   a. Politician #1: "The Fed always messes up the economy by playing around with the money supply. It should just pick a policy and stick to it."

   b. Politician #2: "We've got to do something new and different to get the economy growing again."

   c. Politician #3: "The economy is moving into a recession again. It's time to cut taxes and increase government spending."

   d. Politician #4: "Well, it looks like government policy caused another recession. We've got to decide how much taxes and spending will be, and live within those limits."

   e. Politician #5: "There's no point in having the government spend more money to create jobs—unemployment won't go any lower anyway."

If your instructor assigns these problems, write your answers above, then tear out this page and hand it in.

Answers

Quick-Check Quiz

Section 1: Keynesian Economics

1. b; 2. d
If you missed either of these questions, you should go back and review Section 1 of Chapter 16.

Section 2: Monetarist Economics

1. c; 2. e; 3. a
If you missed any of these questions, you should go back and review Section 2 of Chapter 16.

Section 3: New Classical Economics

1. e; 2. d; 3. e
If you missed any of these questions, you should go back and review Section 3 of Chapter 16.

Section 4: Comparison and Influence

1. a; 2. d; 3. c; 4. d; 5. d; 6. b; 7. c
If you missed any of these questions, you should go back and review Section 4 of Chapter 16.

Practice Questions and Problems

Section 1: Keynesian Economics

1. Keynesian
2. do not
3. is not
4. do

Section 2: Monetarist Economics

1. Milton Friedman
2. consumption; investment
3. short-term
4. price level
5. does
6. do not
7. one; two
8. Recognition
9. Reaction
10. effect
11. worse
12. rules
13. money supply
14. lags

Section 3: New Classical Economics

1. vertical; price; output
2. were
3. are
4. rational; perfect
5. adaptively; rationally
6. does
7. nonlabor
8. unexpected
9. prices
10. inflation

Section 4: Comparison and Influence

1. shortcomings
2. Keynesian
3. Monetarists; new classical

Thinking About and Applying Macroeconomic Viewpoints: New Keynesian, Monetarist, and New Classical

I. The Roots of "Freshwater" Economists

1. M, N
2. N
3. N
4. M, N
5. M, N
6. N
7. N, M
8. M
9. M, N

II. Comparing and Contrasting New Keynesians, Monetarists, and New Classical Economists

N	Fiscal and monetary policies can change the equilibrium level of real GDP only if those changes are unexpected.
M	Monetary and fiscal policies should be set according to formal rules.
K	Wages and prices are inflexible.
N	When real wages are lower, people voluntarily substitute nonlabor activities for employment.
K	The private sector is an important source of shifts for aggregate demand.
M	Money affects income and consumption directly.
M, N	The economy tends toward equilibrium at the level of potential real GDP.
M	Since economic policy acts with a long and variable lag, government should not attempt discretionary monetary and fiscal policies.
K	The economy is subject to disequilibrium in labor and goods markets.
M, N	Wages are flexible.
N	Expectations are formed using all available information, not just past experience.

M, N	Any predictable expansionary fiscal or monetary policy affects only prices.
K, N	Fiscal and monetary policies should aim for a low, stable rate of inflation.
M, N	In the long run, real GDP will be at a level consistent with the natural level of unemployment.
K	Government intervention is necessary to achieve high employment and low, stable inflation.

Chapter 17

MACROECONOMIC LINKS BETWEEN COUNTRIES

FUNDAMENTAL QUESTIONS

1. How does a change in the exchange rate affect the prices of goods traded between countries?

   Changes in exchange rates change the prices people must pay for imported products. When the domestic currency depreciates (decreases in value) against another currency, foreign goods become more expensive for domestic buyers and domestic goods become less expensive for foreign buyers. When the domestic currency appreciates (increases in value) against another currency, foreign goods become less expensive for domestic buyers and domestic goods become more expensive for foreign buyers.

   A few examples will help make this clearer. Let's say that yesterday the U.S. dollar exchange rate for the Japanese yen was $1 = ¥200. Today, the exchange rate changed to $1 = ¥300. The dollar has appreciated relative to the yen, since a dollar will buy more yen than before. A Japanese VCR that costs ¥60,000 in Japan sold for $300 yesterday (¥60,000/¥200 per $) but costs only $200 today (¥60,000/¥300 per $): foreign goods become less expensive to domestic buyers when a currency appreciates. On the other hand, a bushel of wheat that sells for $3 in the United States cost buyers in Japan ¥600 yesterday ($3 × ¥200 per $) but costs them ¥900 today ($3 × ¥300 per $): domestic goods become more expensive to foreign buyers when a currency appreciates.

   Let's say that yesterday the U.S. dollar exchange rate for the euro was $1 = e3. Today, the exchange rate changed to $1 = e2. The dollar has depreciated relative to the euro, since a dollar will buy fewer euros than before. A German BMW that costs e60,000 in Germany sold for $20,000 yesterday (e60,000/e3 per $) but costs $30,000 today (e60,000/e2 per $): foreign goods become more expensive to domestic buyers when a currency depreciates. On the other hand, a bushel of wheat that sells for $3 in the United States cost buyers in Germany e9 yesterday ($3 × e3 per $), but costs them only e6 today ($3 × e2 per $): domestic goods become less expensive to foreign buyers when a currency depreciates.

2. Why don't similar goods sell for the same price all over the world?

   Before we answer this question, let's look at why we would expect similar goods to sell at the same price. Let's suppose that gold sells for $350 per ounce in Philadelphia and for $400 per ounce in New York today. You (and many other people) could make a profit through **arbitrage** by buying gold in Philadelphia, driving to New York, and selling the gold there. But if you and others do this, the demand for gold in Philadelphia will increase, pulling the price of gold above $350, while in New York the supply of gold will increase, pushing the price of gold below $400.

Arbitrage moves the prices of gold in Philadelphia and New York toward the same price; arbitrage will continue until gold has the same price in both cities.

In world markets, we would expect the same sort of process to work: arbitrage should make the cost of a good the same in all countries. If gold costs $400 per ounce in the United States, and the exchange rate between U.S. dollars and euros is $1 = e5, gold should cost e2,000 ($400 × e5 per $) in France. If gold doesn't cost e2,000, then there are opportunities for arbitrage, which will eventually bring the price of gold to the same value in both New York and Paris. When monies have the same purchasing power in different markets, there is **purchasing power parity (PPP)**.

In reality, prices around the world frequently differ from purchasing power parity. A McDonald's Big Mac may cost $2.20 in New York but cost the equivalent of $3.15 in Paris. Deviations from PPP occur for the following reasons:

a. Goods are not identical in different countries. Although McDonald's tries hard to make Big Macs identical around the world, the atmosphere of eating on Seventh Avenue in New York isn't the same as on the Champs Élysées.

b. Information is costly. A Parisian would have to make an international phone call to find out the price of a Big Mac today in New York.

c. Shipping costs affect prices. The cost of mailing a Big Mac from New York to Paris is more than the price difference.

d. Tariffs and other restrictions on trade affect prices. If the French government has a tax on imported hamburgers, the cost to the Parisian will be higher.

3. What is the relationship between inflation and changes in the exchange rate?

Exchange rates tend to change with differences in inflation rates between countries. Starting with purchasing power parity, if prices in the United States go up 10 percent faster than they do in France, the dollar must depreciate by 10 percent to restore PPP.

4. How do we find the domestic currency return on a foreign bond?

In addition to buying and selling goods between countries, the world economy also trades financial instruments like stocks and bonds. To be able to decide whether buying a U.S. bond or buying a Japanese bond is the better choice, you need to calculate the domestic currency return on the Japanese bond to find how much the interest paid in yen is expected to be worth in dollars in the future; you already know the return in dollars for the U.S. bond, since it pays interest in dollars. The domestic currency return on the Japanese bond is the interest rate paid by the bond plus the percentage change in the exchange rate. For example, if the Japanese bond pays 4 percent interest and the exchange rate between the dollar and the yen stays constant, the domestic currency return is still 4 percent. If instead the yen is expected to appreciate by 3 percent per year, buying the Japanese bond gives you a 7 percent return: the 4 percent interest plus the 3 percent increase in the value of the yen.

5. What is the relationship between domestic and foreign interest rates and changes in the exchange rate?

We have already looked at the idea of purchasing power parity and how arbitrage can bring prices of internationally traded goods into line. The same idea can be applied to international financial investments. **Interest rate parity (IRP)** occurs when the domestic currency return is the same for investments in different countries. When interest rate parity does not hold, arbitrageurs can make a profit by buying financial assets in one country and simultaneously selling similar assets in another country. In the process, exchange rates will change to make domestic currency returns move toward equality.

6. Why don't similar financial assets yield the same return all over the world?

   The reasons why interest rate parity doesn't always hold are similar to some of the reasons why purchasing power parity doesn't always hold: financial assets are not identical in different countries (some investments are riskier than others and a **risk premium** must be paid), there are government controls on international financial transactions (similar to other restrictions on international trade), and there are differences in tax structures (similar in effects to tariffs).

7. How does fiscal policy affect exchange rates?

   Fiscal policy affects exchange rates through its effects on interest rates. When the U.S. government increases borrowing to finance a larger deficit, U.S. interest rates rise relative to foreign interest rates. Investments in U.S. bonds become more attractive to foreigners, who increase their demand for dollars to buy U.S. bonds. The increased demand for dollars causes the dollar to appreciate. The dollar appreciation in turn reduces U.S. exports (they've become more expensive to foreigners) and increases U.S. imports (they've become cheaper for U.S. buyers). If the government decreases borrowing, all the changes go in the opposite direction.

8. How does monetary policy affect exchange rates?

   Monetary policy also affects exchange rates through interest rates. If the money supply is increased to finance a larger deficit, nominal interest rates will rise in the United States because of increased inflation caused by the increase in the money supply. To maintain PPP, the dollar must depreciate to counteract the increased inflation. IRP will also be maintained, since the depreciation of the dollar will counterbalance the increased inflation rate and higher nominal interest rates. If both PPP and IRP are maintained, U.S. monetary policy will not affect the amounts of U.S. imports and exports.

9. What can countries gain by coordinating their macroeconomic policies?

   We have seen that the macroeconomic policies followed by one nation can affect other nations through changes in exchange rates and changes in imports and exports. By coordinating their macroeconomic policies, countries have a better chance of attaining their policy goals, have greater access to economic information, and can achieve better outcomes than they could by acting on their own.

Key Terms

arbitrage
open economy

purchasing power parity (PPP)
interest rate parity (IRP)

capital controls
risk premium

Quick-Check Quiz

Section 1: Prices and Exchange Rates

1. When one currency increases in value relative to other currencies, we say that the currency has
   a. depreciated.
   b. appreciated.
   c. diminished.
   d. expanded.
   e. been redevalued.

2. When one currency decreases in value relative to other currencies, we say that the currency has
   a. depreciated.
   b. appreciated.
   c. diminished.
   d. expanded.
   e. been revalued.

3. If the exchange rate between U.S. dollars and euros changes from $.15 to e1 to $.20 = e1, the euro has
   a. depreciated.
   b. appreciated.
   c. diminished.
   d. expanded.
   e. been redevalued.

4. If the exchange rate between U.S. dollars and euros changes from $.15 = e1 to $.20 = e1, the U.S. dollar has
   a. depreciated.
   b. appreciated.
   c. diminished.
   d. expanded.
   e. been redevalued.

5. Arbitrage is
   a. simultaneously buying different goods in the same market.
   b. the condition that exists when average wages buy the same market basket of goods in different countries.
   c. simultaneously buying in a market where the price is low and selling in a market where the price is high to profit from the price differential.
   d. the condition under which monies have the same purchasing power in different markets.
   e. the settlement by outside mediators of disputes concerning foreign exchange.

6. Purchasing power parity (PPP) is
   a. simultaneously buying different goods in the same market.
   b. the condition that exists when average wages buy the same market basket of goods in different countries.
   c. simultaneously buying in a market where the price is low and selling in a market where the price is high to profit from the price differential.
   d. the condition under which monies have the same purchasing power in different markets.
   e. the settlement by outside mediators of disputes concerning foreign exchange.

7. Which of the following is *not* a reason why purchasing power parity (PPP) may not exist?
   a. different wages in different countries
   b. costly information
   c. goods that are not identical in different countries
   d. tariffs and legal restrictions on international trade
   e. shipping costs

8. Which of the following statements is true?
   a. When the domestic currency depreciates, foreign goods become cheaper for domestic buyers.
   b. When the domestic currency appreciates, foreign goods become more expensive for domestic buyers.
   c. When a foreign currency depreciates, American goods become cheaper for foreign buyers.
   d. When a foreign currency depreciates, American goods become more expensive for foreign buyers.
   e. When the domestic currency depreciates, American goods become more expensive for foreign buyers.

9. Price differences across countries are smallest
   a. the more dissimilar the goods being sold in different countries.
   b. the harder it is to gather information about prices.
   c. the higher the shipping costs.
   d. the less restrictive the government barriers to trade.
   e. the higher the tariffs on goods and services.

Section 2: Interest Rates and Exchange Rates

1. When deciding whether to buy a bond denominated in a foreign currency or a domestic bond, the buyer must take into account
   a. only the interest rate on the domestic bond.
   b. only the interest rate on the foreign bond.
   c. only the interest rates on both domestic and foreign bonds.
   d. the interest rates on the foreign and domestic bonds and the expected changes in the exchange rate.
   e. the interest rates on the foreign and domestic bonds and the current exchange rate.

2. Interest rate parity exists when the domestic interest rate equals the
   a. foreign interest rate.
   b. exchange rate.
   c. expected change in the exchange rate.
   d. foreign interest rate plus the expected change in the exchange rate.
   e. expected change in the foreign bond price.

3. When foreign-issued assets are subject to political risks, buyers must be paid
   a. in their own domestic currency.
   b. in another country's currency.
   c. a risk premium.
   d. below-market interest rates.
   e. interest rates based only on IRP.

4. Suppose the interest rate on a Japanese bond is 8 percent. The current exchange rate is ¥107.20 = $1. The expected exchange rate when the bond matures is ¥107.90 = $1. If interest rate parity holds, what is the domestic currency return?
   a. 8 percent
   b. .6 percent
   c. 8.65 percent
   d. 7.35 percent
   e. .65 percent

Section 3: Policy Effects

1. An increase in U.S. government borrowing will
   a. increase real interest rates in the United States and cause the dollar to depreciate.
   b. increase real interest rates in the United States and cause the dollar to appreciate.
   c. decrease real interest rates in the United States and cause the dollar to depreciate.
   d. decrease real interest rates in the United States and cause the dollar to appreciate.
   e. leave real interest rates and the value of the dollar unchanged.

2. A decrease in U.S. government borrowing will
   a. increase real interest rates in the United States and cause the dollar to depreciate.
   b. increase real interest rates in the United States and cause the dollar to appreciate.
   c. decrease real interest rates in the United States and cause the dollar to depreciate.
   d. decrease real interest rates in the United States and cause the dollar to appreciate.
   e. leave real interest rates and the value of the dollar unchanged.

3. An increase in the U.S. money supply growth rate will
   a. increase real interest rates in the United States and cause the dollar to appreciate.
   b. increase nominal interest rates in the United States and cause the dollar to appreciate.
   c. affect exchange rates but not affect international trade if PPP holds.
   d. affect international trade but not affect exchange rates if PPP holds.
   e. affect neither international trade nor exchange rates if PPP holds.

4. Which of the following is *not* true when the money supply growth rate changes and both PPP and IRP hold?
   a. The expected change in the exchange rate equals the interest rate differential between domestic and foreign bonds.
   b. The expected change in the exchange rate equals the expected inflation differential between domestic and foreign countries.
   c. The interest rate differential between domestic and foreign bonds equals the expected inflation differential between domestic and foreign countries.
   d. All of the above are true when PPP and IRP hold.

5. A change in policy that lowers the budget deficit
   a. makes the dollar appreciate and causes net exports to decline.
   b. makes the dollar appreciate and causes net exports to increase.
   c. makes the dollar depreciate and causes net exports to decline.
   d. makes the dollar depreciate and causes net exports to increase.
   e. makes U.S. goods more expensive.

Section 4: International Policy Coordination

1. Which of the following is *not* a reason why countries would benefit from coordinating their macroeconomic policies?
   a. Coordination could make reaching the goals of macroeconomic policy easier.
   b. Nations have access to more information.
   c. Coordination could help nations attain goals they couldn't reach on their own.
   d. Policymakers in most countries now agree on economic theories and appropriate policies.
   e. Overall economic performance would improve.

2. Which of the following is *not* an obstacle to international coordination of macroeconomic policy?
   a. disagreement on goals
   b. disagreement on current economic conditions
   c. disagreement on appropriate policies
   d. use of different currencies

Practice Questions and Problems

Section 1: Prices and Exchange Rates

1. An economy that trades goods and financial assets with the rest of the world is _____ .
2. We say that a currency has appreciated when its value _____ (increases, decreases) relative to other currencies; we say that a currency has depreciated when its value _____ (increases, decreases) relative to other currencies.
3. Yesterday the exchange rate between the U.S. dollar and the British pound was £1 = $1.50. Today the exchange rate between the U.S. dollar and the British pound is £1 = $2.00.
   a. Yesterday the exchange rate was $1 = _____ .
   b. Today the exchange rate is $1 = _____ .
   c. The pound has _____ (appreciated, depreciated) relative to the dollar.
   d. The dollar has _____ (appreciated, depreciated) relative to the pound.
   e. A British Rolls-Royce costs £150,000. Yesterday the Rolls-Royce would have cost an American _____ ; today the Rolls-Royce costs _____ . The dollar has _____ (appreciated, depreciated) relative to the pound, making the Rolls-Royce _____ (more, less) expensive to Americans.

f. An American Boeing airliner costs $60 million. Yesterday the Boeing would have cost a British airline _____ ; today the Boeing costs _____ . The dollar has _____ (appreciated, depreciated) relative to the pound, making the Boeing _____ (more, less) expensive to the British airline.

4. When the domestic currency depreciates, domestic goods become _____ expensive to foreign buyers and foreign goods become _____ expensive to domestic buyers.

5. When the domestic currency appreciates, domestic goods become _____ expensive to foreign buyers and foreign goods become _____ expensive to domestic buyers.

6. Let's say that the exchange rate between dollars and pounds is $1.50 = £1 and that an ounce of gold sells for £300 in London.
   a. What must the price of gold in New York be for purchasing power parity to hold? _____
   b. If gold sells for $400 in New York and £300 in London, would you buy gold in New York or in London to make a profit from arbitrage? _____
   c. If the inflation rate in the United States is 10 percent this year and there is no inflation in Britain, what will the exchange rate be in a year if purchasing power parity is maintained?
   _____

7. Let's say that the exchange rate between dollars and euros is $.50 = e1 and that an ounce of gold sells for $300 in New York.
   a. What must the price of gold in Berlin, Germany, be for purchasing power parity to hold?
   _____
   b. If gold sells for $400 in New York and e400 in Berlin, would you buy gold in New York or Berlin to make a profit from arbitrage? _____
   c. If the inflation rate in the United States is 20 percent this year and there is no inflation in Germany, what will the exchange rate be in a year if purchasing power parity is maintained?
   _____

8. A _____ is a tax on goods that are traded internationally.

9. The dollar _____ against currencies that have a higher inflation rate than the dollar and _____ against currencies that have a lower inflation rate.

Section 2: Interest Rates and Exchange Rates

1. The domestic currency return from a foreign bond equals the foreign _____ plus the percentage change in the _____ . Differences in inflation rates are one reason why the _____ may change.

2. When similar financial assets from different countries have the same interest rate when measured in the same currency, we have _____ .

3. When the domestic interest rate equals the foreign interest rate plus the expected change in the exchange rate, we have _____.

4. List three factors that may create deviations from interest rate parity.

_____

_____

_____

5. Let's say that the interest rate on U.S. government bonds is 10 percent and the interest rate on similar bonds issued by the Japanese government is 15 percent. Interest rate parity holds between the United States and Japan.

   a. What do people expect to happen to the exchange rate between the U.S. dollar and the Japanese yen?

   _____

   _____

   _____

   _____

   b. Do people expect the dollar to appreciate or depreciate? Why?

   _____

   _____

   _____

   _____

   c. If the expected change in the exchange rate is caused only by differences in the expected exchange rate, do people expect inflation to be higher in the United States or in Japan?

   _____

   _____

   _____

   _____

6. If interest rate parity holds and people expect higher inflation in Mexico than in Argentina, will interest rates be higher in Mexico or in Argentina? Why?

   _____

7. Write the equation for the domestic currency return. _____

8. Quotas on the amount of foreign exchange that can be bought and sold and high reserve requirements on foreign-owned bank deposits are examples of _____.

9. The extra return offered by a foreign-issued asset to compensate for political risk is called a _____.

10. A Norwegian bond offers a 15 percent interest rate. The current exchange rate is NOK 6.8955 = $1. When the bond matures, the expected exchange rate is NOK 6.8675 = $1. If interest rate parity holds, what is the domestic currency return on this bond? _____ The Norwegian krone has _____ (appreciated, depreciated).

Section 3: Policy Effects

1. An increase in government spending financed by increased borrowing tends to _____ (raise, lower) real interest rates in the United States, causing the dollar to _____ (appreciate, depreciate).

2. A decrease in government spending leading to decreased borrowing tends to _____ (raise, lower) real interest rates in the United States, causing the dollar to _____ (appreciate, depreciate).

3. When the dollar appreciates, people in other countries will tend to buy _____ (more, fewer) U.S. products and people in the United States will _____ (increase, decrease) their purchases of imported goods.

4. If your objective as a government policymaker is to increase U.S. net exports (exports minus imports), will increasing or decreasing government borrowing be more likely to help? Explain why.
   _____
   _____
   _____
   _____

5. An increase in the growth rate of the money supply will _____ (increase, decrease) the expected inflation differential between domestic and foreign countries.

6. If PPP and IRP both hold, then the change in the expected inflation differential will equal both the expected change in the _____ rate and the _____ rate differential between domestic and foreign bonds.

Section 4: International Policy Coordination

1. Two organizations promoting economic coordination and communication are the IMF and the OECD. What do these acronyms stand for?
   IMF: _____
   OECD: _____

2. List the countries that are members of the Group of 7 (or G7).

3. List three ways that countries can coordinate their economic policies.

4. List three obstacles to increased coordination of macroeconomic policies.

Thinking About and Applying Macroeconomic Links Between Countries

I. The Dollar and U.S. Interest Rates

Analysts and traders expect U.S. interest rates to increase. If they are correct, we would expect the dollar to _____ (appreciate, depreciate) against foreign currencies.

The changes in exchange rates would _____ (benefit, harm) U.S. investors in foreign stocks and bonds. A stronger dollar would _____ (enhance, reduce) their capital gains.

II. Investing Abroad

Recent Mexican governments have reduced the role of the government in controlling Mexico's economy. If there is less government interference in Mexico, we would expect U.S. investors to see less _____ risk. Mexican bonds would become _____ (more, less) attractive, and eventually the prices of these bonds would _____ (rise, fall) and the interest rate would _____ (increase, decrease).

Chapter 17 Homework Problems

Name _____

1. People sometimes think that the same products ought to sell for equivalent prices in different countries. What do economists call that idea?

2. List four reasons why the same goods actually sell for different prices in different countries.

3. The inflation rate in the United States is running around 3 percent, while the inflation rate in Japan is running around 10 percent. If purchasing power parity holds, what will happen to the exchange rate between the U.S. dollar and the Japanese yen?

4. The exchange rate between U.S. dollars and euros has changed from 1.2 e = $1 to 1.3 e = $1. Your are an American tourist about to fly to Germany, where you have signed a contract to pay 78,000 e for a new Mercedes. Are you happy or unhappy about the change in the exchange rate, and why?

5. You are an American tourist on vacation in Scotland. Wandering around Edinburgh, you find a small shop selling Shetland wool sweaters for £40. Before you left, you saw a very similar sweater in a shop in New York selling for $100. The exchange rate between the British pound and the U.S. dollar is £1 = $1.59.

   a. How many dollars does the sweater in Edinburgh cost?

   b. You decide that you can make some money by buying 20 sweaters in Edinburgh and selling them for $100 to your friends back home. You have just decided to engage in what economic practice? How much money do you expect to make from it?

   c. You have to buy an extra suitcase (for £30) to carry all those sweaters. When you get to the Edinburgh airport, you discover you have to pay £150 in excess baggage charges for the extra suitcase. How much potential profit do you have left?

   d. When you land back in New York, you discover that the United States has a tariff of $22 per sweater on Shetland wool sweaters imported into the United States. After you pay the tariff, how much profit do you make? Was it worth your time and effort?

If your instructor assigns these problems, write your answers above, then tear out this page and hand it in.

Answers

Quick-Check Quiz

Section 1: Prices and Exchange Rates

1. b; 2. a; 3. b; 4. a

If you answered c, d, or e to any of these questions, review Section 1.a of Chapter 17 in the text before going on: you need to become familiar with the terminology of foreign exchange.

If you answered a when the right answer was b, or b when the right answer was a, you know the correct terms but have the directions reversed; that's easy to do with foreign exchange problems. Go back through the examples in Sections 1 and 1.a of Chapter 17, go through the examples in the answers to Fundamental Questions 1 and 2 on pages 345–346 of this Study Guide, and then try the questions again.

5. c; 6. d; 7. a; 8. d; 9. d

If you missed any of questions 5 through 9, you should go back and review Section 1 of Chapter 17.

Section 2: Interest Rates and Exchange Rates

1. d; 2. d; 3. c; 4. c

If you missed any of these questions, you should go back and review Section 2 of Chapter 17.

Section 3: Policy Effects

1. b; 2. c; 3. c; 4. d; 5. d

If you missed any of these questions, you should go back and review Section 3 of Chapter 17.

Section 4: International Policy Coordination

1. d; 2. d

If you missed either of these questions, you should go back and review Section 4 of Chapter 17.

Practice Questions and Problems

Section 1: Prices and Exchange Rates

1. open
2. increases; decreases
3. a. £.67
   b. £.50
   c. appreciated (A pound buys *more* dollars than before.)
   d. depreciated (A dollar buys *fewer* pounds than before.)
   e. $225,000; $300,000; depreciated; more
      If the Rolls-Royce costs £150,000 and each pound cost an American $1.50 yesterday, the cost of the Rolls-Royce in dollars is £150,000 × $1.50 per pound = $225,000. If the Rolls-Royce costs £150,000 and each pound cost an American $2.00 today, the cost of the Rolls-Royce in dollars is £150,000 × $2.00 per pound = $300,000.
   f. £40 million; £30 million; depreciated; less
      If the Boeing airliner costs $60 million and the exchange rate was $1.50 per pound yesterday, the cost of the Boeing in pounds is $60 million/$1.50 per pound = £40 million. If the Boeing airliner

costs $60 million and the exchange rate is $2.00 per pound today, the cost of the Boeing in pounds is $60 million/$2.00 per pound = £30 million.
4. less; more
5. more; less
6. a. $450
   This is just the dollar value of £300 (£300 × $1.50 per pound).
   b. New York
   The price in dollars of gold is $400 in New York and $450 in London (answer a). For arbitrage to work, you must buy in the lower-price market and sell in the higher-price market.
   c. $1.65 = £1
   The number of dollars needed to buy a pound will increase by 10 percent of the old exchange rate [$1.50 + ($1.50 × 10 percent)].
7. a. e600
   b. Berlin
   e400 is equivalent to $200 (e400 × $.50 per e), so gold is cheaper in Berlin.
   c. $.60 = e1
   The number of dollars needed to buy a e will increase by 20 percent of the old exchange rate [$.50 + ($.50 × 20 percent)].
8. tariff
9. appreciates; depreciates

Section 2: Interest Rates and Exchange Rates

1. interest rate; exchange rate; exchange rate
2. interest rate parity
3. interest rate parity
4. government controls
   political risk
   different tax structures
5. a. Since IRP holds even though the present interest rates are different, there must be an expected change in the exchange rate between dollars and yen.
   b. People expect the dollar to appreciate relative to the yen: that's why people are willing to buy bonds denominated in dollars even though the interest rate is lower.
   c. Inflation is expected to be 5 percent higher in Japan than in the United States. The higher interest rate in Japan compensates people for the expected decrease in the value of the yen.
6. Interest rates will be higher in Mexico to compensate for the decrease in the value of the Mexican peso caused by inflation.
7. $i_\$ = i^F + \dfrac{E_2 - E_1}{E_1}$
8. capital controls
9. risk premium
10. $i_\$ = i^F + \dfrac{E_2 - E_1}{E_1}$

   $= .15 + \dfrac{6.8675 - 6.8955}{6.8955}$

   $= .1459394$ or 14.59 percent; appreciated

Section 3: Policy Effects

1. raise; appreciate
   More demand for borrowing increases interest rates; higher interest rates increase the demand for the dollar, raising the exchange rate.
2. lower; depreciate
   The same logic as above applies here, but in the opposite direction.
3. fewer; increase
4. Decreasing government borrowing would be expected to lower interest rates in the United States, causing a dollar depreciation and increased exports and lower imports.
5. increase
   Higher money growth usually leads to higher inflation.
6. exchange; interest

Section 4: International Policy Coordination

1. IMF: International Monetary Fund
   OECD: Organization for Economic Cooperation and Development
2. Canada France
   Germany Italy
   Japan United Kingdom
   United States
3. setting joint goals
   exchanging information
   forming and executing policy cooperatively
4. disagreements over goals
   disagreements over current economic conditions
   disagreements over macroeconomic theory

Thinking About and Applying Macroeconomic Links Between Countries

I. The Dollar and U.S. Interest Rates

appreciate; benefit; reduce

II. Investing Abroad

political; more; rise; decrease

Sample Test I
Chapters 12–17
(*Economics* Chapters 12–17)

1. When an increase in government spending increases interest rates and leads to a decline in investment, this is commonly referred to as
   a. the principle of Ricardian equivalence.
   b. the wealth effect.
   c. the real balance effect.
   d. the crowding-out effect.
   e. the balanced-budget effect.

2. The 1990s were characterized by
   a. increases in the national debt and the federal deficit as a percentage of U.S. GDP.
   b. large U.S. budget surpluses.
   c. a decline in the federal deficit as a percentage of U.S. GDP.
   d. a decline in U.S. interest payments as a percentage of government expenditures.
   e. rising U.S. net exports.

3. During a recession,
   a. tax revenues tend to rise and government spending tends to decline.
   b. the multiplier effect of an increase in government spending is diminished.
   c. tax revenues tend to fall and government spending tends to rise.
   d. automatic stabilizers become ineffective.
   e. transfer payments tend to be reduced.

4. Which tax system serves as an automatic stabilizer?
   a. regressive taxation
   b. proportional taxation
   c. lump-sum taxation
   d. marginal taxation
   e. progressive taxation

5. If government spending rises by $500 and taxes go up by $500, then, other things being equal,
   a. the government will create a fiscal deficit.
   b. crowding-out of private investment will occur.
   c. aggregate expenditures will rise.
   d. consumption spending will fall.
   e. equilibrium real GDP will remain unchanged.

6. When money is used to avoid the requirement of a double coincidence of wants, it serves as a
   a. store of value.
   b. medium of exchange.
   c. standard of deferred payment.
   d. unit of account.
   e. form of credit.

7. The U.S. dollar is accepted as money by Americans because it
   a. is fully backed by gold.
   b. constitutes commodity money.
   c. has an intrinsic value that exceeds its face value.
   d. is backed by silver certificates.
   e. has a fiduciary value.

8. M1 is the narrowest definition of the money supply because it
   a. excludes checking account deposits.
   b. primarily emphasizes the use of money as a store of value.
   c. consists only of coinage and currency in circulation.
   d. is the most accurate measure of purchasing power.
   e. includes only the most liquid of assets.

9. The Eurocurrency market is characterized by all of the following statements *except* which one?
   a. Transactions are less risky than in the domestic banking system.
   b. No deposit insurance is required.
   c. The spread is narrower than in the domestic banking system.
   d. Deposits and loans are denominated in a currency other than the currency of the country where the bank is located.
   e. The majority of transactions are denominated in Eurodollars.

10. If total deposits in the banking system equal $1,500,000 and the deposit expansion multiplier equals 5, then total required reserve holdings must be
    a. $7,500,000.
    b. $1,500,000.
    c. $1,200,000.
    d. $300,000.
    e. $150,000.

11. Suppose that Mr. Boyes deposits $5,000 in his local bank. The bank must hold 10 percent of all deposits on reserve. How much new money can this one bank create as a result of Mr. Boyes's deposit?
    a. $500
    b. $4,500
    c. $5,000
    d. $45,000
    e. $50,000

12. If the reserve requirement is 0.4, then an increase in excess reserves by $200,000 could expand the money supply by as much as
    a. $50,000.
    b. $80,000.
    c. $150,000.
    d. $200,000.
    e. $500,000.

13. When the Federal Reserve sells U.S. government bonds in the open market, then, other things being equal,
    a. the federal funds rate will decline.
    b. total reserves in the banking system will decline.
    c. the reserve requirement will rise.
    d. there is potential for the money supply to increase.
    e. the velocity of money will rise.

14. The money supply curve is a function of
    a. the interest rate.
    b. the demand for money.
    c. the policy actions of the Federal Reserve.
    d. the price level.
    e. investment spending.

15. Suppose the Federal Reserve engages in an open market operation that causes the money supply to increase. Other things being equal, this will result in
    a. an increase in aggregate demand; both the price level and real GDP will rise.
    b. a decrease in investment spending and an increase in the interest rate.
    c. a decrease in money demand.
    d. an increase in the aggregate supply curve; the price level will decrease and real GDP will rise.
    e. a decrease in the money supply.

Use the following figures to answer questions 16 and 17.

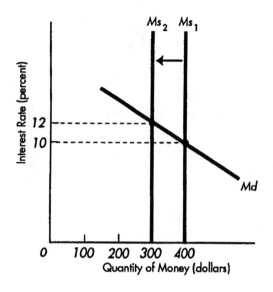
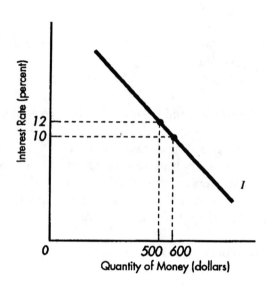
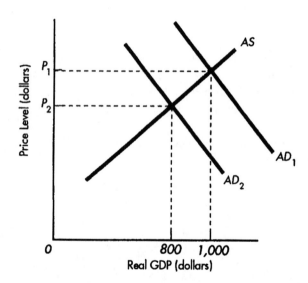

16. Other things being equal, if the money supply is reduced from Ms_1 to Ms_2, then
    a. there will be an excess supply of money at an interest rate of 10 percent.
    b. there will be a $100 decrease in investment expenditures.
    c. equilibrium real GDP will rise from $800 to $1,000.
    d. bond prices will rise, causing a 2 percent drop in the interest rate.
    e. the equilibrium price level will rise.

17. Suppose the shift from Ms_1 to Ms_2 was the result of an open market operation that created a reduction in the banking system's excess reserves of $50. If banks are always fully loaned up and Ms_2 is the new equilibrium money supply, then the deposit expansion multiplier for this economy must be
    a. 0.5.
    b. 1.0.
    c. 2.0.
    d. 5.0.
    e. 10.0.

18. When the money market is in equilibrium, then, other things being equal,
    a. money demand equals money supply.
    b. $V \cdot M > P \cdot Y$.
    c. the quantity of money demanded is no longer a function of the interest rate.
    d. the velocity of money will be zero.
    e. there will be an excess supply of government bonds.

19. Along the long-run Phillips curve,
    a. expected inflation is constant.
    b. there is a tradeoff between unemployment and inflation.
    c. the reservation wage is constant.
    d. equilibrium real GDP equals the natural rate of unemployment.
    e. aggregate supply is a horizontal line.

20. If workers expect more inflation than actually occurs,
    a. the short-run Phillips curve will shift to the left.
    b. the observed unemployment rate will exceed the natural rate of unemployment.
    c. there will be an immediate downward adjustment of the reservation wage.
    d. there will be demand-pull inflation.
    e. the Phillips curve will take the shape of a vertical line.

21. The belief that the Phillips curve may be vertical both in the short run and in the long run is consistent with the theory of
    a. time inconsistency.
    b. regressive expectations.
    c. adaptive expectations.
    d. rational expectations.
    e. Ricardian equivalence.

22. If tax revenues equal $400 billion, government borrowing equals $50 billion, and money growth equals $70 million, then government spending must equal
    a. $280 billion.
    b. $380 billion.
    c. $400 billion.
    d. $420 billion.
    e. $520 billion.

23. Monetarists would argue that
   a. the long-run Phillips curve is downward-sloping.
   b. wages and prices do not respond to changes in aggregate expenditures.
   c. time-consistent monetary and fiscal policy rules are necessary for stable economic growth.
   d. only discretionary government policy can lower the natural rate of unemployment.
   e. the aggregate supply is horizontal.

24. Assume that a British investor purchases a one-year U.S. government bond that offers a yield of 4 percent. Further suppose that a comparable British government bond would pay 6 percent interest. What must be the expected change in the pound/dollar exchange rate during the same one-year time period for interest rate parity to hold?
   a. The pound must appreciate by 2 percent against the dollar.
   b. The pound must depreciate by 10 percent against the dollar.
   c. The dollar must appreciate by 2 percent against the pound.
   d. The dollar must depreciate by 10 percent against the pound.
   e. The pound must depreciate by 6 percent against the dollar.

25. Suppose a cassette tape costs $10 in New York and e18 in Frankfurt, Germany. Then purchasing power parity would imply an exchange rate of
   a. $1 = e1.8.
   b. $1 = e1.
   c. e1 = $1.8.
   d. e1 = $0.8.
   e. $1 = e2.

Answers to Sample Test

1. d (Chapter 12, Section 1.e; *Economics* Chapter 12)
2. a (Chapter 12, Section 2.c; *Economics* Chapter 12)
3. c (Chapter 12, Section 2.d; *Economics* Chapter 12)
4. e (Chapter 12, Section 2.d; *Economics* Chapter 12)
5. c (Chapter 13, Section 1.c; *Economics* Chapter 13)
6. b (Chapter 13, Section 1.a; *Economics* Chapter 13)
7. e (Chapter 13, Section 1.b; *Economics* Chapter 13)
8. e (Chapter 13, Section 1.b; *Economics* Chapter 13)
9. a (Chapter 13, Section 2.c; *Economics* Chapter 13)
10. d (Chapter 13, Section 3.b; *Economics* Chapter 13)
11. b (Chapter 13, Section 3.b; *Economics* Chapter 13)
12. e (Chapter 13, Section 2.b; *Economics* Chapter 13)
13. b (Chapter 14, Section 2.b; *Economics* Chapter 14)
14. c (Chapter 14, Section 3.a; *Economics* Chapter 14)
15. a (Chapter 14, Section 3.b; *Economics* Chapter 14)
16. b (Chapter 14, Section 3.b; *Economics* Chapter 14)
17. c (Chapter 14, Section 3.b; *Economics* Chapter 14)
18. a (Chapter 14, Section 3.b; *Economics* Chapter 14)
19. d (Chapter 15, Section 1.b; *Economics* Chapter 15)
20. b (Chapter 15, Section 2.a; *Economics* Chapter 15)
21. d (Chapter 15, Section 2.b; *Economics* Chapter 15)
22. e (Chapter 15, Section 5.a; *Economics* Chapter 15)
23. c (Chapter 16, Section 2.b; *Economics* Chapter 16)
24. c (Chapter 17, Section 2.b; *Economics* Chapter 17)
25. a (Chapter 17, Section 1.b; *Economics* Chapter 17)

Sample Test II
Chapters 12–17
(*Economics* Chapters 12–17)

1. Suppose that a recessionary gap exists. An appropriate fiscal policy would be to
   a. reduce the fiscal deficit.
   b. lower taxes.
   c. increase interest rates.
   d. lower the money supply.
   e. decrease government spending.

2. If other things are equal, then the effect of an increase in income taxes on GDP is magnified
   a. the steeper the aggregate supply curve.
   b. the stronger the crowding-out effect.
   c. the larger *MPS + MPI*.
   d. the lower the inflation rate.
   e. the larger the recessionary gap.

3. If someone earning $10,000 pays $1,000 in income taxes and someone earning $25,000 pays $2,000 in income taxes, the tax structure is
   a. progressive.
   b. proportional.
   c. balanced.
   d. unfair.
   e. regressive.

4. Automatic stabilizers
   a. increase aggregate expenditures when the economy is in an expansion.
   b. are effective only in conjunction with discretionary fiscal policy.
   c. cause larger budget deficits during recessions.
   d. magnify business cycle fluctuations.
   e. are stronger when the personal income tax is regressive.

5. Suppose that the government tries to close a GDP gap through increased fiscal borrowing. This is likely to lead to
   a. a lower national debt.
   b. a depreciation of the domestic currency.
   c. higher interest rates.
   d. an increase in domestic net exports.
   e. a decrease in domestic saving.

6. The idea that government debt financing causes individuals to save more and to consume less today because of expected future tax increases is called
   a. the crowding-out effect.
   b. the Ricardian equivalence effect.
   c. the balanced-budget effect.
   d. the automatic-stabilizer effect.
   e. the real balance effect.

7. The role of money as a medium of exchange results from
   a. a reduction in transaction costs compared to barter exchanges.
   b. a reduction in information costs compared to credit exchanges.
   c. a reduction in exchange rate risk compared to credit exchanges.
   d. a reduction in liquidity compared to barter exchanges.
   e. a reduction in inflation risk compared to barter exchanges.

Consider the following table for questions 8 and 9.

	Billions
ATS accounts	$ 50
Currency	500
Small-denomination time deposits	110
NOW accounts	240
Savings accounts	195
Large-denomination time deposits	145
Demand deposits	360

8. What is M1?
   a. $790
   b. $860
   c. $1,150
   d. $1,260
   e. $1,455

9. M3 exceeds M2 by
   a. $0.
   b. $145.
   c. $255.
   d. $450.
   e. $535.

10. Composite currencies
    a. constitute a weighted average of a country's official and black-market exchange rates.
    b. are used exclusively for sales transactions between industrial and developing countries.
    c. are composed of the international reserves of various industrial countries.
    d. are used as a medium of exchange in most European countries.
    e. serve to reduce foreign exchange rate risk compared to single currencies.

11. Required reserves are equal to
    a. a bank's demand deposits.
    b. the inverse of the deposit expansion multiplier.
    c. total reserves minus excess reserves.
    d. cash reserves minus new loans.
    e. the reserve requirement times excess reserves.

12. Suppose that the reserve requirement equals 0.20 and total reserves in the banking system equal $120 billion. What is the total amount of bank deposits if the banking system is completely loaned up?
    a. $0 billion
    b. $24 billion
    c. $96 billion
    d. $120 billion
    e. $600 billion

Suppose that First Federal Bank has demand deposits of $4,500,000, total reserves of $1,000,000, and required reserves of $450,000.

13. What is the deposit expansion multiplier in this scenario?
    a. 0.1
    b. 1.0
    c. 2.0
    d. 4.5
    e. 10

14. What is the maximum amount of money by which First Federal Bank can increase the money supply, given the scenario in question 13?
    a. $0
    b. $100,000
    c. $550,000
    d. $2,475,000
    e. $5,500,000

15. If other things are equal, the real GDP will decline when
    a. the reserve requirement falls.
    b. government bonds are sold by the Fed.
    c. the discount rate is lowered.
    d. interest rates fall.
    e. the velocity of money increases.

16. Suppose that the current price of one U.S. dollar is e1.6. If the Fed has an exchange rate target at a minimum of e1.75 = $1 and it engages in a sterilized intervention, then the Fed will
    a. buy U.S. currency in the foreign exchange market and purchase U.S. government bonds in the domestic open market.
    b. buy euros in the foreign exchange market and sell U.S. government bonds in the domestic open market.
    c. buy U.S. currency in the foreign exchange market and sell U.S. government bonds in the domestic open market.
    d. sell U.S. currency in the foreign exchange market and buy U.S. government bonds in the domestic open market.
    e. sell euros in the foreign exchange market and sell U.S. government bonds in the domestic open market.

17. If interest rates fall,
    a. the money supply will decrease.
    b. money demand will rise.
    c. aggregate demand will fall.
    d. the quantity of money demanded will rise.
    e. the opportunity cost of holding money will rise.

18. If the money supply decreases, we would expect the following:
    a. Decrease in money demand → increase in interest rates → decrease in investment spending.
    b. Increase in the quantity of money demanded → decrease in interest rates → increase in aggregate demand.
    c. Decrease in the quantity of money demanded → decrease in bond prices → decrease in national income.
    d. Increase in interest rates → increase in investment spending → increase in aggregate demand.
    e. Increase in money demand → decrease in the price of bonds → decrease in investment spending.

19. If national income and the price level decline at the same time,
    a. the economy has moved down the short-run Phillips curve.
    b. there is demand-pull inflation.
    c. the Phillips curve has shifted to the right.
    d. the aggregate supply curve has shifted to the right.
    e. there is a tradeoff between inflation and unemployment.

20. A vertical Phillips curve implies that
    a. monetary and fiscal policies have no effect on real GDP.
    b. expectations are formed adaptively.
    c. the aggregate supply curve is horizontal.
    d. government policy suffers from time inconsistency.
    e. the economy is no longer subject to real business cycle fluctuations.

21. If there are long-term wage contracts in place, then in the short run, an unexpected increase in the inflation rate will
    a. raise the unemployment rate.
    b. result in a movement up the downward-sloping Phillips curve.
    c. decrease business revenues.
    d. have no effect on the unemployment rate.
    e. increase the real wage rate.

22. New classical economists
    a. believe that the use of fiscal policy is necessary to stabilize the economy.
    b. advocate the use of monetary policy to attain long-term economic growth.
    c. disagree with the Keynesian view of a vertical aggregate supply curve.
    d. believe that the economy tends toward the natural rate of unemployment.
    e. advocate lower income tax rates to stimulate the economy.

23. If other things are equal, an increase in government spending financed by money creation will lead to
    a. a decrease in domestic net exports.
    b. lower domestic inflation.
    c. arbitrage opportunities for speculators.
    d. an increase in domestic interest rates.
    e. a depreciation of the domestic currency.

24. Suppose that at the beginning of the year a Lexus 400 sells for $42,750 in Houston, Texas, and for SF60,000 in Zurich, Switzerland. Over the year, there is an inflation rate of 5 percent in the United States and zero percent inflation in Switzerland. If PPP holds at all times, what must be the exchange rate at the end of the year?
    a. $0.78 = SF1
    b. $0.75 = SF1
    c. $1.33 = SF1
    d. $5.0 = SF1
    e. $0.05 = SF1

25. Other things being equal, if the U.S. dollar appreciates against the British pound,
    a. U.S. net exports will rise relative to British net exports.
    b. the British inflation rate will fall relative to the U.S. inflation rate to maintain PPP.
    c. the U.S. interest rate will fall relative to the British interest rate to maintain IRP.
    d. the U.S. money supply will grow relative to the British money supply.
    e. demand for U.S. goods and services will rise relative to the demand for British goods and services.

Answers to Sample Test

1. b (Chapter 12, Section 1.a; *Economics* Chapter 12)
2. d (Chapter 12, Section 1.a; *Economics* Chapter 12)
3. e (Chapter 12, Section 2.d; *Economics* Chapter 12)
4. c (Chapter 12, Section 2.d; *Economics* Chapter 12)
5. c (Chapter 12, Section 2.c; *Economics* Chapter 12)
6. b (Chapter 12, Section 1.d; *Economics* Chapter 12)
7. a (Chapter 13, Section 1.a; *Economics* Chapter 13)
8. c (Chapter 13, Section 1.b; *Economics* Chapter 13)
9. b (Chapter 13, Section 1.b; *Economics* Chapter 13)
10. e (Chapter 13, Section 1.c; *Economics* Chapter 13)
11. c (Chapter 13, Section 3.a; *Economics* Chapter 13)
12. e (Chapter 13, Section 3.a; *Economics* Chapter 13)
13. e (Chapter 13, Section 3.b; *Economics* Chapter 13)
14. c (Chapter 13, Section 3.b; *Economics* Chapter 13)
15. b (Chapter 14, Section 2.b; *Economics* Chapter 14)
16. a (Chapter 14, Section 2.c; *Economics* Chapter 14)
17. d (Chapter 14, Section 3.a; *Economics* Chapter 14)
18. c (Chapter 14, Section 3.b; *Economics* Chapter 14)
19. a (Chapter 15, Section 1.b; *Economics* Chapter 15)
20. a (Chapter 15, Section 4.a; *Economics* Chapter 15)
21. b (Chapter 15, Section 2.a; *Economics* Chapter 15)
22. d (Chapter 16, Section 3.a; *Economics* Chapter 16)
23. e (Chapter 17, Section 3.b; *Economics* Chapter 17)
24. b (Chapter 17, Section 3.c; *Economics* Chapter 17)
25. c (Chapter 17, Section 2.b; *Economics* Chapter 17)

Chapter 18

ECONOMIC GROWTH

FUNDAMENTAL QUESTIONS

1. What is economic growth?

   Economists define **economic growth** as an increase in real national income, usually measured in terms of the percentage increase in real gross national product (GNP) or real gross domestic product (GDP). An alternative way of defining economic growth, one that more clearly shows growth's effects on individual people, is to look at growth as the percentage increase in the **per capita real GDP:** to look at changes in real GDP per person in the economy. After all, if real GDP increases 5 percent at the same time population increases 5 percent, real GDP may be higher, but the people in the economy are no better off than before: the increase in output is only enough to keep everyone at the same level as before. In this case, per capita real GDP would show no growth.

   Although growth in per capita real GDP shows us how much is available to consume per person, it does not tell us everything about people's standards of living; we also need to look at income distribution and the quality of life. If all of the increase in output goes to a small proportion of the people within a country, most people's standard of living will be unchanged. If economic growth is accompanied by large decreases in environmental quality (more pollution, less wilderness, and so forth), many people may feel that their quality of life has decreased rather than increased.

2. How are economic growth rates determined?

   Economic growth means a shift rightward of the aggregate supply curve, increasing the potential output of the economy. A country's economic growth rate is determined by the factors that determine the aggregate supply curve: the amount of productive resources available and technology. The faster the growth of productive resources and technological advancement, the higher a country's growth rate will be.

3. What is productivity?

   Productivity is one way to look at the impact of advances in **technology** on economic growth. Productivity is the ratio of output produced to the amount of input used. Improvements in technology mean that productivity increases as we find new and better ways to use inputs to produce output. More specifically, **total factor productivity** (TFP) is a nation's output divided by its stock of labor and capital. Economic growth is the sum of the growth rate of total factor productivity and the growth rate of available resources.

4. Why has U.S. productivity changed?

The growth rate of total factor productivity (TFP) in the United States has decreased over the last several decades. Between 1948 and 1965, TFP grew at an average annual rate of about 2 percent. Since the 1970s, TFP growth has averaged less than 1 percent per year. Several changes in the U.S. economy help account for this drop, including a drop in the quality of the U.S. labor force; a drop-off in technological innovation, as shown by the decrease in the number of **patents** issued to U.S. firms; increases in energy prices; and the shift from manufacturing to service industries.

Key Terms

economic growth
rule of 72

per capita real GDP
technology

total factor productivity (TFP)
patent

Quick-Check Quiz

Section 1: Defining Economic Growth

1. Economic growth is defined as an increase in
    a. nominal GDP.
    b. real GDP.
    c. real national inputs.
    d. nominal national inputs.
    e. real government expenditures.

2. Economic growth is usually measured as the
    a. absolute increase in real GNP or GDP.
    b. nominal increase in real GNP or GDP.
    c. percentage increase in real GNP or GDP.
    d. marginal increase in real GNP or GDP.
    e. total increase in real GNP or GDP.

3. For a country with a constant rate of growth, the time required for real GDP to double can be found by using the rule of
    a. net interest.
    b. 100.
    c. 10.
    d. 72.
    e. total interest.

4. Per capita real GDP is real GDP divided by
   a. nominal national income.
   b. real GNP.
   c. 72.
   d. government expenditures.
   e. population.

Section 2: The Determinants of Growth

1. In terms of the aggregate demand–aggregate supply model, economic growth is shown as a(n)
   a. rightward shift in the aggregate demand curve.
   b. rightward shift in the aggregate supply curve.
   c. leftward shift in the aggregate demand curve.
   d. leftward shift in the aggregate supply curve.
   e. upward shift in both aggregate demand and aggregate supply.

2. An abundance of natural resources
   a. is always necessary for economic growth.
   b. is necessary for economic growth only in capitalist countries.
   c. is necessary for economic growth only in developing countries.
   d. has no effect on economic growth.
   e. can contribute to economic growth but is not necessary for growth.

3. Growth in a country's capital stock is tied to
   a. increases in the amounts of natural resources available.
   b. current and future saving.
   c. improvements in technology.
   d. increases in the amount of labor available.
   e. decreases in the labor force participation ratio.

4. Which of the following is *not* one of the determinants of economic growth?
   a. the size and quality of the labor force
   b. the amount of capital goods available
   c. technology
   d. natural resources
   e. the shape of the aggregate demand curve

Section 3: Productivity

1. Total factor productivity is the ratio of
   a. a firm's marginal revenue to its marginal cost.
   b. a firm's total revenues to its total costs.
   c. a nation's total income divided by its total output.
   d. a nation's output to its stock of labor and capital.
   e. a nation's labor supply to its capital stock.

2. Economic growth is the sum of
   a. total factor productivity and resources.
   b. total factor productivity and marginal factor productivity.
   c. growth in total factor productivity and growth in resources.
   d. real GDP and national output.
   e. GNP and GDP.

3. From 1948 to the early 1990s, total factor productivity in the United States
   a. increased at a constant rate.
   b. decreased at a constant rate.
   c. increased, but at a slower and slower rate.
   d. increased, but at a faster and faster rate.
   e. decreased, but at an uneven rate.

4. Which of the following is *not* one of the reasons why U.S. labor quality may have fallen in recent years?
   a. reduced quality of education
   b. increased numbers of inexperienced workers in the work force as the baby boomers entered the work force
   c. increased numbers of inexperienced workers in the work force as more women and immigrants entered the work force
   d. changes in attitudes toward work
   e. increases in the number of days lost to illness

Practice Questions and Problems

Section 1: Defining Economic Growth

1. Economic growth is an increase in _____ , usually measured as a percentage change in _____ or _____ .

2. Small differences in rates of growth are magnified over time because growth is _____ .

3. In 1999, the real GNP of the country of Lalaland was 200 million lals; in 2000, the real GNP was 210 million lals. What was the growth rate in Lalaland in 2000?
   a. 10 million
   b. 10 percent
   c. 5 percent
   d. 4.76 percent
   e. .05 percent

4. The income of the town of Kennebunkport has been growing by 3 percent per year. If this growth continues into the future, how long will it take until the town's income has doubled?
   a. about 33 years
   b. about 24 years
   c. about 2 years
   d. about 3 years
   e. about 216 years

5. Per capita real GDP is _____ divided by _____ .

6. The table below shows the GDP and population in 1999 and 2000 in Aaaland and Zeeland (all figures are in millions).

Country	1999 Real GDP	1999 Population	2000 Real GDP	2000 Population
Aaaland	20,000	25	20,600	25
Zeeland	40,000	40	42,000	41

a. Calculate the growth rates in GDP and in GDP per capita for the two countries.

Aaaland: GDP growth rate: _____

   GDP per capita growth rate: _____

Zeeland: GDP growth rate: _____

   GDP per capita growth rate: _____

b. Which country is growing faster? Explain.

_____

_____

7. Looking at growth rates in GNP or GDP per capita does not give you a complete picture of the standard of living in different countries. What important factors are not included in the GNP or GDP per capita figures?

_____

_____

Section 2: The Determinants of Growth

1. Economic growth shifts the aggregate _____ (demand, supply) curve to the _____ (right, left).

2. The long-run growth of the economy rests on growth in productive resources such as _____ , _____ , and _____ and on advances in _____ .

3. The size of a country's labor force is determined by the _____ and the _____ of the population in the labor force.

4. Growth in a country's capital stock depends on current and future _____ .

5. Technology is ways of combining _____ to produce _____ .

6. What are two factors that cause developing countries to lag behind in the development and implementation of new technology?

_____

_____

Section 3: Productivity

1. Productivity is the ratio of _____ to the amount of _____ .

2. _____ is the nation's real GDP divided by its stock of labor and capital.

3. In the United States, labor receives about 70 percent of national income and capital receives about 30 percent. If total factor productivity increases by 1 percent, labor increases by 1 percent, and capital increases by 3 percent, by what percentage will national income increase? _____

4. A _____ is a legal document that gives an inventor the legal rights to an invention.

5. List four factors that may help explain why productivity in the United States has grown more slowly in recent years.

   _____
   _____
   _____
   _____

Thinking About and Applying Economic Growth

I. Quality of Life and Economic Growth

One of the issues discussed in this chapter has been the difficulties of using standard measures of economic growth (growth in GDP or growth in GDP per capita) to show changes in the well-being of people. The effects on economic well-being of growth in GDP per capita does not take into account the distribution of income or quality-of-life issues such as pollution. When economic growth increases pollution, most people would agree that people are not really as much better off as the economic growth statistics show. Conversely, increases in the quality of life may not show up in the economic growth figures.

Since the middle 1960s, people have become more concerned about the environment and pollution. One of the ways the U.S. government has responded to this concern is by passing laws requiring businesses to install pollution control equipment. As a result of these laws and other factors, the air and water in most of the United States are substantially cleaner now than they were ten or fifteen years ago. Although most of us would agree that cleaner air and water improve our quality of life, this improvement does not show up in the economic growth statistics. In fact, environmental improvements can result in lower measured economic growth. Let's take a look at the reasons for this.

1. Suppose that the Best-Yet Whatchamacallit Company has saved $1 million. Best-Yet was planning to use the money to buy a machine that would produce an additional $2 million worth of whatchamacallits every year for ten years. However, the government just passed a law requiring Best-Yet to buy $1 million worth of pollution control equipment to eliminate the horrible-smelling green smoke that the factory emits. Figure out the following:

   a. Effect on real GDP of an extra $2 million worth of whatchamacallits produced per year: _____

b. Effect on real GDP of elimination of horrible-smelling green smoke:

_____

2. Buying the whatchamacallit machine will _____ (raise, lower) total factor productivity.

3. Buying the pollution control equipment will _____ (raise, lower) total factor productivity.

4. Compare the timing of the decline in TFP growth in the United States and the environmental movement in the United States. Is there any possible connection? If there is, do you think productivity has really slowed down as much as the statistics show?

_____

_____

_____

_____

II. Government Policy and Growth

Government policies that hold down interest rates have adverse effects on economic growth in developing countries. Although low interest rates are intended to make it cheaper for local businesses to invest in new capital goods, they have the effect of drying up the supply of savings, since savers can get a higher return by taking their money out of the country or by making less productive investments on their own. Similar policies are sometimes followed in other economic sectors, with similarly bad results.

For example, many developing countries require farmers to sell their crops to the government, which resells the food to city dwellers. To keep the city dwellers happy, the prices charged for food are set very low, as are the prices paid to farmers. Think about the farmers' opportunity costs of growing food for sale, and predict what is likely to happen to the food supply in countries adopting this policy.

_____

_____

_____

_____

Chapter 18   Homework Problems

Name _____

1. a. What economic statistic would you look at to judge whether a country's economy has been growing over time?

   b. What economic statistic would you look at to judge whether the individual people in a country have had a rising standard of living?

2. How can you show economic growth in the aggregate demand–aggregate supply model, and what causes economic growth?

3. What changes in the U.S. economy can explain why productivity grew much more slowly from 1973 to the late 1990s than it did in previous years?

4. The population of the island of South Hamilton is growing at 5 percent per year. The real GDP of South Hamilton is growing at 8 percent per year. How many years will it take before the per capita GDP of the residents of South Hamilton doubles?

5. You have been hired by the United Nations to measure the economic well-being of the residents of two islands, East Podunk and West Podunk. You have the following data:

	East Podunk	West Podunk
1995 GDP	$247,000,000	$136,000,000
2000 GDP	$298,000,000	$175,000,000
1995 population	28,670	14,786
2000 population	30,421	17,172

Use all this information to evaluate which country is doing better economically.

If your instructor assigns these problems, write your answers above, then tear out this page and hand it in.

Answers

Quick-Check Quiz

Section 1: Defining Economic Growth

1. b; 2. c; 3. d; 4. e
If you missed any of these questions, you should go back and review Section 1 of Chapter 18.

Section 2: The Determinants of Growth

1. b; 2. e; 3. b; 4. e
If you missed any of these questions, you should go back and review Section 2 of Chapter 18.

Section 3: Productivity

1. d; 2. c; 3. e; 4. e
If you missed any of these questions, you should go back and review Section 3 of Chapter 18.

Practice Questions and Problems

Section 1: Defining Economic Growth

1. real national income; GNP; GDP
2. compounded
3. c is correct. The growth rate is calculated this way:

$$\text{Growth rate} = \frac{\text{change in real GDP over year}}{\text{real GDP in beginning year}} \times 100$$

$$\text{For Lalaland, growth rate} = \frac{(210 - 200)}{200} \times 100 = 5 \text{ percent}$$

   If you chose answer a, you found the amount of growth, not the growth rate. If you chose answer b, you must have thought that the actual change was the same as the percentage change. If you chose answer d, you used the GDP in the ending year (2000) rather than the GDP in the beginning year (1999). If you chose answer e, you forgot to multiply by 100 to convert the answer into a percentage.

4. b is correct. You should use the rule of 72 to find the length of time to double income. Divide 72 by the percentage growth rate to find the time to double. In this case, 72/3 = 24, or 24 years to double the town's income.

   If you chose answer a, you forgot about the effect of compounding. The rule of 72 is just a shorthand way to look at compound growth. If you chose answer c or d, you need to review Sections 1.a.1 and 1.a.2. If you chose answer e, you multiplied the growth rate times 72 instead of dividing the growth rate into 72.

5. real GDP; population
6. a. Aaaland: GDP growth rate: 3 percent
   GDP per capita growth rate: 3 percent

   Zeeland: GDP growth rate: 5 percent
   GDP per capita growth rate: 2.4 percent

To calculate the GDP growth rate, see Section 1, question 3 above. To calculate the GDP per capita growth rate, you first need to calculate GDP per capita in both years; then you find the growth rate the same way you found the growth rate for GDP.

Aaaland: GDP per capita in 1999 is 20,000/25 = 800
           GDP per capita in 2000 is 20,600/25 = 824

GDP per capita growth rate = (24/800) × 100 = 3 percent

Zeeland: GDP per capita in 1999 is 40,000/40 = 1,000
           GDP per capita in 2000 is 42,000/41 = 1,024

GDP per capita growth rate = (24/1,000) × 100 = 2.4 percent

 b. Which country is growing faster depends on which statistic you want to look at. Aaaland's GDP per capita is growing faster, but Zeeland's GDP is growing faster. The size of Zeeland's economy is growing faster, but the average standard of living in Aaaland is growing faster.

7. income distribution
   quality of life

Section 2: The Determinants of Growth

1. supply; right
2. labor; capital; natural resources; technology
3. working-age population; participation
4. saving
5. resources; output
6. low levels of education
   limited financial resources (capital)

Section 3: Productivity

1. output produced; inputs
2. Total factor productivity
3. 2.6 percent
   Growth is growth in TFP plus growth in each resource × that resource's share of national income. For this case, growth = 1 (TFP growth) + .7 (1 percent growth in labor × labor's .7 share of national income) + .9 (3 percent growth in capital × capital's .3 share of national income).
4. patent
5. lower-quality labor force
   fewer technological innovations
   higher energy prices
   shift from manufacturing to service industries

Thinking About and Applying Economic Growth

I. Quality of Life and Economic Growth

1. a. increases real GDP by $2 million (assuming that the resources used, such as the $1 million in savings, would not otherwise be used elsewhere in the economy)
   b. no effect on real GDP (since green smoke is not bought and sold through markets)

2. raise

   Buying the whatchamacallit machine increases output by $2 million and the capital stock by $1 million. Output is in the numerator of the TFP equation, and capital is in the denominator. Since the numerator (the top part) of the ratio increased by more than the denominator (the bottom part), TFP will increase.

3. lower

   Buying the pollution control equipment increases the capital stock but does not increase output (as measured by GDP). Since the numerator is unchanged and the denominator increased, the ratio is smaller: investing in pollution control equipment makes TFP decrease.

4. The timing of the decline in TFP growth matches the timing of increases in investments in pollution control equipment. Although the amount spent on pollution control is not large enough to explain all of the decrease in the growth of TFP, it may account for some of the drop. Since we have a cleaner environment, pollution control equipment is doing something worthwhile, even though it does not show up in the standard economic statistics.

II. Government Policy and Growth

If the price paid for food crops is low enough, farmers will decide to do something else with their resources than grow food crops. They may switch to cash crops sold for export or just take more leisure, growing only enough to feed themselves and their families. Either way, the amount of food produced for sale to city dwellers will drop substantially. The low prices charged to city dwellers will not help them much when there is no food available for sale.

Chapter 19

DEVELOPMENT ECONOMICS

FUNDAMENTAL QUESTIONS

1. **How is poverty measured?**

   Although most of us have an idea of what it means to be poor, measuring poverty is not easy, partly because there are two different ways of looking at poverty. Poverty can be defined in an *absolute* sense: you are poor if your income is below a specified level. Poverty can also be defined in a *relative* sense: if your income is much less than the income of those around you, you feel poor. In the United States, for example, the poverty level is calculated by the federal government; in 1999, a family of four was poor if its income was less than $16,895. Most of the people in the world would feel quite well off if they received that high an income.

   When comparing countries, the usual measure of people's standard of living is per capita GNP. The World Bank uses a per capita GNP of less than $760 as its standard for poverty. Other measures aim at the quality of life in different countries, using measures such as life expectancy, infant mortality, literacy, and other things that reflect a people's standard of living.

2. **Why are some countries poorer than others?**

   Although the industrialized, "First World" countries have shown that economic growth and development are possible and that countries can maintain a high average standard of living, most "Third World" countries have not been able to follow in their footsteps. Several common factors have been found in many developing countries that help explain their lack of growth. These factors can be grouped into political obstacles and social obstacles.

   Political obstacles include a lack of skilled government officials, political instability and risks of **expropriation,** corruption, and constraints imposed on governments by special-interest groups. Social obstacles include cultural attitudes that discourage business and entrepreneurial activities, and rapid population growth, which can reduce the amount of capital per worker and can divert resources away from uses that promote economic growth.

3. **What strategies can a nation use to increase its economic growth?**

   In terms of trade with other nations, most developing countries have a natural comparative advantage only in **primary products** such as agricultural products and minerals. Countries whose governments have wanted to encourage economic development have tried to shift resources from primary sectors to industrialized, manufacturing sectors in the belief that industrialization is necessary for economic development.

   The two basic industrialization strategies followed by developing countries are known as inward-oriented development (followed by most developing countries) and outward-oriented development (followed by South Korea, Taiwan, Hong Kong, and Singapore). Inward-oriented development focuses on **import substitution:** developing a domestic manufacturing sector to produce goods that replace imports. Outward-oriented development focuses on **export substitution:** developing a domestic manufacturing sector that can produce goods for export. In general, the countries that have chosen outward-oriented strategies have been more successful.

4. How are savings in one nation used to speed development in other nations?

   In any country, savings are used to pay for investments in capital goods. Developing countries typically have such low levels of income that saving is difficult if not impossible. In order to buy capital goods, these countries must use other countries' savings. Foreign investment in developing countries can be by private sources or in the form of foreign aid from other governments. Foreign investment can increase economic growth by creating new jobs, transferring modern technology, or stimulating exports.

5. What microeconomic issues are involved in the transition from socialism?

   Prices and incomes must be removed from government determination. Instead, markets determine prices and incomes. Government-owned businesses must be **privatized** (transferred to the private sector). Because these changes can lead to temporary unemployment and rising prices, the government must provide a social safety net during the transition period.

6. What macroeconomic issues are involved in the transition from socialism?

   Macroeconomic stabilization must be achieved before microeconomic reforms can be undertaken effectively. To achieve stabilization, **monetary overhangs** must be eliminated, free **currency convertibility** must be implemented, and credit must be allocated on a market basis. The objective of monetary policy is a low, stable rate of inflation. Fiscal policy should avoid larger budget deficits.

Key Terms

expropriation
primary product
import substitution
export substitution
terms of trade
dual economy

foreign direct investment
portfolio investment
commercial bank loan
trade credit
foreign aid
bilateral aid

multilateral aid
privatize
monetary overhang
currency convertibility

Quick-Check Quiz

Section 1: The Developing World

1. According to the World Bank, a country is below the poverty level if its per capita GNP is less than
   a. $14,763.
   b. $6,550.
   c. $2,100.
   d. $760.
   e. $155.

2. Which of the following is *not* one of the standard ways to measure the economic progress of a country?
   a. per capita GNP
   b. life expectancy at birth
   c. percentage of the population involved in natural resource production
   d. infant mortality
   e. literacy rate

Section 2: Obstacles to Growth

1. Political obstacles to growth include all of the following *except*
   a. government workers' lack of administrative skills.
   b. political instability.
   c. lack of property rights protection.
   d. control by the military.
   e. corruption.

2. Social obstacles to growth include all of the following *except*
   a. decision-making systems based on tradition.
   b. a lack of entrepreneurs.
   c. capital shallowing caused by rapid population growth.
   d. reduced savings caused by large numbers of children.
   e. property rights structures that prevent expropriation.

3. Expropriation is
   a. government seizure of assets, typically without adequate compensation to the owners.
   b. government purchase of assets at their market price.
   c. seizure of the government by the military.
   d. restriction of immigration to discourage immigrant entrepreneurs.
   e. restriction of immigration to encourage local entrepreneurs.

4. In many developing countries, entrepreneurs are usually
   a. immigrants or descendants of recent immigrants.
   b. native residents from the traditional leadership groups.
   c. low-ranking members of the military.
   d. members of groups supporting traditional values that discourage change.
   e. people who believe that poverty is a virtue.

Section 3: Development Strategies

1. The economic development strategy aimed at replacing imports with domestically manufactured goods is known as
   a. replacement oriented.
   b. substitution oriented.
   c. inward oriented.
   d. outward oriented.
   e. domestically oriented.

2. The economic development strategy aimed at exporting domestically manufactured goods is known as
   a. replacement oriented.
   b. substitution oriented.
   c. inward oriented.
   d. outward oriented.
   e. domestically oriented.

3. An economy with two sectors that show very different levels of development is called a
   a. dual economy.
   b. double-level economy.
   c. differentiated economy.
   d. split-level economy.
   e. divided economy.

Section 4: Foreign Investment and Aid

1. Which of the following is *not* a form of private foreign investment?
   a. multilateral aid
   b. foreign direct investment
   c. portfolio investment
   d. commercial bank loans
   e. trade credit

2. Which of the following is *not* one of the benefits of foreign investment?
   a. creation of new jobs
   b. transfer of technology
   c. increased earnings from exports
   d. reduced need for education
   e. transfer of information

Section 5: Economies in Transition from Socialism

1. The process of transforming state-owned enterprises to private ownership is called
   a. privatization.
   b. reorganization.
   c. restoration.
   d. transmogrification.
   e. resale.

2. For a market system to make efficient decisions, prices must be
   a. fixed at an efficient level by government.
   b. adjusted by government to move the economy toward efficiency.
   c. free to react to changes in demand and supply.
   d. free of the constraints of demand and supply.
   e. limited to changes within a small range.

3. A social safety net must be provided during the transition to capitalism because
   a. the transition may upset the balance in people's lives.
   b. government workers may experience mental illness.
   c. political refugees from socialism may overwhelm the market.
   d. the transition will cause temporary unemployment and higher prices.
   e. capitalism needs to be protected from any remaining socialists within the country.

4. The large amounts of money that households in a socialist economy may have accumulated because there was little available that they wanted to buy is called a
   a. monetary hangover.
   b. resource surplus.
   c. monetary surplus.
   d. real balance.
   e. monetary overhang.

5. During the transition, a low, stable rate of inflation should be achieved through the use of
   a. fiscal policy.
   b. direct price controls.
   c. indirect price controls.
   d. monetary policy.
   e. controls on wages and output.

6. Which of the following statements regarding the sequencing of reforms is correct?
   a. Macroeconomic reform is necessary before conversion to a market system.
   b. Conversion to a market system is necessary before attempting macroeconomic reform.
   c. Because microeconomic reforms tend to reinforce one another, they generally should be carried out simultaneously.
   d. Both a and c are correct.
   e. Both b and c are correct.

Practice Questions and Problems

Section 1: The Developing World

1. Poverty can be defined in a(n) _____ sense, for example, by a specified minimum amount of income, or in a(n) _____ sense, for example, by how one's income compares with the average income in one's area.

2. The World Bank uses a _____ of less than $760 as its standard for defining poverty. This standard is a(n) _____ (relative, absolute) measure of poverty.
3. Life expectancy, infant mortality rates, and other similar measures are called _____ measures of economic progress.

Section 2: Obstacles to Growth

1. Obstacles to growth can be grouped into _____ and _____ obstacles.
2. To encourage private investment and economic development, governments must protect _____ .
3. _____ is the seizure of private property without compensation by the government.
4. Societies that make decisions based on tradition usually lack _____ , who are willing to take risks to gain profits.
5. Explain why each of the following effects of rapid population growth can have a negative effect on economic growth:

    a. capital shallowing: _____

    b. age dependency: _____

    c. investment diversion: _____

6. According to the World Bank, population growth rates above _____ percent act as a brake on economic development.

Section 3: Development Strategies

1. Most economic development efforts aim at replacing exports of _____ products like minerals or agricultural products with manufactured products.
2. The amount of exports that must be exchanged for some amount of imports is the _____ .
3. Inward-oriented development strategies focus on building an _____ (import, export) substitution manufacturing sector.
4. Outward-oriented development strategies focus on building an _____ (import, export) substitution manufacturing sector.
5. Countries using _____ (inward, outward)-oriented development strategies have shown higher growth rates.
6. A _____ product is a product in the first stage of production, which often serves as an input in the production of some other good.

7. _____ refers to replacing imported manufactured goods with domestic goods.
8. The argument that specializing in the production and export of primary products will not produce rapid growth in developing countries is called the _____ argument. This argument calls for an _____ -oriented strategy.
9. A single economy with industries at very different levels of development is called a _____ economy.
10. _____ -oriented economies have had higher growth rates than _____ -oriented economies.

Section 4: Foreign Investment and Aid

1. Foreign _____ (aid, investment) is a gift or low-cost loan made to developing countries from official sources, whereas foreign _____ (aid, investment) comes from private sources.
2. Match the forms of foreign investment with the definitions.
   foreign direct investment   portfolio investment
   commercial bank loans   trade credit
   bilateral aid   multilateral aid

   a. _____ : foreign aid that flows from one country to another
   b. _____ : the extension of a period of time before an importer must pay for goods or services purchased
   c. _____ : the purchase of a physical operating unit in a foreign country
   d. _____ : the purchase of securities
   e. _____ : aid provided by international organizations supported by many nations
   f. _____ : a loan at market rates of interest, often involving a syndicate of lenders

3. The largest and most important multilateral aid institution is the _____ .
4. The agency that coordinates and plans foreign aid programs in the United States is the _____ .
5. List three reasons why foreign investment may benefit a developing country.

   _____
   _____
   _____

Section 5: Economies in Transition from Socialism

1. The transformation of a socialist economy into a capitalist economy requires the creation of _____ to make decisions about resource allocation.

2. For a market system to be able to make efficient production and consumption decisions, _____ must be free to fluctuate.

3. The move from socialism to a market system requires that state-owned enterprises (SOEs) be _____.

4. To ease the effects of unemployment and rising prices, governments undergoing the transition from socialism to capitalism must provide an effective _____.

5. Unless it's absorbed, a large monetary overhang in the transition to capitalism is likely to result in _____.

6. Currency convertibility requires that a country's domestic currency be easily converted into _____.

7. During the transition, monetary policy should aim at the creation of a _____ (low, high), stable rate of inflation.

8. During the transition, fiscal policy must aim at reducing subsidies from government to _____ and at collecting _____ taxes.

9. Socialist economies usually don't have explicit taxes—sales taxes or income taxes, for example. Explain how socialist governments obtain revenues without these taxes.

_____

_____

_____

10. Economists generally agree that macroeconomic reform must provide a stable, _____ (low-inflation, high-inflation) environment before microeconomic reform can be successful.

11. In general, microeconomic reforms should be carried out _____ (simultaneously, one at a time).

Thinking About and Applying Development Economics

I. Foreign Aid: Food or Money?

The "Economically Speaking" section for this chapter looks at world efforts to relieve the effects of famine and also discusses the effects of different forms of aid. Let's look a little more closely at this issue.

The graphs below reproduce the graphs in the section, except that hypothetical numbers have been added to let us go further with the analysis. The left graph shows the effects of giving foreign aid in the form of food; the right graph shows the effects of giving people enough money to buy the same amount of food as they would have received in aid.

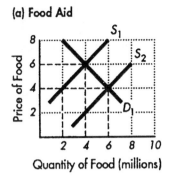
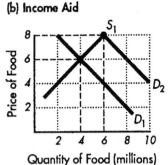

1. On the left graph, the supply shifts to the right by the amount of food given in aid. How much is this?

   Amount of food aid: _____

2. What effects on price and quantity produced did the food aid have on the local farmers? (Hint: Supply curve S_1 shows the amounts supplied by local farmers at different prices.)

   Effect on price: _____

   _____

   Effect on quantity produced: _____

   _____

3. What effects on price and quantity produced did cash aid have (the right graph) on the local farmers?

   Effect on price: _____

   _____

   Effect on quantity produced: _____

   _____

4. Which policy (food aid, cash aid) is likely to encourage farmers to produce more food in the long run? _____

5. Much foreign aid has been provided to developing countries in the form of various products that they could produce on their own. Use your analysis above to generalize about which foreign aid policy will have more beneficial effects for the receiving country: giving aid in the form of *physical products* or giving *cash aid* that people in the developing country can spend themselves.

   _____

6. Which policy (cash aid, physical products) creates more economic benefits for the country that *provides* the aid? _____

II. China's "Economic Czar"

In the July 12, 1993, edition, the *Wall Street Journal* reported on actions taken by China's "economic czar," Zhu Rongji:

> Over the weekend, he . . . raised interest rates and unveiled a plan to tighten central control over China's banks. The measures are aimed at cooling off China's overheated economy. Inflation is currently running at 20 percent in China's cities.
>
> Analysts said that Mr. Zhu appears to be trying to bring China's overheated economy in for a soft landing . . . a sharp downturn could lead to widespread unemployment. (p. A8)

1. Based on the information above. Zhu Rongji's economic measures are aimed at _____ (macroeconomic, microeconomic) reform.

2. Do his actions fit the recommendations discussed in this chapter for helping transform China's socialist economy? Explain your answer.

Chapter 19   Homework Problems

Name _____

1. a. According to the U.S. government, how much income did a family of four need to have in the United States to escape poverty in 1999?

    b. According to the World Bank, what was the minimum per capita GNP that a country needed to escape poverty in 1999? How much would this be for a family of four?

    c. Are the figures above absolute or relative measures of poverty?

2. List some of the political obstacles that developing countries face in trying to grow.

3. List some of the social obstacles that developing countries face in trying to grow.

4. Portugal is one of the least-developed countries in western Europe, although its people are far above the World Bank's poverty standard. The *Wall Street Journal* described the controversy surrounding a large minivan plant that Ford and Volkswagen were jointly building in Portugal.
    Supporters argued that "foreign investment, particularly in the car industry, can help build up local suppliers and train workers."
    On the other hand, "Critics contend that Portugal ought to build on traditional strengths such as pulp and paper, textiles and tourism," and they question whether "high-tech plants run by foreigners are the best development strategy."
    Use what you have learned in this chapter, especially the lessons learned from the successes of the newly industrialized countries, to evaluate the arguments of the supporters and the critics, and decide who is probably correct.

5. How must price determination be changed for a country to make the transition from socialism?

6. What should be the objectives of fiscal and monetary policies for countries making the transition from socialism?

If your instructor assigns these problems, write your answers above, then tear out this page and hand it in.

Answers

Quick-Check Quiz

Section 1: The Developing World

1. d; 2. c
If you missed either of these questions, you should go back and review Section 1 of Chapter 19.

Section 2: Obstacles to Growth

1. d; 2. e; 3. a; 4. a
If you missed any of these questions, you should go back and review Section 2 of Chapter 19.

Section 3: Development Strategies

1. c; 2. d; 3. a
If you missed any of these questions, you should go back and review Section 3 of Chapter 19.

Section 4: Foreign Investment and Aid

1. a; 2. d
If you missed either of these questions, you should go back and review Section 4 of Chapter 19.

Section 5: Economies in Transition from Socialism

1. a; 2. c; 3. d; 4. e; 5. d; 6. d
If you missed any of these questions, you should go back and review Section 5 of Chapter 19.

Practice Questions and Problems

Section 1: The Developing World

1. absolute; relative
2. GNP per capita; absolute
3. quality-of-life

Section 2: Obstacles to Growth

1. political; social
2. private property rights
3. Expropriation
4. entrepreneurs
5. a. An increase in the number of workers leads to a decrease in capital per worker.
   b. When there are many children in a society, resources must be used to support them.
   c. When there are growing numbers of children in a society, investment needs to be used for health care and education facilities, leaving less investment in directly productive uses.
6. 2

Section 3: Development Strategies

1. primary
2. terms of trade
3. import
4. export
5. outward
6. primary
7. Import substitution
8. deteriorating terms of trade; inward
9. dual
10. Outward; inward

Section 4: Foreign Investment and Aid

1. aid; investment
2. a. bilateral aid
   b. trade credit
   c. foreign direct investment
   d. portfolio investment
   e. multilateral aid
   f. commercial bank loans
3. World Bank
4. U.S. Agency for International Development
5. creation of new jobs
   transfer of technology
   foreign exchange earnings

Section 5: Economies in Transition from Socialism

1. markets
2. prices
3. privatized
4. social safety net
5. inflation
6. foreign currencies
7. low
8. firms. explicit
9. The main source of funds for socialist governments is an implicit tax on labor: workers are paid less than the value of their output, and the government keeps the difference.
10. low-inflation
11. simultaneously

Thinking About and Applying Development Economics

I. Foreign Aid: Food or Money?

1. Amount of food aid: 4 million
   The supply curve is shifted to the right by the amount of the food given in aid. At any price (say 2, for example), the quantity supplied is 4 million more than before.

2. Effect on price: Price dropped from 6 to 4, lowering the price not only for buyers, but also for local farmers.
Effect on quantity produced: Because the price was lower, fewer farmers could afford to keep producing for sale in the market. The *local* quantity supplied at a price of 4 dropped to 2 million, found from the original supply curve. People had more to eat because of the aid (6 million instead of 4 million), but not as much more as the amount of the aid (4 million), because local farmers had to reduce their output.
3. Effect on price: Price increased from 6 to 8.
Effect on quantity produced: Because the increase in demand raised the market price, local farmers could supply more to the market. Their output went up from 4 million to 6 million.
4. cash aid (because it encourages an expansion of local production)
5. cash aid (Aid in the form of cash is likely to be better than aid in a form that replaces local production.)
6. physical products
Look at the situation from the point of view of an American farmer. You have to pay taxes to provide the funds for foreign aid, so will you be better off if the money goes to farmers in the receiving country or if it is used to buy the output of American farmers? When foreign aid is used to buy the products of the giving country, that country receives more benefits, even though such aid is not as worthwhile to the receiving country.

II. *China's "Economic Czar"*

1. macroeconomic
2. They fit the idea that macroeconomic reform should try to create a stable, low rate of inflation.

Sample Test Chapters 18–19
(*Economics* Chapters 18–19)

1. The percentage increase in a country's real GDP is generally referred to as
   a. inflation.
   b. a real business cycle.
   c. economic growth.
   d. industrial development.
   e. technological expansion.

2. Suppose Kenya's real GDP is Sh120 billion as of 1997. How long would it take Kenya to double its national income if the economy grows at 7.5 percent per year?
   a. 0.6 year
   b. 1.67 years
   c. 7.5 years
   d. 9.6 years
   e. 72 years

3. If real GDP is growing, per capita real GDP
   a. must be growing at the same rate.
   b. will fall if population growth exceeds real GDP growth.
   c. will fall if population growth is less than real GDP growth.
   d. will fall if there is a deterioration in the nonmonetary quality of life.
   e. will grow at a larger rate if the inflation rate is less than real GDP growth.

4. If other things are equal, a more-educated labor force will result in
   a. a leftward shift of the horizontal aggregate supply curve.
   b. a rightward shift of the aggregate demand curve.
   c. a higher unemployment rate.
   d. a leftward shift of the downward-sloping Phillips curve.
   e. a rightward shift of the vertical aggregate supply curve.

5. A country's total factor productivity is equal to
   a. economic growth minus the growth rate of labor and capital inputs.
   b. the percentage change in real GDP.
   c. the sum of labor, capital, and natural resource growth.
   d. growth in per capita real GDP plus the growth rate of labor and capital.
   e. the ratio of the economy's resource inputs to its real output.

6. Which of the following statements is true?
   a. Technological progress depends on the abundance of natural resources.
   b. The slowdown in U.S. economic growth since the 1960s may be the result of a decrease in the average level of education.
   c. The lower the standard of living, the larger the percentage of GDP spent on current consumption.
   d. The size of a country's labor force is vitally important for economic growth.
   e. The opportunity cost of increased current saving is a decline in future consumption.

7. Assume that labor's share of real GDP is 60 percent and capital's share is 40 percent. If total factor productivity is growing at 5 percent per year, the labor force is growing at an annual rate of 3.5 percent, and capital grows at 4 percent per year, then what must be the annual growth rate of real national income?
   a. 12.5 percent
   b. 8.7 percent
   c. 6.7 percent
   d. 3.7 percent
   e. 1.3 percent

8. Developing countries
   a. are largely dependent on manufacturing as a means of economic growth.
   b. are characterized by a relative scarcity in natural resources.
   c. tend to have high populations in urban areas.
   d. are classified by the level of per capita GDP.
   e. are located exclusively south of the equator.

9. As a relative measure, poverty can be measured by all of the following *except*
   a. the life expectancy at birth.
   b. the literacy rate.
   c. the percentage change in real GDP.
   d. the availability of public health care.
   e. the quality-of-life index.

10. What key determinant of economic growth is missing in many developing countries?
    a. high birthrates
    b. restrictions on foreign trade
    c. immigrant entrepreneurs
    d. secure property rights
    e. foreign aid

11. Which of the following development strategies is most successful in achieving economic growth?
    a. exporting domestically manufactured goods
    b. closing off the domestic economy by imposing severe trade restrictions
    c. replacing imports with domestically manufactured goods
    d. concentrating on the production of primary products
    e. establishing a dual economy

12. The deteriorating terms-of-trade argument has been used to justify
    a. outward-oriented development strategies.
    b. the existence of dual economies.
    c. the need for foreign direct investment in developing countries.
    d. free trade strategies.
    e. inward-oriented development strategies.

13. The main export of developing countries tends to be
    a. agricultural products.
    b. unskilled labor.
    c. capital equipment.
    d. raw materials.
    e. subsistence goods.

14. The Agency for International Development provides development assistance for
    a. Asian countries only.
    b. African countries only.
    c. developing countries in general.
    d. only those countries with per capita real GDP below $765.
    e. the eastern European nations only.

15. Which of the following is an example of foreign aid?
    a. trade credit
    b. cash grants
    c. foreign direct investment
    d. technology transfers
    e. commercial bank loans

16. All of the following are *microeconomic* issues involved in the transition from socialism *except*
    a. privatizing state-owned enterprises.
    b. a social safety net provided to individuals.
    c. the free convertibility of the currency.
    d. the freeing of prices and incomes from state control.
    e. All of the choices are microeconomic issues involved in the transition to capitalism.

17. When prices are freed from state control, which of the following is the normal response?
    a. a lack of opportunity costs
    b. a decrease in the availability of goods and services after an initial increase in output
    c. an increase in the availability of goods and services after an initial fall in output
    d. a complete lack of effect on the economy
    e. none of the above

18. For microeconomic reform to succeed, what must be delivered by macroeconomic reform?
    a. a monopolistic environment
    b. a purely competitive environment
    c. a high-inflationary environment
    d. a stable-low-inflationary environment
    e. No macroeconomic reform is needed for microeconomic reform to succeed.

Answers to Sample Test

1. c (Chapter 18, Section 1.a; *Economics* Chapter 18)
2. d (Chapter 18, Section 1.a; *Economics* Chapter 18)
3. b (Chapter 18, Section 1.b; *Economics* Chapter 18)
4. e (Chapter 18, Section 2.a; *Economics* Chapter 18)
5. a (Chapter 18, Section 3.a; *Economics* Chapter 18)
6. c (Chapter 18, Section 2.b; *Economics* Chapter 18)
7. b (Chapter 18, Section 3.a; *Economics* Chapter 18)
8. d (Chapter 19, Section 1; *Economics* Chapter 19)
9. c (Chapter 19, Section 1.b; *Economics* Chapter 19)
10. d (Chapter 19, Section 2.a; *Economics* Chapter 19)
11. a (Chapter 19, Section 3.c; *Economics* Chapter 19)
12. e (Chapter 19, Section 3.c; *Economics* Chapter 19)
13. d (Chapter 19, Section 3.a; *Economics* Chapter 19)
14. c (Chapter 19, Section 4.c; *Economics* Chapter 19)
15. b (Chapter 19, Section 4.c; *Economics* Chapter 19)
16. c (Chapter 19, Section 5.a.1; *Economics* Chapter 19)
17. c (Chapter 19, Section 5.a.2; *Economics* Chapter 19)
18. d (Chapter 19, Section 5.c; *Economics* Chapter 19)

Chapter 20
(*Economics* Chapter 35)

WORLD TRADE EQUILIBRIUM

FUNDAMENTAL QUESTIONS

1. What are the prevailing patterns of trade between countries? What goods are traded?

   Trade occurs because specialization in production, based on **comparative advantage,** leads to increased output. Countries specialize in those products for which their opportunity costs are lower than costs in other nations; countries then trade what they produce beyond their own consumption and receive other countries' products in return.

   The bulk of world trade occurs within industrialized countries; trade between industrialized countries and developing countries accounts for most of the rest. Canada is the largest buyer of U.S. exports, and Japan is the largest source of U.S. imports. Petroleum, motor vehicles, and petroleum products are the goods that have the largest trading volume, although world trade occurs across a great variety of products.

2. What determines the goods a nation will export?

   A nation exports those goods for which it has a comparative advantage over other nations—that is, those goods for which its opportunity costs are lower than the opportunity costs of other nations. The **terms of trade**—how much of an exported good must be given up to obtain one unit of an imported good—are limited by the domestic opportunity costs of the trading countries.

3. How are the equilibrium price and the quantity of goods traded determined?

   As with most other markets, demand and supply determine the equilibrium price and quantity. For internationally traded goods, the **export supply curve** shows how much countries are willing to export at different world prices. The **import demand curve** shows how much countries are willing to import at different world prices. The international equilibrium price and quantity traded equal the point at which the export supply curve and the import demand curve intersect.

4. What are the sources of comparative advantage?

   There are two major sources of comparative advantage: productivity differences and factor abundance. Productivity differences come from differences in labor productivity and human capital, and from differences in technology. Factor abundance affects comparative advantage because countries have different resource endowments. The United States, with a large amount of high-quality farmland, has a comparative advantage in agriculture.

   Productivity differences and factor abundance explain most, but not all, trade patterns. Other sources of comparative advantage are human skills differences, product life cycles, and consumer preferences. Consumer preferences explain **intraindustry trade,** in which countries are both exporters and importers of a product. Some consumers prefer brands made in their own country; others prefer foreign brands.

Key Terms

absolute advantage
comparative advantage
terms of trade
export supply curve
import demand curve
intraindustry trade

Quick-Check Quiz

Section 1: An Overview of World Trade

1. The bulk of world trade occurs
   a. in the Eastern trading area.
   b. among developing countries.
   c. among industrial countries.
   d. between developing and industrial countries.
   e. between industrial countries and the Eastern trading area.

2. The United States imports the most from
   a. Canada.
   b. Germany.
   c. Japan.
   d. Mexico.
   e. Russia.

3. The United States exports the most to
   a. Canada.
   b. Germany.
   c. Japan.
   d. Mexico.
   e. Russia.

4. The most heavily traded good in the world is
   a. crude petroleum.
   b. airplanes.
   c. automobiles.
   d. televisions.
   e. wheat.

Section 2: An Example of International Trade Equilibrium

1. A nation has an absolute advantage in producing a good when
   a. it can produce a good more efficiently than can other nations.
   b. the opportunity cost of producing a good, in terms of the forgone output of other goods, is lower than that of other nations.
   c. it can produce a good less efficiently than can other nations.
   d. the opportunity cost of producing a good, in terms of the forgone output of other goods, is higher than that of other nations.
   e. the nation's export supply curve is below its import demand curve.

2. A nation has a comparative advantage in producing a good when
   a. it can produce a good for a lower input cost than can other nations.
   b. the opportunity cost of producing a good, in terms of the forgone output of other goods, is lower than that of other nations.
   c. it can produce a good for a higher input cost than can other nations.
   d. the opportunity cost of producing a good, in terms of the forgone output of other goods, is higher than that of other nations.
   e. the nation's export supply curve is below its import demand curve.

3. The terms of trade are the
   a. price of your country's currency in terms of another country's currency.
   b. price of another country's currency in terms of your country's currency.
   c. amount of an export good that must be given up to obtain one unit of an import good.
   d. amount of an import good that must be given up to obtain one unit of an export good.
   e. amount of imports divided by the amount of exports.

4. Limits on the terms of trade are determined by the
   a. difference between domestic and world prices.
   b. domestic opportunity costs of production within one country.
   c. opportunity costs in each country.
   d. ratio of the domestic price to the world price.
   e. ratio of the world price to the domestic price.

5. The export supply and import demand curves for a country measure the
   a. international surplus and shortage, respectively, at different world prices.
   b. international shortage and surplus, respectively, at different world prices.
   c. domestic surplus and shortage, respectively, at different world prices.
   d. domestic shortage and surplus, respectively, at different world prices.
   e. domestic surplus and shortage, respectively, at different exchange rates.

Section 3: Sources of Comparative Advantage

1. The productivity-differences explanation of comparative advantage stresses
   a. differences in labor productivity among countries.
   b. the advantage that comes to a country that is the first to develop and produce a product.
   c. the relative amounts of skilled and unskilled labor in a country.
   d. differences in the amounts of resources countries have.
   e. differences in tastes within a country.

2. The factor-abundance explanation of comparative advantage stresses
   a. differences in labor productivity among countries.
   b. the advantage that comes to a country that is the first to develop and produce a product.
   c. the relative amounts of skilled and unskilled labor in a country.
   d. differences in the amounts of resources countries have.
   e. differences in tastes within a country.

3. The human-skills explanation of comparative advantage stresses
   a. differences in labor productivity among countries.
   b. the advantage that comes to a country that is the first to develop and produce a product.
   c. the relative amounts of skilled and unskilled labor in a country.
   d. differences in the amounts of resources countries have.
   e. differences in tastes within a country.

4. The product-life-cycle explanation of comparative advantage stresses
   a. differences in labor productivity among countries.
   b. the advantage that comes to a country that is the first to develop and produce a product.
   c. the relative amounts of skilled and unskilled labor in a country.
   d. differences in the amounts of resources countries have.
   e. differences in tastes within a country.

5. The consumer-preferences explanation of comparative advantage stresses
   a. differences in labor productivity among countries.
   b. the advantage that comes to a country that is the first to develop and produce a product.
   c. the relative amounts of skilled and unskilled labor in a country.
   d. differences in the amounts of resources countries have.
   e. differences in tastes within a country.

Practice Questions and Problems

Section 1: An Overview of World Trade

1. The country that imports the most from the United States is _____ ; the country that exports the most to the United States is _____ .
2. World trade is _____ (distributed across many, dominated by only a few) products.
3. The product that accounts for the most world trade is _____ .
4. Use Table 1 in the text to answer the following questions.
   a. Trade just within industrial countries accounts for _____ percent of world trade.
   b. Trade just within the developing countries accounts for _____ percent of world trade.

Section 2: An Example of International Trade Equilibrium

1. _____ (Comparative, Absolute) advantage is based on the relative opportunity costs of producing goods in different countries.
2. _____ (Comparative, Absolute) advantage occurs when a country can produce a good more efficiently than can other nations.
3. The _____ are the amount of an export good that must be given up to obtain one unit of an import good.
4. The _____ (export supply, import demand) curve is derived from the domestic surplus at different world prices.
5. The _____ (export supply, import demand) curve is derived from the domestic shortage at different world prices.
6. The table below shows the number of hours of labor needed to produce a ton of mangos and a ton of papayas in Samoa and in Fiji.

	Samoa	Fiji
Mangos	2	6
Papayas	1	2

   a. The country that has an absolute advantage in producing mangos is _____ .
   b. The country that has an absolute advantage in producing papayas is _____ .
   c. The opportunity cost of 1 ton of papayas in Samoa is _____ .
   d. The opportunity cost of 1 ton of papayas in Fiji is _____ .
   e. The country that has a comparative advantage in papayas is _____ .
   f. The opportunity cost of 1 ton of mangos in Samoa is _____ .
   g. The opportunity cost of 1 ton of mangos in Fiji is _____ .
   h. The country that has a comparative advantage in mangos is _____ .
   i. The limits on the terms of trade are 1 ton of mangos for between _____ and _____ tons of papayas.

7. The graphs on the next page show the soybean markets in the United States and in France (we assume that no other country in the world is involved in trade in soybeans).

   a. Before doing an analysis, let's look at the soybean markets in the two countries. The price in the United States without trade is _____ per bushel; in France it is _____ per bushel. Because market prices reflect opportunity costs, the country that has a comparative advantage in soybean production and should export soybeans is _____ .
   b. On graph (c) on the following page, draw in the import demand and export supply curves for the United States and France.

(a) United States

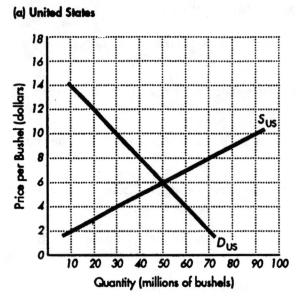

(b) France

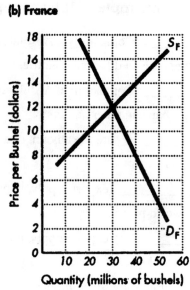

(c) World

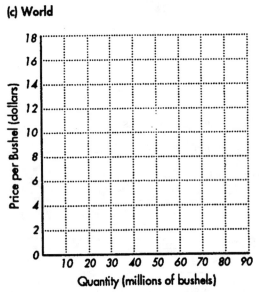

c. The equilibrium world price of soybeans is _____ per bushel. The quantity traded is _____ bushels.

d. The United States produced _____ bushels of soybeans and consumed _____ bushels. The United States is an _____ (exporter, importer) of soybeans.

e. France produced _____ bushels of soybeans and consumed _____ bushels. France is an _____ (exporter, importer) of soybeans.

f. In the problem above, what is the effect of trade on the price of soybeans in the United States? _____
France? _____

Section 3: Sources of Comparative Advantage

1. Name the comparative-advantage theory that matches each explanation of comparative advantage listed below.

    a. Differences in labor productivity among countries: _____

    b. The advantage that comes to a country that is the first to develop and produce a product: _____

    c. The relative amounts of skilled and unskilled labor in a country: _____

    d. Differences in the amounts of resources countries have: _____

    e. Differences in tastes within a country: _____

2. The productivity-differences theory of comparative advantage is known as the _____ model.

3. The factor-abundance theory of comparative advantage is known as the _____ model.

4. Differences in consumer tastes within a country explain _____, in which a country is both an exporter and an importer of a differentiated product.

Thinking About and Applying World Trade Equilibrium

I. World Trade Equilibrium

The graphs on the following page show the domestic markets for wheat in the United States, Canada, Argentina, and Russia.

1. Draw the import demand and export supply curves for the four countries; then sum the import demand and export supply curves for the four countries to draw the world import demand and export supply curves on graph e.

(a) United States

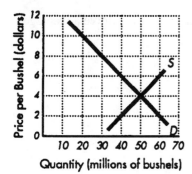
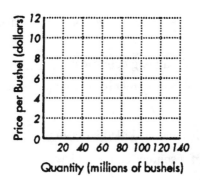

(b) Canada

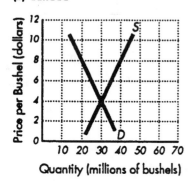
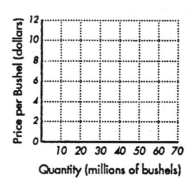

(c) Argentina

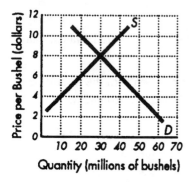
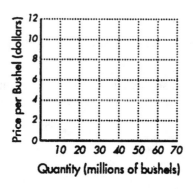

(e) World

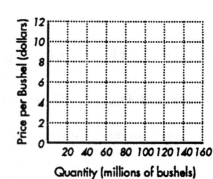

(d) Russia

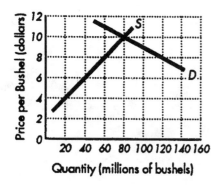
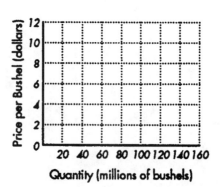

2. The equilibrium world price is _____ ; the quantity traded is _____ bushels.
3. The United States produced _____ bushels and consumed _____ bushels. The United States is a(n) _____ (exporter, importer, nontrader) of wheat.
4. Canada produced _____ bushels and consumed _____ bushels. Canada is a(n) _____ (exporter, importer, nontrader) of wheat.
5. Argentina produced _____ bushels and consumed _____ bushels. Argentina is a(n) _____ (exporter, importer, nontrader) of wheat.
6. Russia produced _____ bushels and consumed _____ bushels. Russia is a(n) _____ (exporter, importer, nontrader) of wheat.

II. Triangular Trade

Many people complain about the trade imbalance between the United States and Japan. Economists generally don't worry much about trade imbalances with specific countries; they believe that trade between any two countries need not balance as long as each country's trade with all countries taken together is roughly balanced. Let's look a little further at this idea.

The graphs on the following page show the domestic markets for bananas, oranges, and sugar in Guatemala, Honduras, and Costa Rica.

1. Draw the import demand and export supply curves for the three countries for each product; then sum the import demand and export supply curves for each product to draw the world import demand and export supply curves on the world graphs.

418 / Chapter 20 (*Economics* Chapter 35)

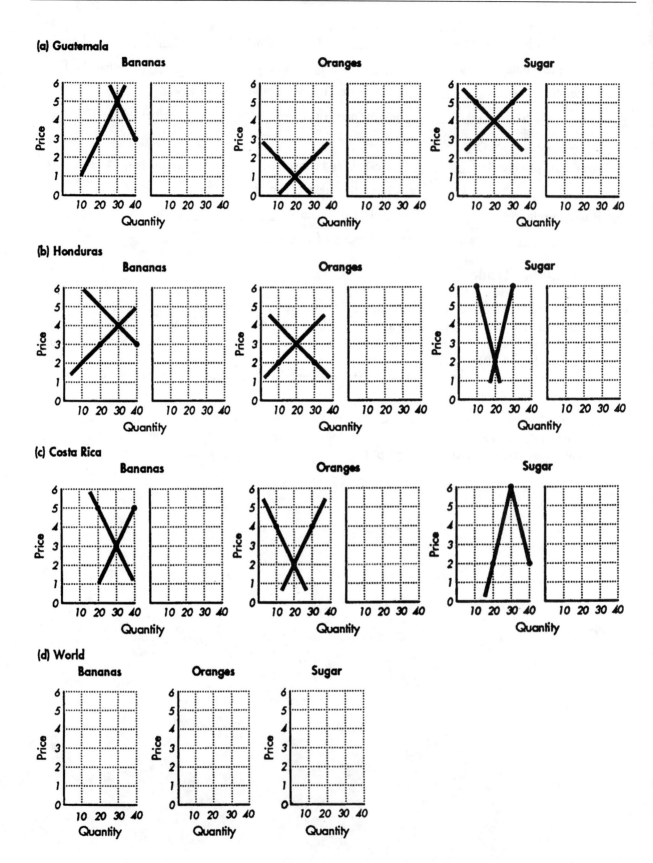

2. Find the equilibrium world price and quantity traded for each product, the amounts produced and consumed of each product in each country, and the status of each country as an importer, exporter, or nontrader.

	World Price	Quantity Traded
Bananas	$ _____	_____
Oranges	_____	_____
Sugar	_____	_____

	Amount Produced	Amount Consumed	Status
Guatemala			
Bananas	_____	_____	_____
Oranges	_____	_____	_____
Sugar	_____	_____	_____
Honduras			
Bananas	_____	_____	_____
Oranges	_____	_____	_____
Sugar	_____	_____	_____
Costa Rica			
Bananas	_____	_____	_____
Oranges	_____	_____	_____
Sugar	_____	_____	_____

3. On the diagram below, put in the amounts of dollars flowing between each pair of countries, and which product and how much of it flows between each pair of countries.

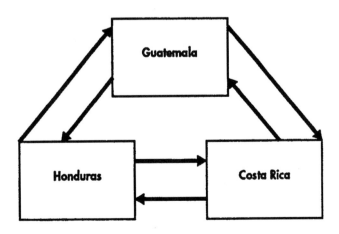

Chapter 20 (*Economics* Chapter 35)   Homework Problems

Name _____

1. Compare and contrast the concepts of absolute advantage and comparative advantage. Which is the determining factor in determining what products a country should produce?

2. If Japan exports television sets to the United States, this results in a(n) _____ (increase, decrease) in the price of television sets in the United States and a(n) _____ (increase, decrease) in the price of television sets in Japan. If the United States exports beef to Japan, this results in a(n) _____ (increase, decrease) in the price of beef in the United States and a(n) _____ (increase, decrease) in the price of beef in Japan.

3. In the past, many developing countries were anxious to adopt the high-technology production techniques used by the industrial countries. Knowing the sources of comparative advantage, can you see how adopting high-technology production techniques may work against developing countries?

4. How does the theory of comparative advantage explain the fact that the United States exports cars to Germany and also imports cars from Germany?

5. A recent edition of the *Wall Street Journal* reported that Chile has pushed ahead of the United States as the world's largest producer of copper. The article notes:

> Chile has great advantages: Its new mines tap such high grade ore and are so huge and cost efficient that they would be very profitable even if copper prices slumped to 61 cents a pound, as they did from 1984 until 1986. Some, but not all U.S. mines could survive. Most in Africa, Australia, Canada and the former Soviet Union wouldn't stand a chance....
>
> [A] combination of better ore and looser environmental regulations elsewhere has all but dried up exploration in the U.S.... "It's not that we're more lenient here," says Gustavo Lagos, director of the mining center at the Universidad Catolica de Chile. "There are no people in Atacama and no scenery to destroy."

  a. According to the article, does Chile have an absolute advantage in copper production? A comparative advantage? Defend your answers.

  b. Which theory of the sources of comparative advantage applies here?

If your instructor assigns these problems, write your answers above, then tear out this page and hand it in.

Answers

Quick-Check Quiz

Section 1: An Overview of World Trade

1. c; 2. a; 3. a; 4. e

If you missed any of these questions, you should go back and review Section 1 in Chapter 20 (*Economics*, Chapter 35).

Section 2: An Example of International Trade Equilibrium

1. a; 2. b; 3. c; 4. c; 5. c

If you missed any of these questions, you should go back and review Section 2 in Chapter 20 (*Economics*, Chapter 35).

Section 3: Sources of Comparative Advantage

1. a; 2. d; 3. c; 4. b; 5. e

If you missed any of these questions, you should go back and review Section 3 in Chapter 20 (*Economics*, Chapter 35).

Practice Questions and Problems

Section 1: An Overview of World Trade

1. Canada; Canada
2. distributed across many
3. motor vehicles
4. a. 47
   b. 15

Section 2: An Example of International Trade Equilibrium

1. Comparative
2. Absolute
3. terms of trade
4. export supply
5. import demand
6. a. Samoa (Mangos cost only 2 hours of labor in Samoa; they cost 6 hours of labor in Fiji.)
   b. Samoa (Papayas cost only 1 hour of labor in Samoa; they cost 2 hours of labor in Fiji.)
   c. ½ ton of mangos (Mangos take twice as much labor time as papayas in Samoa, so you can produce half as many mangos in the same amount of time.)
   d. ⅓ ton of mangos (Mangos take three times as much labor time as papayas in Fiji, so you can produce one-third as many mangos in the same amount of time.)
   e. Fiji (Fiji has the lower opportunity cost: it has to give up only ⅓ ton of mangos to get a ton of papayas, whereas Samoa has to give up ½ ton.)
   f. 2 tons of papayas (Papayas take half as much labor time as mangos in Samoa, so you can produce twice as many papayas in the same amount of time.)

g. 3 tons of papayas (Papayas take one-third as much labor time as mangos in Fiji, so you can produce three times as many papayas in the same amount of time.)
h. Samoa (Samoa has the lower opportunity cost: it has to give up only 2 tons of papayas to get a ton of mangos, whereas Fiji has to give up 3 tons.)
i. 2; 3

7. a. $6; $12; the United States
   b.

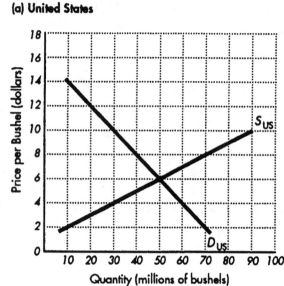
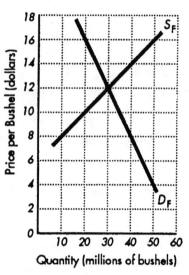
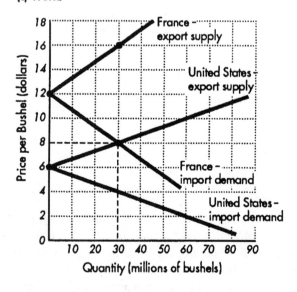

   c. $8; 30 million
   d. 70 million; 40 million; exporter
   e. 10 million; 40 million; importer
   f. The price went up from $6 to $8; the price went down from $12 to $8.

Section 3: Sources of Comparative Advantage

1. a. productivity differences
   b. product life cycle
   c. human skills
   d. factor abundance
   e. consumer preferences
2. Ricardian
3. Heckscher-Ohlin
4. intraindustry trade

Thinking About and Applying World Trade Equilibrium

I. World Trade Equilibrium

1. See the solution on page 426.
   The domestic prices before trade vary between $4 (United States and Canada) and $10 (Russia). Russia will begin demanding imports if the world price is below $10; if the price goes below $8, Argentina also will demand imports. The United States and Canada will begin supplying exports if the world price goes above $4; if the price goes above $8, Argentina also will supply exports. Graph (e) shows the amounts these countries will supply (export) and demand (import) at various prices.
2. $8; 60 million
3. 70 million; 30 million; exporter
4. 40 million; 20 million; exporter
5. 30 million; 30 million; nontrader
6. 60 million; 120 million; importer

II. Triangular Trade

1. See the solution on page 427.

(a) United States

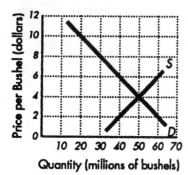 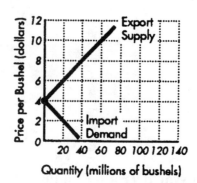

(b) Canada

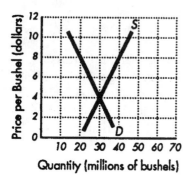 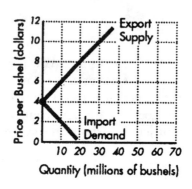

(c) Argentina

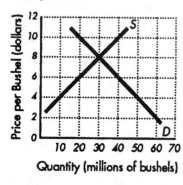 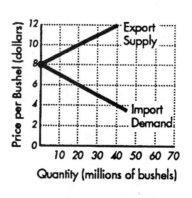

(e) World

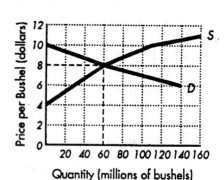

(d) Russia

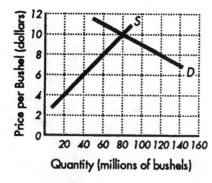 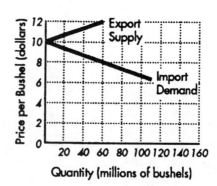

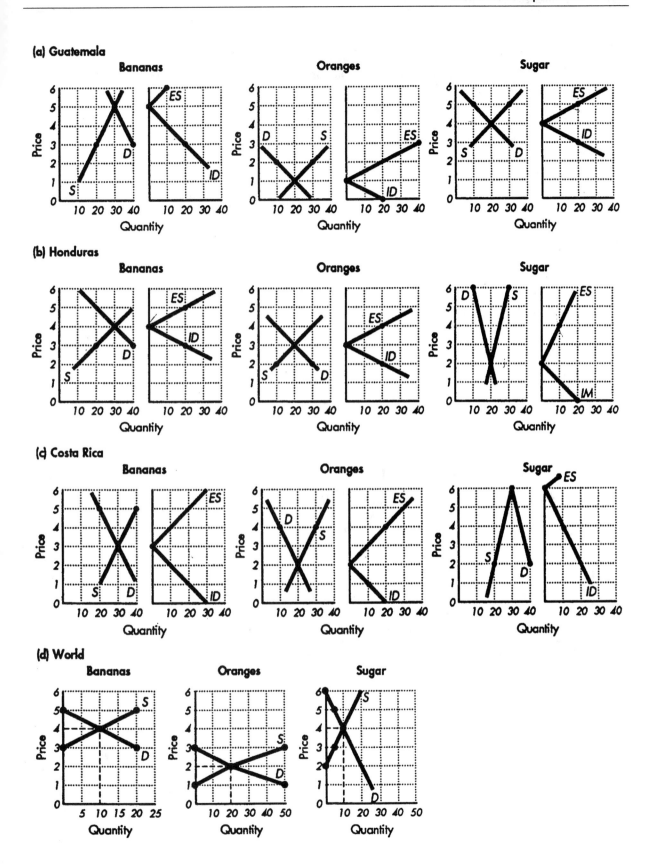

2.

	World Price	Quantity Traded
Bananas	$4	20
Oranges	2	20
Sugar	4	10

	Amount Produced	Amount Consumed	Status
Guatemala			
Bananas	25	35	Importer
Oranges	30	10	Exporter
Sugar	20	20	Nontrader
Honduras			
Bananas	30	30	Nontrader
Oranges	10	30	Importer
Sugar	25	15	Exporter
Costa Rica			
Bananas	35	25	Exporter
Oranges	20	20	Nontrader
Sugar	25	35	Importer

3.

Chapter 21
(*Economics* Chapter 36)

INTERNATIONAL TRADE RESTRICTIONS

FUNDAMENTAL QUESTIONS

1. Why do countries restrict international trade?

    Most countries follow some sort of **commercial policy** to influence the direction and volume of international trade. Despite the costs to domestic consumers, countries frequently try to protect domestic producers by restricting international trade. Lobbying for trade restrictions is an example of the rent-seeking activities discussed in the chapter on government and public choice.

    To help hide the special-interest nature of most trade restrictions, several arguments commonly are used. These include saving domestic jobs, creating fair trade, raising revenue through tariffs, protecting key defense industries, allowing new industries to become competitive, and giving **increasing-returns-to-scale industries** an advantage over foreign competitors. Although a few of these arguments have some validity, most have little or no merit.

2. How do countries restrict the entry of foreign goods and promote the export of domestic goods?

    Several tactics are used for these purposes. **Tariffs,** or taxes on products imported into the United States, protect domestic industries by raising the price of foreign goods. Quotas restrict the amount or value of a foreign product that may be imported; **quantity quotas** limit the amount of a good that may be imported, and **value quotas** limit the monetary value of a good that may be imported. **Subsidies,** payments made by the government to domestic firms, both encourage exports and make domestic products cheaper to foreign buyers. In addition, a wide variety of other tactics, among them health and safety standards, are used to restrict imports.

3. What sorts of agreements do countries enter into to reduce barriers to international trade?

    Groups of countries can establish **free trade areas,** where member countries have no trade barriers among themselves, or **customs unions,** where member countries not only abolish trade restrictions among themselves but also set common trade barriers on nonmembers. The United States, Mexico, and Canada established a free trade area in 1994. The best-known customs union is the European Economic Community (EEC), composed of most of the countries in western Europe. Because they do not include all countries, free trade areas can result in both **trade diversion,** which reduces efficiency, and **trade creation,** which allows a country to obtain goods at lower cost.

Key Terms

commercial policy
strategic trade policy
increasing-returns-to-scale
   industry

tariff
quantity quota
value quota
subsidies

free trade area
customs union
trade diversion
trade creation

Quick-Check Quiz

Section 1: Arguments for Protection

1. The basic objective of commercial policy is to
   a. promote free and unrestricted international trade.
   b. protect domestic consumers from dangerous, low-quality imports.
   c. protect domestic producers from foreign competition.
   d. protect foreign producers from domestic consumers.
   e. promote the efficient use of scarce resources.

2. Using trade restrictions to save domestic jobs
   a. usually costs consumers much more than the job saved is worth.
   b. usually just redistributes jobs from other industries to the protected industry.
   c. may provoke other countries to restrict U.S. exports.
   d. does all of the above.
   e. does only b and c above.

3. Some arguments for trade restrictions have economic validity. Which of the following arguments has *no* economic validity?
   a. the infant industry argument
   b. the national defense argument
   c. the government revenue creation from tariffs argument
   d. the creation of domestic jobs argument
   e. All of the above have some economic validity.

4. The objective of strategic trade policy is to
   a. protect those industries needed for national defense.
   b. provide domestic decreasing-cost industries an advantage over foreign competitors.
   c. develop economic alliances with other countries.
   d. carefully develop free trade areas to counteract customs unions.
   e. increase government revenues through tariffs.

Section 2: Tools of Policy

1. A tariff is a
   a. tax on imports or exports.
   b. government-imposed limit on the amount of a good that can be imported.
   c. government-imposed limit on the value of a good that can be imported.
   d. payment by government to domestic producers.
   e. payment by government to foreign producers.

2. A subsidy is a
   a. tax on imports or exports.
   b. government-imposed limit on the amount of a good that can be imported.
   c. government-imposed limit on the value of a good that can be imported.
   d. payment by government to domestic producers.
   e. payment by government to foreign producers.

3. A quantity quota is a
   a. tax on imports or exports.
   b. government-imposed limit on the amount of a good that can be imported.
   c. government-imposed limit on the value of a good that can be imported.
   d. payment by government to domestic producers.
   e. payment by government to foreign producers.

4. A value quota is a
   a. tax on imports or exports.
   b. government-imposed limit on the amount of a good that may be imported.
   c. government-imposed limit on the value of a good that may be imported.
   d. payment by government to domestic producers.
   e. payment by government to foreign producers.

5. Which of the following are *not* used to restrict trade?
   a. health and safety standards
   b. government procurement regulations requiring domestic purchasing
   c. subsidies
   d. cultural and institutional practices
   e. All of the above are used to restrict trade.

Section 3: Preferential Trade Agreements

1. An organization of nations whose members have no trade barriers among themselves but are free to fashion their own trade policies toward nonmembers is a
   a. customs union.
   b. trade group.
   c. international cartel.
   d. free trade area.
   e. international economic alliance.

2. An organization of nations whose members have no trade barriers among themselves but impose common trade barriers on nonmembers is a
   a. customs union.
   b. trade group.
   c. international cartel.
   d. free trade area.
   e. international economic alliance.

3. Trade diversion occurs when a preferential trade agreement
   a. allows a country to buy imports from a nonmember country at a lower price than that charged by member countries.
   b. reduces economic efficiency by shifting production to a higher-cost producer.
   c. allows a country to obtain goods at a lower cost than is available at home.
   d. reduces trade flows between nonmember countries.
   e. increases economic efficiency by shifting production to a higher-cost producer.

4. Trade creation occurs when a preferential trade agreement
   a. allows a country to buy imports from a nonmember country at a lower price than that charged by member countries.
   b. reduces economic efficiency by shifting production to a higher-cost producer.
   c. allows a country to obtain goods at a lower cost than is available at home.
   d. reduces trade flows between nonmember countries.
   e. increases economic efficiency by shifting production to a higher-cost producer.

Practice Questions and Problems

Section 1: Arguments for Protection

1. The main reason governments restrict foreign trade is to protect _____ producers from _____ competition.

2. Governments can generate revenues by restricting trade through _____ ; this is a common tactic in _____ (industrial, developing) countries.

3. The argument that new industries should receive temporary protection is known as the _____ argument.

4. Strategic trade policy aims at identifying industries with _____ and giving them an advantage over their foreign competitors.

5. Using trade restrictions to protect domestic jobs usually costs consumers _____ (more, less) money than the jobs are worth to the workers holding them.

6. Trade restrictions usually _____ (create more, redistribute) domestic jobs within the economy.

Section 2: Tools of Policy

1. Tariffs are _____ on imports or exports. In the United States, tariffs on _____ (imports, exports) are illegal under the Constitution.
2. Quotas can be used to set limits on the _____ or _____ of a good allowed to be imported into a country.
3. List three trade barriers to trade besides tariffs and quotas.

   _____

   _____

   _____

4. The graph below shows the U.S. market for tangerines. The world price for tangerines is $10 per bushel. On the graph, mark the quantity demanded and quantity supplied by U.S. sellers when the price is $10.

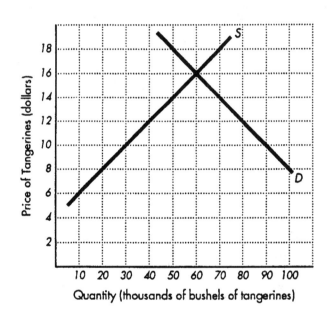

   a. If the United States does not restrict imports of tangerines, it will import _____ tangerines at the price of _____ .
   b. Suppose the United States imposes a $4 per bushel tariff on imported tangerines. On the graph above, mark the quantity demanded and the quantity supplied by U.S. sellers when the price is $14. The United States would import _____ tangerines at a price of _____ .
   c. With the $4 tariff, _____ tangerines will be produced in the United States, and U.S. growers will receive _____ per bushel.

5. The graph below shows the U.S. market for tangerines again. The world price for tangerines is again $10 per bushel.

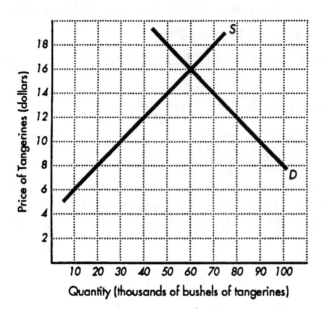

a. Suppose the United States imposes a quota of 40,000 bushels on imported tangerines. On the graph, mark the price at which the United States will import 40,000 tangerines. The price is _____ .

b. With a quota of 40,000, _____ tangerines will be produced in the United States. U.S. tangerine growers will receive _____ for each bushel sold.

Section 3: Preferential Trade Agreements

1. A(n) _____ is a group of nations whose members have no trade barriers among themselves but impose common trade barriers on nonmembers.

2. A(n) _____ is a group of nations whose members have no trade barriers among themselves but have their own trade policies toward nonmembers.

3. The European Union (formerly known as the European Economic Community) is a(n) _____ . List the six original member countries and the six that joined later.

Original Members	Later Members
_____	_____
_____	_____
_____	_____
_____	_____
_____	_____
_____	_____

Thinking About and Applying International Trade Restrictions

I. Rent Seeking in the Automobile Industry

Table 1 in the text shows the costs to consumers and the gains to producers from trade restrictions on various imports into the United States.

1. Look through Table 1. Can you find any industry for which the benefits of trade restrictions (producer gains) are larger than the costs (total consumer losses)?

   _____

2. Let's take a look at some of the reasons why trade restrictions cause net losses to the United States. Look back at problem 5 on page 434, the problem with an import quota on tangerines. Before the quota was imposed, foreign tangerine growers received _____ for the tangerines they sold in the United States. After the quota, foreign tangerine growers received _____ for the tangerines they sold in the United States. Do you think U.S. producers got to keep all the extra money U.S. consumers spent for tangerines after the quota was imposed? Explain your answer.

   _____

   _____

   _____

3. a. Look back to Table 1 in your text again, and find the consumer losses and producer gains from trade restraints on automobiles. Consumer losses are _____ . Producer gains are _____ .

   b. In a good year, auto sales in the United States are around 10 million. U.S. consumers are paying _____ extra per car, and U.S. automakers are receiving _____ extra per car, as a result of trade restraints.

4. The most significant restriction on auto imports into the United States has been the voluntary export restraint agreement between the United States and Japan, whereby the Japanese agreed to set a quota on exports of automobiles to the United States and each Japanese automaker was given a specific number of cars that could be exported. Explain why the export quotas help prevent competition among Japanese automakers.

   _____

   _____

   _____

5. Use the ideas you learned in the chapter on government and public choice to explain why the U.S. government would encourage restrictions on importing Japanese autos, even though the restrictions cost U.S. car buyers large amounts of money. (*Hint:* Look at the title of this problem.)

_____

_____

_____

_____

II. Tax Effects of Import Restrictions

According to *Newsweek:*

> Lower-income families are hit hardest by trade restrictions, because they spend a far greater share of their earnings at the store. In 1989, for example, households earning more than $50,000 laid out 3.3 percent of their disposable incomes on clothing, but households in the $20,000-to-$30,000 bracket spent 4.6 percent— and families earning $10,000 to $15,000 spent 5.4 percent. The quotas and tariffs that force import prices up to protect U.S. apparel jobs don't matter much in Beverly Hills, but they put a big dent in pocketbooks in Watts. (July 12, 1993, p. 45)

Let's look more closely at the effects of tariffs and quotas on apparel on different income groups. Assuming that 20 percent of the price of clothing is due to tariffs and quotas, calculate the dollar cost of tariffs and quotas on families making the incomes given below. Then calculate the percentage of its income each family pays due to tariffs and quotas.

1. Family income = $50,000

    Cost: _____

    Percentage of income: _____

2. Family income = $25,000

    Cost: _____

    Percentage of income: _____

3. Family income = $10,000

    Cost: _____

    Percentage of income: _____

4. Tariffs and quotas on clothing are equivalent to a _____ (progressive, proportional, regressive) tax.

Chapter 21 (*Economics* Chapter 36)   Homework Problems

Name _____

1. Government policy aimed at influencing international trade flows is called _____ .

2. Generally speaking, protection from foreign competition benefits _____ at the expense of _____ .

3. List five barriers to international trade.

4. The North American Free Trade Agreement (NAFTA) created a free trade area within the United States, Canada, and Mexico. Who benefits and who is hurt by this agreement?

5. Table 1 in the text shows that consumer losses (in the form of higher prices and fewer goods and services) far outweigh producer gains when domestic industries are protected from foreign competition. Clearly, U.S. consumers would be better off if the United States unilaterally eliminated barriers to trade. Instead, U.S. policy has been to negotiate trade treaties. Why doesn't the United States unilaterally eliminate trade restrictions instead of bothering with trade treaties? (*Hint:* Remember what you learned about rent seeking and public choice theory in Chapter 5.)

If your instructor assigns these problems, write your answers above, then tear out this page and hand it in.

Answers

Quick-Check Quiz

Section 1: Arguments for Protection

1. c; 2. d; 3. d; 4. b

If you missed any of these questions, you should go back and review Section 1 in Chapter 21 (*Economics*, Chapter 36).

Section 2: Tools of Policy

1. a; 2. d; 3. b; 4. c; 5. e

If you missed any of these questions, you should go back and review Section 2 in Chapter 21 (*Economics*, Chapter 36).

Section 3: Preferential Trade Agreements

1. d; 2. a; 3. b; 4. c

If you missed any of these questions, you should go back and review Section 3 in Chapter 21 (*Economics*, Chapter 36).

Practice Questions and Problems

Section 1: Arguments for Protection

1. domestic; foreign
2. tariffs; developing
3. infant industry
4. decreasing costs
5. more
6. redistribute

Section 2: Tools of Policy

1. taxes; exports
2. quantity; value
3. subsidies
   government procurement regulations requiring domestic purchasing
   health and safety standards
   cultural or institutional barriers

4.

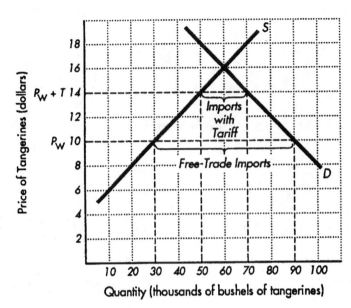

a. 60,000; $10 (At a world price of $10, the United States demands 90,000 bushels but produces only 30,000 bushels. The difference [90,000 – 30,000] is how much the United States will import.)
b. 20,000; $14 (The tariff raises the price of tangerines in the United States to $14 [the $10 world price + the $4 tariff]. At this price, U.S. consumers demand 70,000 tangerines, and U.S. producers supply 50,000, leaving 20,000 to be imported.)
c. 50,000; $14

5.

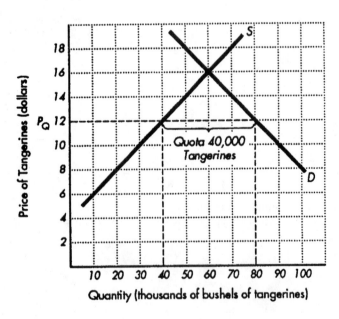

a. $12 (The quota limits imports to 40,000. From the U.S. supply and demand curves, the price where the difference between U.S. demand and U.S. supply is 40,000 is at $12 per bushel: U.S. consumers buy 80,000 bushels, and U.S. producers supply 40,000 bushels.)
b. 40,000; $12

Section 3: Preferential Trade Agreements

1. customs union
2. free trade area
3. customs union

Original Members	Later Members
France	United Kingdom
West Germany	Ireland
Italy	Denmark
Belgium	Greece
Netherlands	Spain
Luxembourg	Portugal

Thinking About and Applying International Trade Restrictions

I. Rent Seeking in the Automobile Industry

1. no (Except for peanuts, where the gains are estimated to equal the losses, the losses to consumers are larger than the gains to producers.)
2. $10; $12; no; some of the extra money U.S. consumers paid went to foreign sellers of tangerines, who received a higher price.
3. a. $5,800,000,000; $2,600,000,000
   b. $580; $260
4. Cartels try to raise prices by cutting back output. From the point of view of an individual firm in a cartel, cutting price to expand sales is usually profitable; such cheating contributes to the eventual collapse of most cartels. By using the Japanese government to enforce limits on output, Japanese car makers were able to raise prices without worrying about any cheating their competitors might do.
5. Trade restraints are an example of rent-seeking behavior. Import quotas on automobiles transfer wealth from consumers (a relatively small amount from many car buyers) to automakers and auto workers (a relatively large amount to each one). The cost to car buyers is hidden in the price of the automobile and so does not provoke consumer resentment against politicians who vote for restraints. The automakers and auto workers, of course, know who is responsible for their added wealth and reward cooperative politicians with campaign contributions and votes.

II. Tax Effects of Import Restrictions

1. $330 (3.3 percent of $50,000 = $1,650 spent on clothing; 20 percent of $1,650 = $330); 0.66 percent ($330/$50,000 = .0066 = 0.66 percent)
2. $165 (4.6 percent of $25,000 = $1,150 spent on clothing; 20 percent of $1,150 = $230); 0.92 percent ($230/$25,000 = .0092 = 0.92 percent)
3. $108 (5.4 percent of $10,000 = $540 spent on clothing; 20 percent of $540 = $108); 1.08 percent ($108/$10,000 = .0108 = 1.08 percent)
4. regressive (The percentage of income paid in the "tax" is highest for low-income families and then decreases for higher-income families.)

Chapter 22
(*Economics* Chapter 37)

EXCHANGE-RATE SYSTEMS AND PRACTICES

FUNDAMENTAL QUESTIONS

1. How does a commodity standard fix exchange rates between countries?

   A commodity standard exists when exchange rates are based on the values of different currencies in terms of some commodity. The **gold standard,** in general use between 1880 and 1914, fixed the value of countries' currencies in terms of how much currency was needed to buy an ounce of gold. Fixing the value of currencies in terms of gold also fixes the relative value of all currencies to one another. For example, if the value of an ounce of gold is 20 U.S. dollars and its value is also 200 Mexican pesos, then a U.S. dollar has the same value as 10 Mexican pesos. As long as countries fix the value of their currencies in terms of some commodity, the relative values of those currencies stay the same.

2. What kinds of exchange-rate arrangements exist today?

   The gold standard ended with World War I. Since then, many exchange-rate systems have been tried. At the present time, nations use a variety of exchange-rate arrangements, including fixed exchange rates, freely floating exchange rates, and **managed floating exchange rates.**

3. How is equilibrium determined in the foreign-exchange market?

   Equilibrium is determined in foreign-exchange markets the same way it's determined in other markets: by the intersection of supply and demand curves. The demand for a currency, such as the U.S dollar, comes from the desire of people in other countries to buy things in the United States; the supply of U.S. currency to the foreign-exchange market comes from U.S. residents' desire to buy things from foreign countries.

4. How do fixed and floating exchange rates differ in their adjustment to shifts in supply and demand for currencies?

   With floating exchange rates, the foreign-exchange market adjusts automatically to shifts in supply and demand, the same way perfectly competitive markets for products adjust. With fixed exchange rates, a government can try to maintain the fixed rate through intervention in the foreign-exchange market, although this is unlikely to work unless the shifts in supply and demand are temporary. A **fundamental disequilibrium** usually requires a currency devaluation.

5. What are the advantages and disadvantages of fixed and floating exchange rates?

   Fixed exchange rates require that a nation match its macroeconomic policies to those of the country or countries to which its currency is pegged; this limits a country's ability to set its own policies. Floating exchange rates allow countries to follow their own macroeconomic policies.

6. What determines the kind of exchange-rate system a country adopts?

   Countries in general can choose what kind of exchange-rate system they want to use. The choice seems to depend on four characteristics: the size of the country (in terms of economic output), the nature of the **economy** (how large a fraction of the GNP is devoted to international trade), the country's experience with inflation, and trade diversification.

Key Terms

gold standard
gold exchange standard
reserve currency
International Monetary Fund (IMF)
World Bank
foreign exchange market intervention
devaluation
equilibrium exchange rates
managed floating exchange rates
appreciate
depreciate
fundamental disequilibrium
speculators
open economy
multiple exchange rates

Quick-Check Quiz

Section 1: Past and Current Exchange-Rate Arrangements

1. Which of the following describes a gold standard?
   a. a currency that is used to settle international debts and that is held by governments to use in foreign exchange market interventions
   b. an exchange-rate system in which each nation fixes the value of its currency in terms of gold but buys and sells the U.S. dollar rather than gold to maintain fixed exchange rates
   c. the buying or selling of currencies by a government or central bank to achieve a specified exchange rate
   d. the exchange rates that are established in the absence of government foreign exchange market intervention
   e. a system whereby national currencies are fixed in terms of their value in gold, thus creating fixed exchange rates between currencies

2. Which of the following describes a gold exchange standard?
   a. a currency that is used to settle international debts and that is held by governments to use in foreign exchange market interventions
   b. an exchange-rate system in which each nation fixes the value of its currency in terms of gold but buys and sells the U.S. dollar rather than gold to maintain fixed exchange rates
   c. the buying or selling of currencies by a government or central bank to achieve a specified exchange rate
   d. the exchange rates that are established in the absence of government foreign exchange market intervention
   e. a system whereby national currencies are fixed in terms of their value in gold, thus creating fixed exchange rates between currencies

3. Which of the following describes a reserve currency?
   a. a currency that is used to settle international debts and that is held by governments to use in foreign exchange market interventions
   b. an exchange-rate system in which each nation fixes the value of its currency in terms of gold but buys and sells the U.S. dollar rather than gold to maintain fixed exchange rates
   c. the buying or selling of currencies by a government or central bank to achieve a specified exchange rate
   d. the exchange rates that are established in the absence of government foreign exchange market intervention
   e. a system whereby national currencies are fixed in terms of their value in gold, thus creating fixed exchange rates between currencies

4. Which of the following describes foreign exchange market intervention?
   a. a currency that is used to settle international debts and that is held by governments to use in foreign exchange market interventions
   b. an exchange-rate system in which each nation fixes the value of its currency in terms of gold but buys and sells the U.S. dollar rather than gold to maintain fixed exchange rates
   c. the buying or selling of currencies by a government or central bank to achieve a specified exchange rate
   d. the exchange rates that are established in the absence of government foreign exchange market intervention
   e. a system whereby national currencies are fixed in terms of their value in gold, thus creating fixed exchange rates between currencies

5. Which of the following describes equilibrium exchange rates?
   a. a currency that is used to settle international debts and that is held by governments to use in foreign exchange market interventions
   b. an exchange-rate system in which each nation fixes the value of its currency in terms of gold but buys and sells the U.S. dollar rather than gold to maintain fixed exchange rates
   c. the buying or selling of currencies by a government or central bank to achieve a specified exchange rate
   d. the exchange rates that are established in the absence of government foreign exchange market intervention
   e. a system whereby national currencies are fixed in terms of their value in gold, thus creating fixed exchange rates between currencies

6. The Bretton Woods system
   a. created the International Monetary Fund and the World Bank.
   b. set a gold exchange standard.
   c. used the U.S. dollar as a reserve currency.
   d. tried to maintain exchange rates through foreign exchange market intervention.
   e. was and did all of the above.

Section 2: Fixed or Floating Exchange Rates

1. Currency appreciation is
   a. a decrease in the value of a currency under floating exchange rates.
   b. an increase in the value of a currency under floating exchange rates.
   c. a decrease in the value of a currency under fixed exchange rates.
   d. an increase in the value of a currency under fixed exchange rates.
   e. resetting the pegged value of a currency.

2. Currency depreciation is
   a. a decrease in the value of a currency under floating exchange rates.
   b. an increase in the value of a currency under floating exchange rates.
   c. a decrease in the value of a currency under fixed exchange rates.
   d. an increase in the value of a currency under fixed exchange rates.
   e. resetting the pegged value of a currency.

3. Which of the following statements about fixed and floating exchange rates is false?
   a. Fixed exchange rates put pressure on a nation to manage its macroeconomic policy in concert with other nations.
   b. Floating exchange rates put pressure on a nation to manage its macroeconomic policy in concert with other nations.
   c. Speculators are more likely to be a problem under fixed exchange rates than under floating exchange rates.
   d. Fixed exchange rates can force a devaluation in the event of fundamental disequilibrium.
   e. Floating exchange rates adjust automatically to changes in demand and supply.

Section 3: The Choice of an Exchange-Rate System

1. Economically, an open economy is one in which
   a. no trade with other countries take place.
   b. there are no trade restraints.
   c. a large fraction of the country's GDP is devoted to internationally traded goods.
   d. exchange rates are freely floating, with no government intervention in foreign-exchange markets.
   e. other nations may freely invest.

2. Which of the following circumstances would make it likely that a country would choose a fixed exchange rate?
   a. The country is large, in terms of GDP.
   b. The country has an open economy.
   c. The country's inflation experience has diverged from its trading partners'.
   d. The country has a very diversified trading pattern.
   e. Both b and d would make it likely that a country would choose a fixed exchange rate.

3. Multiple exchange rates
   a. are impossible.
   b. eventually lead to fixed exchange rates.
   c. eventually lead to a gold standard.
   d. have the same effects as taxes and subsidies.
   e. are easier to administer than a single exchange rate.

Practice Questions and Problems

Section 1: Past and Current Exchange-Rate Arrangements

1. From about 1880 to 1914, most currencies were fixed in value in terms of _____ .

2. The Bretton Woods agreement of 1944 set up two international financial institutions that are still active today. Name the two institutions that match the descriptions below.

   a. Supervises exchange-rate arrangements and lends money to member countries experiencing problems meeting their external financial obligations: _____

   b. Makes loans and provides technical expertise to developing countries: _____

3. A(n) _____ is a deliberate decrease in the official value of a currency.

4. Today, the major industrial countries determine the value of their currencies through _____ .

5. The _____ was introduced in 1999 as the eventual replacement for the currencies of several European countries.

6. Under a gold standard, if gold is worth $35 per ounce in the United States and 175 francs per ounce in France, _____ franc(s) will exchange for $1.

7. Under a gold standard, if gold is worth $20 per ounce in the United States and 10 marks per ounce in Germany, _____ mark(s) will exchange for $1.

Section 2: Fixed or Floating Exchange Rates

1. The U.S. demand for German marks comes from the desire of _____ (U.S., German) citizens for _____ (U.S., German) goods.

2. The U.S. supply of German marks comes from the desire of _____ (U.S., German) citizens for _____ (U.S., German) goods.

3. If U.S. citizens decide that they want to buy more Mercedes-Benz automobiles from Germany, the U.S. _____ (demand for, supply of) marks will _____ (increase, decrease).

4. If German citizens decide they want to buy fewer IBM computers from the United States, the U.S. _____ (demand for, supply of) marks will _____ (increase, decrease).

5. The two graphs below show the current U.S. demand for and supply of German marks. The exchange rate between marks and dollars floats freely.

(a)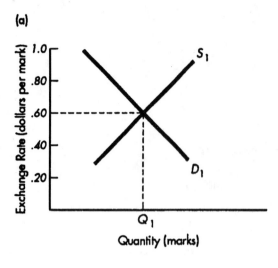

(b)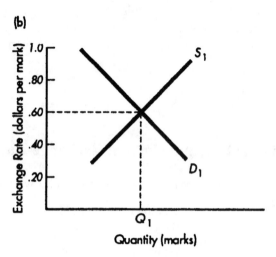

a. The current exchange rate in dollars per mark is _____ .
b. The current exchange rate in marks per dollar is _____ .
c. On graph (a), sketch in a new demand or supply curve (whichever is appropriate) that shows the effects of a decrease in the purchase of German BMW automobiles by U.S. residents.
d. With the change in demand, the dollar _____ (appreciates, depreciates) relative to the mark, and the mark _____ (appreciates, depreciates) relative to the dollar.
e. On graph (b), sketch in a new demand or supply curve (whichever is appropriate) that shows the effects of a decrease in the purchase of Boeing airplanes (made in the United States) by German airlines.
f. With the change in supply, the dollar _____ (appreciates, depreciates) relative to the mark, and the mark _____ (appreciates, depreciates) relative to the dollar.

Section 3: The Choice of an Exchange-Rate System

1. Countries with fixed exchange rates are likely to be _____ (large, small), to be _____ (more open, less open), to trade with _____ (many countries, mostly one country), and to have a _____ (similar, different) inflation history compared with their trading partners.

2. Some countries use _____ exchange rates to provide subsidies for activities they favor and taxes for activities they do not.

3. Section 3.b in the text, on multiple exchange rates, cites Venezuela as a country that was using multiple exchange rates in 1985. Use the exchange rates listed there to find the costs in Venezuelan bolivars (Bs) of the transactions below.

   a. $10,000 interest payment on debt owed by a Venezuelan company to Citibank in New York: _____

   b. $10,000 purchase of drilling supplies by the Venezuelan national oil company: _____

   c. $10,000 purchase of personal computers by the Venezuelan education agency: _____

   d. $10,000 purchase of a Chevrolet by a Venezuelan citizen: _____

Thinking About and Applying Exchange-Rate Systems and Practices

Floating Exchange Rates?

The headline in the *Wall Street Journal* on April 28, 1993, read "U.S. Slows Yen's Rise, Easing Japanese Tension" (page C1). The exchange rate between the dollar and the yen had dropped from 125 yen per dollar in early January 1993 to below 110 yen per dollar in April 1993. (Since then, it has dropped even further, to around 85 yen per dollar in mid-1995.) The article said:

> Marking the Clinton administration's first intervention in the foreign-exchange markets, the Federal Reserve Bank of New York repeatedly sold yen for dollars after the U.S. currency hit a postwar low of 109.25 yen. By late yesterday afternoon in New York, the dollar had risen about 1% against the yen.

1. Explain why the headline is correct when it talks about the yen's "rise" between January and April.

2. Use demand and supply analysis to explain the effect that the Federal Reserve's selling yen for dollars would have on the exchange rate between dollars and yen.

3. How can economists say that both the United States and Japan have adopted floating exchange rates, when the Federal Reserve acts to control exchange rates?

Chapter 22 (*Economics* Chapter 37)   Homework Problems

Name _____

1. Under the gold standard, what determined the exchange rate between two countries' currencies?

2. How are the exchange rates between the dollar and other major currencies determined today?

3. What four characteristics are important in a country's choice of what type of exchange-rate system to use?

4. If the United States and its major trading partners went back on the gold standard, how would they have to change their macroeconomic policy making?

5. Suppose the exchange rate between the U.S. dollar and the British pound is floating. What effect will each of the following have on the demand or supply of dollars, and what will happen to the price of a dollar in pounds (the exchange rate)?

   a. British Airways decides to buy 200 new Boeing 777 airliners.

   b. British Land Rovers become much more popular in the United States.

   c. The U.S. stock market booms, attracting large numbers of British investors.

   d. The Federal Reserve lowers interest rates in the United States, making British bonds more attractive to U.S. investors.

Answers

Quick-Check Quiz

Section 1: Past and Current Exchange-Rate Arrangements

1. e; 2. b; 3. a; 4. c; 5. d; 6. e

If you missed any of these questions, you should go back and review Section 1 in Chapter 22 (*Economics*, Chapter 37).

Section 2: Fixed or Floating Exchange Rates

1. b; 2. a; 3. b

If you missed any of these questions, you should go back and review Section 2 in Chapter 22 (*Economics*, Chapter 37).

Section 3: The Choice of an Exchange-Rate System

1. c; 2. b; 3. d

If you missed any of these questions, you should go back and review Section 3 in Chapter 22 (*Economics*, Chapter 37).

Practice Questions and Problems

Section 1: Past and Current Exchange-Rate Arrangements

1. gold
2. a. International Monetary Fund (IMF)
   b. World Bank
3. devaluation
4. managed floating exchange rates
5. euro
6. 5 (It takes five times as many francs as dollars to buy an ounce of gold [175 francs per ounce/$35 per ounce], so $1 would be equivalent to five times as many francs.)
7. 0.5 mark (It takes half as many marks as dollars to buy an ounce of gold [10 marks per ounce/$20 per ounce], so $1 would be equivalent to half as many marks.)

Section 2: Fixed or Floating Exchange Rates

1. U.S.; German
2. German; U.S.
3. demand for; increase (The Mercedes-Benz factory in Germany wants to be paid in its own currency [marks]. U.S. buyers of German products have to buy marks with dollars. Because we want to buy more marks than before, the demand for marks will increase.)
4. supply of; decrease (IBM in the United States wants to be paid in its own currency [dollars]. German buyers of U.S. products have to sell marks to get dollars. Because they want to sell fewer marks than before, the supply of marks will decrease.)

5.

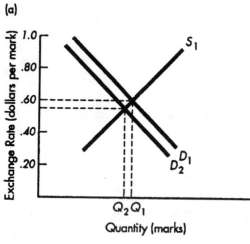
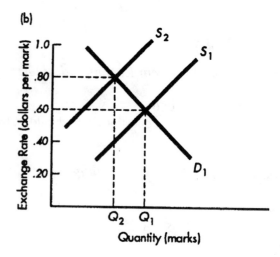

a. 0.60 dollar per mark (It takes $.60 to buy 1 mark, in dollars per mark. You can read this value from the intersection of demand and supply on the graphs.)

b. 1.67 marks per dollar (The exchange rate in marks per dollar is the inverse of the exchange rate in dollars per mark: 1/0.60 = 1.67. Exchange rates can be expressed either way.)

c. U.S. buyers of German products are the demanders of marks (they need to buy marks to pay Germans), so the demand curve will shift. If we buy fewer BMWs, the demand for marks will decrease, as shown on graph (a). The size of the shift on the graph does not matter.

d. appreciates; depreciates (It takes fewer dollars now to buy a mark than it did before [0.55 dollar per mark instead of 0.60], so that the dollar is more valuable relative to the mark. And it now takes 1.82 marks to buy a dollar [1/0.55]. It takes more marks now to buy a dollar than before, so the mark is less valuable relative to the dollar.)

e. German buyers of U.S. products are the sellers of marks (they need to sell marks to get dollars to pay Americans), so the supply curve will shift. If they buy fewer Boeing planes, the supply of marks will decrease, as shown on graph (b). The size of the shift on the graph does not matter.

f. depreciates; appreciates (It takes more dollars now to buy a mark than it did before [0.80 dollar per mark instead of 0.60], so the dollar is less valuable relative to the mark. And it now takes only 1.25 marks to buy a dollar [1/0.80]. It takes fewer marks now to buy a dollar than before, so the mark is more valuable relative to the dollar.)

Section 3: The Choice of an Exchange-Rate System

1. small; more open; mostly one country; similar
2. multiple
3. a. Bs43,000 (The exchange rate for interest payments on foreign debt was Bs4.30 per dollar, so buying $10,000 cost Bs43,000 [$10,000 times 4.30].)
   b. Bs60,000 (The exchange rate for the national petroleum company was Bs6.00 per dollar, so buying $10,000 cost Bs60,000 [$10,000 times 6.00].)
   c. Bs75,000 (The exchange rate for government agencies was Bs7.50 per dollar, so buying $10,000 cost Bs75,000 [$10,000 times 7.50].)
   d. Bs144,000 (The exchange rate for other transactions was the free-market rate of Bs14.40 per dollar, so buying $10,000 cost Bs144,000 [$10,000 times 14.40].)

Thinking About and Applying Exchange-Rate Systems and Practices

Floating Exchange Rates?

1. The yen "rose" (appreciated) during that time because the number of yen needed to buy a dollar decreased, making the yen more valuable relative to the dollar. A U.S. product that cost $1 would have cost a Japanese buyer 125 yen in January but only about 110 yen in April.
2. Looking at the markets for dollars and yen, selling yen and buying dollars would have increased the supply of yen, lowering the price of yen; it also would have increased the demand for dollars, raising the price of dollars.
3. At any moment, the Federal Reserve (or other central bank) can affect exchange rates to a limited extent. What limits the Fed's actions in this case is its limited supply of yen to sell. Most of the time, the exchange rate is determined by market demand and supply.

Sample Test
Chapters 20–22
(*Economics* Chapters 35–37)

1. What determines which goods a country will specialize in?
   a. Its opportunity costs of production are equal to those of other countries.
   b. Its opportunity costs of production are higher than those of other countries.
   c. Its degree of subsidization is greater than that of other countries.
   d. Its opportunity costs of production are lower than those of other countries.
   e. Its product quality is higher than that of other countries.

Refer to the following table to answer questions 2–6. The data indicate that both Japan and Taiwan produce camcorders and clothing; Japan can make 20 camcorders or 4 units of clothing in a day, and Taiwan can make 10 camcorders or 10 units of clothing in a day.

	Camcorders	Clothing
Japan	20	4
Taiwan	10	10

2. Japan has an absolute advantage in producing
   a. camcorders.
   b. clothing.
   c. both camcorders and clothing.
   d. neither camcorders nor clothing.
   e. clothing and an absolute disadvantage in producing camcorders.

3. Japan has a comparative advantage in producing
   a. camcorders.
   b. clothing.
   c. both camcorders and clothing.
   d. neither camcorders nor clothing.
   e. clothing and an absolute disadvantage in producing camcorders.

4. What is the opportunity cost of one camcorder in Japan?
   a. 4 units of clothing
   b. 10 units of clothing
   c. $1/5$ unit of clothing
   d. 1 unit of clothing
   e. $1/2$ unit of clothing

Copyright © Houghton Mifflin Company. All rights reserved.

5. What is the opportunity cost of one unit of clothing in Japan?
   a. 20 camcorders
   b. 10 camcorders
   c. 1 camcorder
   d. $\frac{1}{5}$ camcorder
   e. $\frac{1}{20}$ camcorder

6. What are the limits on the terms of trade for one unit of clothing?
   a. between 4 camcorders and 20 camcorders
   b. between 1 camcorder and 10 camcorders
   c. between 1 camcorder and 20 camcorders
   d. between 1 camcorder and 2 camcorders
   e. between $\frac{1}{5}$ camcorder and 1 camcorder

7. What happens when the world price is below the domestic "no-trade" equilibrium price?
   a. The domestic shortage can be eliminated by rationing.
   b. The domestic surplus can be consumed at home.
   c. The domestic shortage can be eliminated by foreign imports.
   d. The quantity demanded is equal to that supplied by the world.
   e. The domestic shortage can be eliminated by foreign imports.

8. Most empirical studies indicate that restrictions on international trade
   a. cause a net increase in jobs in the domestic economy.
   b. promote both exports and imports.
   c. promote imports and restrict exports.
   d. restrict both imports and exports.
   e. harm consumers.

9. In general, protecting domestic producers from foreign competition benefits
   a. both domestic producers and foreign producers.
   b. all groups in the domestic economy.
   c. both domestic producers and domestic consumers.
   d. domestic producers at the expense of domestic consumers.
   e. foreign producers and domestic consumers.

10. The consequences of protection in the affected industry are generally known to be
    a. lower prices for the product, lower profits for owners, and lower wages for workers.
    b. higher prices for the output, lower profits for owners, and lower wages for workers.
    c. higher prices for the product, lower profits for owners, and higher wages for workers.
    d. lower prices for the product, higher profits for owners, and higher wages for workers.
    e. higher prices for the product, higher profits for owners, and higher wages for workers.

11. All of the following are basic principles of the GATT *except* the statement that
    a. barriers to trade should apply equally across all countries.
    b. quotas should be eliminated.
    c. disagreements should be settled through consultation.
    d. developing nations with underutilized comparative advantages should be favored using selectivity.
    e. once tariffs have been lowered, they cannot be increased without compensation to trading partners.

Consider the following figure for questions 12–16.

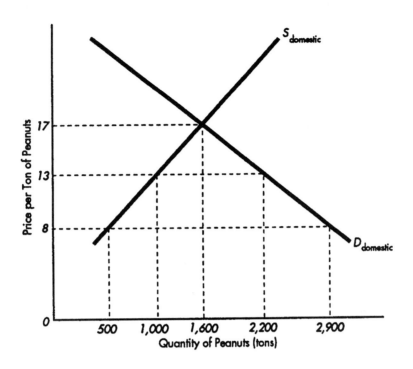

12. Without international trade, the domestic price and equilibrium quantity of peanuts are
    a. $8 per ton and 1,000 tons.
    b. $13 per ton and 1,600 tons.
    c. $8 per ton and 2,900 tons.
    d. $17 per ton and 1,600 tons.
    e. $13 per ton and 2,200 tons.

13. Suppose that the world equilibrium price is $8 per ton and free trade prevails. Then
    a. this country will export 500 tons of peanuts.
    b. there will be a shortage of peanuts, driving prices up.
    c. this country will import 2,400 tons of peanuts.
    d. domestic producers will produce 1,600 tons of peanuts.
    e. consumers will demand no peanuts at a price of $8.

14. Suppose that the world equilibrium price is $8 per ton, and this country imposes a $5 per ton tariff on peanut imports. Then
    a. the equilibrium price must rise to $17.
    b. the price to domestic consumers and producers will be $13.
    c. imports of peanuts will increase by 1,000 tons.
    d. a surplus of 500 tons will be created.
    e. a shortage of 500 tons will be created.

15. Suppose that this country wanted to completely eliminate all imports of peanuts. Given these demand and supply data and a world price of $8, the import tariff per ton of peanuts should be
    a. $3.
    b. $8.
    c. $9.
    d. $5.
    e. $7.

16. The total tariff revenue to the government that imposes a $5 import tariff per ton of peanuts with a world price of $8 is
    a. $1,200.
    b. $6,000.
    c. $5,000.
    d. $2,200.
    e. $2,900.

17. Which of the following is true regarding a comparison between import quotas with import tariffs?
    a. A tariff raises the worldwide equilibrium price.
    b. A quota raises government tax revenue.
    c. With a quota, both domestic and foreign producers enjoy a higher price for products sold in the domestic market.
    d. Quotas benefit consumers of the product.
    e. Quotas increase the quantity of the good available to consumers.

18. Suppose that the price of an ounce of gold is 10 dinars in Bahrain and $400 in the United States. Then the
    a. Bahraini dinar is worth 40 times the value of a U.S. dollar.
    b. Bahraini dinar is worth one-fortieth the value of a U.S. dollar.
    c. U.S. dollar is worth 40 times the value of a Bahraini dinar.
    d. U.S. economy must be 40 times larger than that of Bahrain.
    e. Bahrain economy must be 40 times larger than that of the United States.

19. Suppose that the official gold value of the Portuguese escudo changes from 300 escudos per ounce to 200 escudos per ounce. We can then say that
    a. the Portuguese escudo has been devalued.
    b. the Portuguese escudo has appreciated in value.
    c. gold is now more expensive to purchase in Portugal.
    d. the Portuguese economy is expected to experience rapid inflation.
    e. the Portuguese escudo has depreciated in value because of free-market fluctuations.

Consider the following figure for questions 20 and 21.

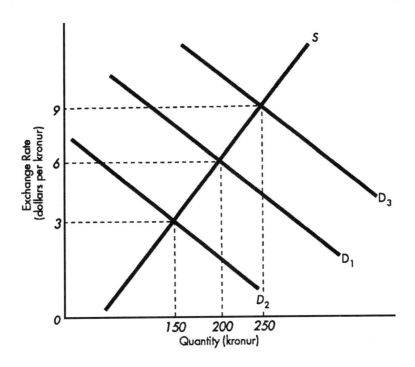

20. Suppose that U.S. residents significantly increase their demand for imported Icelandic sweaters. The greater U.S. demand will
    a. increase the demand for Icelandic kronur from D_1 to D_3 and increase the exchange rate to $9.
    b. decrease the demand for Icelandic kronur from D_1 to D_2 and increase the exchange rate to $6.
    c. increase the demand for Icelandic kronur from D_1 to D_3 and decrease the kronur price to $6.
    d. decrease the demand for Icelandic kronur from D_1 to D_2 and decrease the kronur price to $6.
    e. not affect the foreign exchange market for Icelandic kronur.

21. The demand curves shown for Icelandic kronur are based on _____, and the supply curve shown for Icelandic kronur is based on _____.
    a. economists' preferences for dollars; economists' preferences for dollars
    b. the supply of Icelandic kronur; the supply of Icelandic products
    c. U.S. demand for Icelandic goods; Icelandic demand for U.S. products
    d. Icelandic demand for U.S. products; U.S. demand for Icelandic products
    e. the supply of U.S. dollars in Iceland; the supply of Icelandic kronur in the United States

22. The Bretton Woods System of exchange rates was established
    a. to solidify support for the then-existing gold standard.
    b. to peg the worldwide price of silver to the price of gold.
    c. in Europe before World War II to develop flexible exchange rates.
    d. in the United States in 1944 to develop a gold exchange standard.
    e. by a mechanism that made gold the reserve currency of the system.

23. The International Monetary Fund was created to achieve each of the following purposes *except*
    a. to supervise exchange-rate practices of member countries.
    b. to help finance economic development in poor countries.
    c. to encourage the free convertibility of member countries' currencies.
    d. to lend money to countries that are having difficulty meeting their international payments obligations.
    e. to collect and disburse each country's annual membership fee or quota.

24. The World Bank was created to
    a. help finance economic development in poor countries.
    b. supervise exchange-rate practices of member countries.
    c. encourage the free convertibility of member countries' currencies.
    d. lend money to countries that are having difficulty meeting their international payments obligations.
    e. collect and disburse each country's annual membership fee or quota.

25. In international finance, the term *appreciate* refers to
    a. a decrease in the value of a currency under floating exchange rates.
    b. a decrease in the value of a currency under fixed exchange rates.
    c. an increase in the value of a currency under floating exchange rates.
    d. an increase in the value of a currency under fixed exchange rates.
    e. foreign policy consequences of an accommodative fiscal policy by which one country helps another.

Answers to Sample Test

1. d (Chapter 21, Preview; *Economics* Chapter 35)
2. a (Chapter 21, Section 2.a; *Economics* Chapter 35)
3. a (Chapter 21, Section 2.a; *Economics* Chapter 35)
4. c (Chapter 21, Section 2.a; *Economics* Chapter 35)
5. b (Chapter 21, Section 2.a; *Economics* Chapter 35)
6. b (Chapter 21, Section 2.b; *Economics* Chapter 35)
7. c (Chapter 21, Section 2.b; *Economics* Chapter 35)
8. e (Chapter 22, Section 1.a; *Economics* Chapter 36)
9. d (Chapter 22, Section 1.a; *Economics* Chapter 36)
10. e (Chapter 22, Section 1.a; *Economics* Chapter 36)
11. d (Chapter 22, Section 2.a; *Economics* Chapter 36)
12. d (Chapter 22, Section 2.a; *Economics* Chapter 36)
13. c (Chapter 22, Section 2.a; *Economics* Chapter 36)
14. b (Chapter 22, Section 2.a; *Economics* Chapter 36)
15. c (Chapter 22, Section 2.a; *Economics* Chapter 36)
16. b (Chapter 22, Section 2.a; *Economics* Chapter 36)
17. c (Chapter 22, Section 2.b; *Economics* Chapter 36)
18. a (Chapter 23, Section 1.a; *Economics* Chapter 37)
19. b (Chapter 23, Section 1.d; *Economics* Chapter 37)
20. a (Chapter 23, Section 2.a; *Economics* Chapter 37)
21. c (Chapter 23, Section 2.a; *Economics* Chapter 37)
22. d (Chapter 23, Section 1.b; *Economics* Chapter 37)
23. b (Chapter 23, Section 1.c; *Economics* Chapter 37)
24. a (Chapter 23, Section 1.c; *Economics* Chapter 37)
25. c (Chapter 23, Section 2.b; *Economics* Chapter 37)